Volume 8

THE G. STANLEY HALL
LECTURE SERIES

G. STANLEY HALL, 1844–1924

Volume 8

THE G. STANLEY HALL LECTURE SERIES

Edited by
Ira S. Cohen

1987 HALL LECTURERS

Richard W. Brislin
William E. Cashin
Donald A. Dewsbury
Leonard D. Goodstein
Richard M. Suinn

AMERICAN PSYCHOLOGICAL ASSOCIATION
WASHINGTON, D.C.

Published by the American Psychological Association, Inc.
1200 Seventeenth Street, N.W., Washington, DC 20036

ISBN: 1-55798-035-7
ISSN: 8756-7865

Copies may be ordered from:
Order Department
American Psychological Association
P.O. Box 2710
Hyattsville, MD 20784

Printed in the United States of America

CONTENTS

PREFACE   1
Ira S. Cohen

THE SOCIAL PSYCHOLOGY   5
OF THE WORKPLACE
Leonard D. Goodstein

COMPARATIVE PSYCHOLOGY: 47
CONTEMPORARY VIGOR
CONTINUES A PROUD TRADITION
Donald A. Dewsbury

ABNORMAL PSYCHOLOGY: 87
NEW CHALLENGES
AND BASIC FOUNDATIONS
Richard M. Suinn

INCREASING AWARENESS OF CLASS,   137
ETHNICITY, CULTURE, AND RACE BY
EXPANDING ON STUDENTS' OWN EXPERIENCES
Richard W. Brislin

USING EVALUATION DATA TO IMPROVE   181
COLLEGE CLASSROOM TEACHING
William E. Cashin

PREFACE

There is a myth, tacitly endorsed on so many college campuses, that says that the highest level courses—the advanced graduate courses in specialized areas—are the ones that are complex and difficult to teach. Perhaps this myth has its roots in the reduced teaching course loads that are characteristic of large university research-oriented departments. But these teaching assignments are based not on the complexity of the pedagogical task, but on the other obligations (research, writing, supervision of graduate students' theses and dissertations) that are intrinsic to the mission of those departments. Indeed, it is the inverse that is true: The lower level courses are the difficult ones to teach, with the introductory course perhaps the most challenging in this respect. The Nobelist Harold C. Urey recognized this anomaly when he would periodically accept the challenge of presenting contemporary nuclear physics to high school students in California.

The G. Stanley Hall Lecture Series was established in 1980 to help psychology instructors faced with the formidable task of introducing psychology to the undergraduate in a fashion that was convincing, honest, engaging, and current. There were to be five lectures presented annually at the American Psychological Association (APA) convention and then collected as chapters in a monograph to be published as an annual APA separate. Four of the chapters were to deal with topics typically included in the introductory psychology course; the fifth chapter was to examine a topic of current interest. Each lecturer was asked not only to present an up-to-date review of the latest developments concerning the topic, but also to suggest effective and interesting ways of presenting the topic to undergraduates.

In 1987 the scope of the Series was broadened to include undergraduate teaching in general, rather than a restricted focus on the introductory course. Currently, the lectures are comprised of three on topics usually included in the undergraduate psychology curriculum; a fourth on a less traditional topic of lively, contemporary interest; and a fifth on the teaching–learning process or some other aspect of undergraduate psychology teaching. The lecturers are chosen for their expertise in the assigned area, but equally important is their ability to present the material clearly and interestingly to the nonspecialist and to include workable ideas for classroom demonstrations, exercises, and discussions.

This eighth volume of the Hall Series includes chapters based on the lectures delivered at APA's 1987 annual convention in New York. The volume begins with a chapter by Leonard D. Goodstein on the social psychology of work, followed by chapters by Donald A. Dewsbury on comparative psychology; Richard M. Suinn on abnormal psychology; Richard W. Brislin on social class, culture, ethnicity, and race differences; and William E. Cashin on the use of evaluation data to improve classroom teaching. Psychologists who are knowledgeable in each area and who are experienced teachers were asked to comment on earlier drafts of the manuscripts. These reviews were very helpful, both to the editor and to the authors. As anonymous readers, these people cannot be cited, but their comments contributed significantly to the descriptions that follow.

In the first chapter, Leonard Goodstein emphasizes the organizational rather than the industrial aspects of industrial/organizational psychology. He provides a social psychological approach to work and reviews the theory and research that offer a framework for understanding and changing the workplace. He points out that there are "two independent values that underlie most organizational change efforts: organizational effectiveness (the 'bottom line') and worker satisfaction (humanism)," both of which are clearly appropriate objects of the attention of organizational psychologists. Especially valuable is his review and analysis of the concept of organizational culture and how this phenomenon affects, in a variety of ways, the functioning of the workplace.

In the second chapter, Donald Dewsbury begins by providing a scholarly review of the historical bases for the contemporary view of animal behavior. This contemporary view, he argues, focuses on the adaptive and economically sensitive organism. It stresses the individual and its survival. He then goes on to offer samples of research that are consistent with these contemporary principles—research in such areas as foraging, competition, mating systems, and behavioral development. Dewsbury's chapter provides a current and insightful panoramic survey of animal behavior. It shows how the undergraduate comparative psychology course can be organized around the concepts of adaptation and optimality and suggests ways of making the student appreciate the importance and excitement of the area.

Next, Richard Suinn offers a stimulating review of recent developments in abnormal psychology. His basic premise is that the origins of psychopathology are to be found not only in psychological factors, but also in genetic, biological, familial, and cultural sources. To illustrate this point, he reviews recent studies on the genetics of schizophrenia, communication deviance in families, and the cultural influences in anorexia and bulimia. His analysis of recent trends points to the increasing prominence of cognitive variables (in theories of depression and of stress, for example) and of longitudinal developmental studies (in both high-risk and risk-resistant children, for example). For Suinn, clearly, the study of psychopathology is a provocative study of multiple origins and multiple interactions.

In Chapter 4, Richard Brislin attempts to expand students' awareness of the concepts of social class, ethnicity, culture, and race by leading them through a series of exercises and providing illustrative examples and critical incidents. His illustrations, drawn largely from Eurocentric and Asian groups, reflect an international, cross-cultural perspective. Brislin first explains the concepts of class, ethnicity, culture, and race and then reviews some of the research relating to them. He concludes by considering the four concepts as social categories that people use to think about other people and shows how intergroup relations can be influenced by this category-based thinking.

In the last chapter, William Cashin points out that to improve teaching, one needs models of effective teaching; data about one's present teaching; and, if the teaching falls short of the models, some new strategies to achieve one's instructional goals. The author first discusses various views of effective teaching, emphasizing that there is no single definition that holds for all teaching situations. He then presents a review of the two major techniques for gathering data on teaching effectiveness—traditional observational coding systems and student ratings of instruction. The author has had extensive experience in helping faculty use these evaluation data to improve their teaching. Thus it is not surprising that his comments are direct, practical, and useful. They should be most helpful to the undergraduate teacher.

Each year, the various boards and committees of the American Psychological Association are asked to nominate outstanding psychologists for the next year's series, keeping in mind the criteria of teaching effectiveness as well as subject matter expertise. It is from this pool of nominees that the lecturers are chosen by the Committee on Undergraduate Education. The committee charged with the selection of the G. Stanley Hall Lecturers whose papers appear in this volume included Paul J. Lloyd, Antonio E. Puente, Margaret A. Lloyd, Margaret S. Martin, and Janet R. Matthews. Their efforts are gratefully acknowledged.

Finally, special thanks are also due to Genevieve Whittemore, who handled most of the correspondence with the authors and adroitly arranged for the presentation of the lectures at the 1987 convention. I also wish to thank Vivian Parker Makosky, who offered helpful suggestions; Donna Stewart, who supervised this volume through the production process; and Stephanie Selice, the technical editor who prepared the manuscripts for publication.

Ira S. Cohen

LEONARD D. GOODSTEIN

THE SOCIAL PSYCHOLOGY OF THE WORKPLACE

Since September 1985, Leonard D. Goodstein has been Executive Officer of the American Psychological Association. His 30-year academic career has included faculty appointments at the University of Iowa as Professor of Psychology and Director of the University Counseling Service, the University of Cincinnati as Professor of Psychology and Director of Professional Training in Psychology, Arizona State University as Professor and Chair of Psychology, and a Fulbright-Hayes Senior Lectureship at the Vrije Universiteit in the Netherlands. He then served as President and Chief Executive Officer, and later as Chairman of the Board, of University Associates, a San Diego-based consulting and publishing company.

Goodstein has a BS degree in psychology from the City College of New York and both MA and PhD degrees in psychology from Columbia University. He is a Diplomate in Clinical Psychology from the American Board of Professional Psychology and a Distinguished Practitioner of the American Academies of Practice.

THE SOCIAL PSYCHOLOGY OF THE WORKPLACE

Freud noted long ago that in order to be genuinely mature, one must "lieben und arbeiten": love and work. Most of us spend a great deal of time at work. It is a central human activity—one that provides a structure in daily life, a way of meeting economic needs, a means to a sense of accomplishment, and a basis for developing a measure of self-esteem and personal identity.

Certainly one of the few things the diverse people who take introductory psychology courses have in common is that virtually all of them will be out in the workplace at some time. Yet look at the meager coverage of this vital area in the typical introductory textbook!

Psychology (or at least the authors of introductory texts) seems

I am indebted to several people for their help in bringing this project to completion: Jeanette Treat Goodstein was invaluable in providing conceptual clarity, rigorous editing, and unfailing support; Barbara Ann Leigh, my 1987 undergraduate summer intern, did much of the initial bibliographic research; Rick Sample, the APA Librarian, found most of the materials; Paul Thayer provided consistently useful feedback; and my colleagues Vivian Parker Makosky and Matthew Zalichin provided expert editorial input.

to have heard only half of Freud's message. Of the 15 recent introductory texts I checked, all of them indexed either love or sex or both, whereas only 5 indexed work, and one of those references was to "workaholics" in the chapter on motivation. It may be extreme to conclude as a result of this informal survey that psychology is not yet fully mature. Yet with the exception of two books (Benjamin, Hopkins, & Nation, 1986; Bootzin, Bower, Zajonc, & Hall, 1986), the coverage in introductory texts of the world of work in general and of industrial/organizational (I/O) psychology in particular is as inadequate today as when Thayer (1982) surveyed the field. These inadequacies are confirmed by a recent independent survey (Turnage, 1987). The exceptions in this textbook survey, however, are exemplary in having entire chapters devoted to I/O psychology. In contrast, four of the texts reviewed had entire chapters devoted to sexual behavior! We seem to be making progress slowly.

The Field of I/O Psychology

It is interesting to speculate on the distinction between the industrial and the organizational aspects of I/O psychology in terms of the various activities they encompass. This is a distinction that is not at all clear in the field and one that is difficult to make simply. I suggest that one important difference is that the industrial aspect of I/O psychology has a strong focus on individual behavior in the workplace, whereas the organizational aspect focuses on the behavior of the work group or organization as a functioning unit rather than on the individual worker per se. Though this distinction is not without its inconsistencies and limitations in application, it seems a useful one for the purpose of this discussion.

The activities that are more individual (industrial) in nature include performing job analyses and job classifications, doing testing and personnel selection, conducting time-and-motion studies, and designing and delivering training and development programs. They may also include studying worker motivation and job satisfaction, designing optimal interfaces between humans and machines, and improving worker safety. This individual focus is the more traditional one in I/O psychology, reflecting its roots in differential and experimental psychology and mandating close linkages with engineering psychology, psychometrics, industrial engineering, and personnel management. Other activities are more organizational in nature, such as analyzing organization behavior, examining organization change and organization development (OD), improving the quality of work life (QWL), and developing more participatory management styles in the organization. These activities reflect I/O's roots in social, personality, and clinical/counseling psychology and mandate close linkages with sociology, management science, and operations research.

The emphasis of this chapter, as is obvious from its title, is on the organizational, rather than the industrial, aspects of I/O psychology, although some of the other aspects will be touched on in an organizational context. I have several reasons for this focus. The first and most important is that the concept of the organization as a social system should be the most pervasive aspect of I/O psychology. An understanding of this can touch all our lives, even those of people who never directly experience any other aspect of this field. At the same time, the study of the organization as a social system is the most overlooked aspect of I/O psychology, even in those texts that do provide more than minimal coverage of the field. Second, the industrial aspects of the field were well covered by Thayer (1982) in an earlier lecture in this series and, in any event, tend to have at least some coverage in the texts. Finally, the social psychology of the organization is the area to which I have devoted my own professional efforts for the past dozen years and about which I am the most knowledgeable.

Beginning with an analysis of organizations as social systems—an approach that I have found both provocative and useful in my own work—I will discuss organizational change and review a variety of psychologically based change processes, including organization development, sociotechnical systems interventions, quality circles, and quality of work life. Next I will discuss organizational culture and how the concept of culture will affect the functioning of the I/O psychologist in selection, socialization, training, organizational career development, succession planning, and mentoring. Then I will present a brief case report that illustrates many of these issues.

Organizations as Social Systems

The term "organization" is not easy to define. It is so difficult, in fact, that March and Simon (1958), two leading students of organizations, declined to offer a definition in their classic book. Instead, they noted, "it is easier, and probably more useful, to give examples of formal organizations than to define the term" (p. 1). Undeterred by such advice, I believe that a useful working definition is possible. My own is: *An organization is a group (or groups) of individuals who regularly interact together to achieve some shared explicit purpose or goal through the expenditure of differentiated and coordinated effort.*

My formal definition emphasizes that an organization may involve single or multiple groups. There must also be some regular pattern of activity, a clear goal toward which all are striving, and both a division of labor and some integration of that divided effort. If any of these conditions are lacking, the organization is unlikely to achieve its goal. This definition thus encompasses all business, educational, religious, social, and political organizations regardless of their size and complexity. (I leave it to the reader to decide whether or not this definition is sufficiently inclusive to comprehend the typical American family.) What is most evident about this definition, at least from my point of view, is that it clearly describes the organization as a social system.

All social systems, including organizations, involve the behavior of individuals in regular patterns of activity. This pattern of behaviors needs to be relatively constant, regularly repeated, and interdependent if organizational goals are to be achieved. If the pattern of behavior occurs rarely or unpredictably, there is no organization. This is *not* to say that the goals of the individuals are the same as those of their organization, but rather that the achievement of the individual goals must facilitate the achievement of organizational goals and purposes.

Open-Systems Theory

Open-systems theory (Katz & Kahn, 1978) provides a valuable approach to understanding organizations as social systems. Bertalanffy (1956) originally proposed open-systems theory as a way of seeing social systems as patterns of recurrent activities in which energy (information, raw materials, human resources, and so on) is imported into the system and transformed, with the resulting product then exported back into the environment. Open-systems theory focuses interest on the structure of systems and on the relationships between the structural elements of the systems, especially on the interdependence of these elements as each affects the energy transformation process.

Open-systems theory has been advanced as a clear alternative to closed-systems approaches, that is, systems that operate according to classical Newtonian principles. In contrast to closed systems, open systems maintain themselves through constant commerce—by continual exchanges of energy between the internal and external environments. This continual interaction with the environment means that the system or organization cannot internally determine its desired outcomes. Rather, the external environment will play a major role in such determinations and will incidentally produce a good bit of situational uncertainty.

The functioning of any open system consists of recurring cycles of input, transformation, and output. Although this transformation process is an internal one, both the input and output involve active dealings with the external environment. To function effectively, a system must monitor the external environment to assure that it can adequately manage the input from the environment and that the environment can manage the output from the system.

A manufacturing organization must be able to regularly secure the necessary raw materials, power, machinery, and workers in order to transform these resources into product lines that the environment is willing to accept and able to purchase when available. Similarly, a university has its own cycle: It admits new students at the beginning of each academic year, transforms them into educated persons over a period of several years, and graduates them into an accepting society. In both of these examples, we can observe the cyclic nature of these processes, the need for a match between the input and output characteristics, and the constant exchange with the environment.

An open system can be effective only when it restricts its input to what it can handle and similarly restricts its output to what the environment can accept. Thus the manufacturer must avoid overbuying raw material, overexpanding plant capacity, and overhiring workers on the one hand; and producing more products than there are willing customers for on the other. Similarly, the university must be certain that it has enough teachers and dorm rooms for its student body and that it requires a sufficient level of academic performance of its graduates to give them marketplace credibility.

This open-systems approach highlights two aspects of organizations as social systems: (a) Action in one part of the system predictably leads to action in other parts of the system, and (b) organizations typically are in a state of constant flux as a result of their openness to environmental inputs. The open-systems approach treats organizations like complex living organisms rather than static mechanistic systems. The latter closed-systems approach typifies the bureaucratic approach to organizations.

Weber (1947) coined the term *bureaucracy* as a label for organizations characterized by impersonality and rationality, where rules cover all contingencies; technically expert supervisors act as impartial autocrats; and communications follow a carefully controlled, hierarchical path. Bureaucratic and other closed-system models of organizations tend to heavily emphasize their formal structure, whereas organizations that take the open-systems model approach heavily emphasize their informal structure.

Organizational Structure

Human organizations lack structure in any anatomical sense; rather, they are held together by patterns of behavioral events that give them stability and order. The most important of these patterns are the *role* behaviors of the organization's members, the organization's *norms* prescribing and sanctioning these behaviors, and the *values* in which roles and norms are embedded. Roles are sets of functionally specific, interrelated behaviors generated by interconnected tasks. Such role behaviors are carried out not because of the individual's personal needs but because these behaviors are necessary for system functioning.

In all organizations these roles become quickly accepted and habitual for those who occupy them. Thus, from an open-systems perspective, organizations can be seen as a series of interrelated and overlapping roles. Each of these roles is interdependent with the others, and this allows the organization to maintain its viability—that is, teachers cannot survive without students, supervisors without supervisees, and so on. From such a perspective, organizations are structures of roles.

In a similar vein, Moch (1980) argued that the only real structure of an organization is found in the network of integrated relationships among that organization's workers. Meyer and Rowan (1977) went even further in their theoretical analysis, insisting that the institutional or formal realities of an organization's structure exist more in its myths and ceremonies than in its formal organizational design. Ransom, Hinings, and Greenwood (1980) stated that the process of structuring is a more relevant issue than is the more static and mechanistic concept of structure. All of these writers emphasize the fact that organizations need to be understood in a more dynamic sense than is typically provided by the traditional organization chart.

Once we accept the importance of roles in organizations, we can readily understand why these roles are embedded in strong belief systems about how these roles should be carried out. There are powerful sanctions to maintain what is seen as appropriate role behavior or norms. Statements such as "That's the way we do it around here," "Our way or the highway," and "That's simply not the XYZ way of doing business" are among the most obvious examples of the sanctions brought to bear on organizational deviants. Thus, norms and values are those commonly held beliefs of an evaluative nature that support and maintain role behavior. Values tend to be the more generalized belief systems and norms the more behaviorally specific.

The Informal Organization

These values, norms, and roles coupled with the unstructured pattern of friendship, groupings, and communication networks found in all organizations constitute the informal organization. In contrast, the formal organization is the official blueprint of how work is to be done, but it is never fully realized in the behavior of the organization's members. The formal organization typically tends to ignore the informal organization, whereas the informal structure often serves to protect organizational members from the formal structure or at least to reduce its potency in governing the members' day-to-day behavior.

Exercise 1. Group Norms

Objective. To identify and examine the impact of specific group norms on the behavior of each student as an individual.

Procedures

1. Ask the students individually to list some of the organizations—formal or informal—of which they are current members. These might include dormitory groups, fraternities and sororities, sports teams, clubs, religious groups, and so on.
2. Each student then should select one of these groups in which membership is important to him or her. For that group, the student should list 3–4 norms that he or she believes the group regards as important. These norms might involve membership selection, dress codes, eating behaviors, the manner in which people interrelate, and so on.
3. Small groups of 3–5 students are then formed and asked to share their data informally. Issues that should be addressed in this discussion might include the following:
   (a) Are the norms bound by formal written rules or by less formal expectations?
   (b) What are the sanctions for violations of these norms?
   (c) How are these norms communicated to new members?
   (d) What are the underlying basic assumptions about human nature that are implicit in these norms?
4. Each small group can be asked to report on its most salient observations.

The seminal research project of Roethlisberger and Dickson (1939)—the so-called Hawthorne studies—played a central role in initially identifying the critical importance of the informal organization. This research was intended to assess the impact of a variety of working conditions such as rest periods, pay incentives, and lighting on worker productivity, but its overwhelming significance was that such factors were clearly less important than various psychological factors that emerged. The most important of these was the strong sense of group cohesion and identity that was exhibited by those who were included in each of the several experimental conditions. These groups quickly formed norms about how they would respond to the experimental interventions, norms that affected the behavior and roles of individual workers and thus the outcome of the experiment.

The outcome of the Hawthorne studies is often misrepresented in psychology and other textbooks (Bramel & Friend, 1981) as demonstrating across-the-board increases in productivity regardless of the experimental conditions, primarily as a result of the attention paid to the workers by the experimenters. The true "Hawthorne effect," however, is that these workers—like all of us—developed a group dynamic, one that set the production norms in each of the conditions. This early finding on the importance of the effects of group norms on member behavior has been largely supported by innumerable laboratory and field studies conducted since.

Another seminal study (Coch & French, 1948) found that workers more readily accepted work-rule changes when they had either directly or indirectly participated in planning, a finding that also has been extensively replicated over the years. In the Coch and French study, participation facilitated the development of the new work processes as a group goal that all members accepted and worked toward. It is interesting to note that, whereas participation through representation was effective in producing acceptance, direct participation produced greater and earlier performance changes. Direct participation probably produced better understanding of the nature of the changes and a higher sense of involvement.

Anecdotal Evidence

Both Schrank (1978) and Terkel (1972) provided strong anecdotal support for this general view of work as a social system. Schrank reported on his more than four decades of work at such diverse jobs as laborer, factory worker, plumber, coal miner, farmhand, machinist, union organizer, corporation executive, social service program director, city commissioner, doctoral-level sociologist, and, finally, executive at the Ford Foundation. Based on these highly diverse experiences, he concluded that people work for two basic reasons: because they have to make money and because they want to "schmooze"—to socialize with their work mates and to feel a part of a community in the workplace. According to Schrank, such schmoozing serves as a primary social outlet for many people and is an often neglected aspect of the nature of work and the workplace. Terkel provided additional support for these points in 125 interviews about work and the workplace with workers from all walks of life. Faculty and students with limited nonacademic work experience will find that both of these first-person accounts provide a rich insight into the social psychology of work.

Some Real-World Implications

Of greatest practical importance, however, are the changes in corporate America's attitudes toward the social psychology of the workplace. Buffeted both at home and abroad by foreign competition that appears to produce higher quality goods at lower prices, corporate America has now largely forsaken (at least publicly and momentarily) its traditional analogy of the organization and its members as machine and parts designed to work effectively and efficiently. Instead, many American corporations are accepting the "New Age" view of organizations as "a nested set of open, living systems and subsystems dependent upon the larger environment for survival" (Waldbaum, 1987, p. 19). What is surprising about this quote is not its content—this view has been normative in the organizational psychology literature for several decades—but its source: *The Wall Street Journal.* And it is typical to find such articles in virtually every issue of most American business publications: articles on corporate culture; on the changing values and attitudes of American workers; on the need for greater employee participation in managerial decision making; and on the place of employees as an important (if not the most important) asset of the corporation.

No one—certainly not I—would ever suggest that there are no longer any traditionally managed organizations in America. However, corporate executives have definitely begun to recognize that managing the social psychology of the workplace is a critical element in the success of any organization. Kenneth H. Olsen, Chairman of Digital Equipment Corporation—a leading computer manufacturer of which he is the founder—clearly recognized this in his 1987 commencement address to the Massachusetts Institute of Technology:

> I would also suggest that one of the most satisfying things [about running a business] is to help others to be creative, to take responsibility, to be challenged in their jobs and to be successful is the thing which, if not the most important, is almost the most important (1987, p. F 2).

This view of organizations as social systems has important implications for both the theory and practice of organizational change. As we have seen, the human element is an important consideration in any change effort if that effort is to be successful.

Change and Development

Organizations are in a constant state of change, much to the chagrin of both those who prefer stability to change and those who elect to use a closed-systems model for understanding organizational life. On the other hand, such continual change does satisfy those of us who follow an open-systems approach to understanding organizations and who prefer a bit more excitement in our day-to-day organizational life.

Organizations, at least in my experience, tend to change primarily because of external pressures rather than because of some internal desire or need to change. A few all-too-familiar examples of the kinds of environmental factors requiring organizations to change are when a new competitor snares a significant portion of a firm's market share, an old customer is acquired by a giant conglomerate that is dictating new sales arrangements, or a new invention offers the possibility of changing the existing production technology of the organization. Other examples include new government regulations that affect certain health-care financing programs, or economic and social conditions that create long-term changes in the availability of the labor force. Each of these external changes requires that the organization be alert to early-warning signs and move promptly to make the necessary internal changes required to remain viable in the changing external world.

Resistance to Change

According to the open-systems view of organizations, they tend like living creatures to be homeostatic or continuously working to maintain a steady state. This helps us to understand that organizations require external impetus for initiating change and indeed that change will be resisted even when it is necessary. There are three different levels at which organizational change can occur, each with different patterns of resistance to change, patterns that require different change strategies and techniques. These levels are: (a) changing the *individuals* who work in the organization—that is, their skills, values and attitudes and eventually their behavior, but with such individual behavior change always regarded as instrumental to organizational change; (b) changing various organizational *structures and systems*— reward systems, reporting relationships, work design, and so on; and (c) changing the organizationsl *climate or interpersonal style*—how open people are with each other, how conflict is managed, how decisions are made, and so on (Porter, Lawler, & Hackman, 1975).

According to Lewin (1958), one of the pioneers in the field of the social psychology of organizations, the first step of any change process is *unfreezing* the present pattern of behavior. Depending upon the organizational level of change intended, such unfreezing might involve selectively promoting or terminating employees on the individual level; developing highly experiential training programs about new organizational designs such as matrix management on the structural level; or providing data feedback about how employees feel about certain management practices on the climate level. Regardless of the level involved, however, each of these interventions is intended to make members of the organization address the organization's need for change, heighten their awareness about their own patterns of behavior, and make them open to the change process.

Exercise 2. Resistance to Change

Objective. To identify and explore the common elements of resistance to change on either the personal or organizational level.

Procedures

1. Ask the students to identify a change effort in which they have been personally involved.
   (a) On the organizational level, this could mean a family move to a new community, a move to a new home, an organizational restructuring on the job, a family divorce, and so on.
   (b) On the personal level, this could mean losing weight, stopping smoking, changing majors, and so on.
2. Each student should briefly note the nature of the change activity, how the resistance (if any) was evidenced, and how the resistance was managed.
3. Small groups of 3–5 students can be asked to share this information informally. They can then develop lists of the many forms of resistance and how resistance can be managed, successfully and otherwise.
4. The instructor can then develop a master list from the small groups' output.

The second step, *movement,* involves making the actual changes that will move the organization to another level of response. On the individual level we would expect to see individuals behaving differently, perhaps demonstrating new skills or new supervisory practices. On the structural level, we would expect to see changes in actual organizational structures, reporting relationships, and reward systems that affect how people do their work. Finally, on the climate or interpersonal style level, we would expect to see patterns of behavior indicating greater interpersonal trust and openness and fewer dysfunctional interactions.

The final, *refreezing* stage of the change process involves the stabilization or institutionalization of these changes—through the establishment of systems that make these behavioral patterns "relatively secure against change" (Lewin, 1958). This refreezing stage may involve redesigning the organization's recruitment process to assure that individuals who share the organization's new management style and value system are more likely to be selected. During the refreezing stage, the organization may also ensure that the new behaviors have become the operating norms of work; that the reward system actually reinforces those behaviors; or that there is a new, more participative management style predominating.

According to Lewin (1958), achieving lasting organizational change involves dealing with resistance to change through initially unblocking the present system. This unblocking usually involves some kind of confrontation (Beckhard, 1969) or retraining process. Then there must be planned behavior changes in the desired direction. Finally, deliberate steps need to be taken to cement these changes in place in order to make them semipermanent until the next cycle of change occurs.

Managing Change

The process of change, unfortunately, is not a smooth one, even if one is attentive to Lewin's (1958) model of change. Changing behavior both individually and organizationally means inhibiting habitual responses and producing new and different responses that feel awkward and unfamiliar. It is easy to slip back to the familiar and comfortable.

For example, an organization may intend to manage more participatively. But when confronting a difficult decision, it may not be possible to make a consensus decision, at least not initially. The frustration and impatience to get on with a decision can lead to the organization's early abandonment of the new management style.

In moving from a known present state to a desired future state, organizations must recognize that there is an intervening *transition* state (Beckhard & Harris, 1987) that requires careful management, especially when the planned organization change is large and complex. An important part of this change management is recognizing and accepting the disorganization and temporarily lowered effectiveness that characterize the transition state. Managing these organizational changes may mean using a transition management team composed of a broad cross-section of members of the organization to heighten involvement. Other techniques include using multiple interventions rather than just one (Burke, Clark, & Koopman, 1984), keeping the system open to feedback about the change process, and using symbols and rituals to mark significant achievements.

Organization Development (OD)

Like individuals or families, organizations frequently find themselves in need of help, especially when instituting change. Sometimes they need specific content experts—people who can do things that present employees either cannot do or do not have the time to do, such as design a cafeteria-style benefits program or conduct a market research study. (Such experts are readily available, as a perusal of your local Yellow Pages under "Consultants" will quickly reveal.) Often, however, the organization's problems are not so quickly sorted out. The organization can identify certain dysfunctional behaviors—such as conflict; absenteeism; low productivity; and, particularly, all sorts of difficulties in managing the change process. Here the need is to look beyond the symptoms of organizational distress and seek the root cause in the traditional clinical diagnostic model.

Organization development (OD) was initially a special kind of organizational consultation process (Burke, 1982, 1987) aimed at uncovering such root causes and generally facilitating organizational change. In the organizational assessment and diagnostic phase of the OD process, OD consultants typically collect data using interviews and questionnaires as well as direct observations, and then provide the client organization with feedback on its throughput processes (especially its internal human interactions) based on those data. Finally, in the intervention phase OD consultants use training, structural changes, role negotiations, team building (Dyer, 1987), and process consultation (Schein, 1969) to facilitate change.

Process consultation—the unique OD intervention—involves the consultant's examining the pattern of communications in an organization. This is done most often through direct observation of staff meetings and, at opportune times, through raising questions or making observations about what has been transpiring. The role of the process consultant is to be counternormative—that is, to ask why others never seem to respond to Eve's questions, or why no one ever challenges Fred's remarks when he is clearly off target. Generally speaking, process consultation is intended to identify the true quality of the emperor's new clothes, even when everybody pretends that they are quite elegant.

Argyris (1970) specified three criteria for OD consultants in facilitating organizational change: (a) valid and useful information, (b) informed choice, and (c) internal commitment. By the first criterion, Argyris means that the information the OD consultant has collected and fed back to the client system accurately reflects the feelings, attitudes, and concerns of the organization's members and the changes they would like to see. The second criterion means that the members of the organization, not the consultant, choose what to do about the data, explore the meaning of the data and its implications, and decide how to proceed. The third criterion means that there is commitment to that planned course of action by the members of the organization. OD interventions that meet Argyris's criteria comprise a set of actions or interventions based on the understandings and technologies of social psychology and organizational behavior that are undertaken to improve organizational effectiveness, especially in the management of change.

OD and management. Although OD started as the application by consultants of theory from psychology and organizational behavior, the general management literature and management practices have now adopted many of the concepts, methods, and values inherent in the work of these consultants (Beer & Walton, 1987), a state of affairs that has been greatly aided by the popular writings of Peters and Waterman (1982) and others. Managers now talk about their organizations as open systems (Waldbaum, 1987) and acknowledge the importance and nature of leadership and of organizational culture. Further, managers themselves now design innovative plants, manage participatively, collaborate with unions, use task forces on special projects, and hold off-site team building sessions. As a result, OD consultants now often find themselves in the role of supporting the changes initiated by managers rather than initiating the changes themselves.

Changing world economic conditions require a higher level of commitment from employees for organizational success. Hackman (1986) suggested that this pressure for commitment has led at least some organizations and their managers to shift from a top-down management control process to an employee "self-management" process. This process of self-management, according to Hackman's review, leads to significant increases in work-unit effectiveness in terms of unit productivity, problem-solving capacity, and work-related contribution to individual growth and personal well-being.

The research evidence. What do we know about the impact of these OD interventions on organizations and their effectiveness? In the past few years, the research literature has shown a sharp improvement in both research design and methodological rigor, especially in the development of "hard criteria" such as productivity and quality indices (Nicholas, 1982; Nicholas & Katz, 1985). The findings have been surprisingly positive.

For example, Katzell and Guzzo (1983) reviewed over 200 intervention studies and reported that 87% presented evidence of significant increases in worker productivity as a result of the intervention. Guzzo, Jette, and Katzell's (1985) meta-analysis of 98 of these same studies revealed increases in productivity averaging almost half a standard deviation, impressive enough "to be visible to the naked eye" (p. 289).

The picture with respect to employee satisfaction, however, is not so clear. A different meta-analysis by Macy, Izumi, Hurts, and Norton (1986) of the effects of OD interventions on both performance measures and employee work satisfaction found positive effects on performance but *negative* effects on attitudes, perhaps because of the pressure experienced from the new work group norms about productivity. The positive effects on performance, however, are in keeping with the bulk of prior research. A recent comprehensive review of the entire field of OD (Sashkin & Burke, 1987) concluded, "There is little doubt that, when applied properly, OD has substantial positive effects in terms of performance measures" (p. 215). Thus, it would appear that OD, which began as a values-based effort to improve the workplace and to develop more effective organizations, seems to be more effective with the latter than the former—a matter of concern to some OD practitioners.

Other Approaches to the Workplace

Although OD is probably the most widespread and best understood of the various approaches to understanding the workplace, there are three others that deserve consideration at this juncture, albeit briefly. These are (a) sociotechnical systems approaches, (b) quality circles, and (c) quality of work life. All are based on an open-systems model, at least to some extent. These three approaches may be specialized forms of OD, or OD may be some derivative form of one or more of them. Each of these represents yet another attempt both to describe and to change the social psychology of the workplace.

Sociotechnical systems (STS) approach. One such social psychological approach to understanding and changing the workplace is through sociotechnical systems (STS) thinking (Barko & Passmore, 1986). The STS approach came about through Trist's pioneering work at the Tavistock Institute (Trist & Bamforth, 1951). Trist studied what happened when coal mining procedures in certain British mines were changed. Under the traditional methods, coal was mined by closely knit teams, each made up typically of six workers who were responsible for digging, loading, and excavating the coal from the mine face. The change in mining procedure involved shifting to a "long wall" from the traditional "short wall"; instead of the cohesive leaderless team, the new procedure used a production line of 40 to 50 workers under a single supervisor. Overall productivity declined sharply and miners became severely alienated from their work as the interface between the technical and social aspects of the job was disrupted.

STS concerns itself with enhancing the match between the human organization and its technology while maintaining congruence with the external environment. In contrast, OD typically focuses on enhancing the interface between various human systems, again while maintaining congruence with the external world. Both approaches are concerned with facilitating organizational effectiveness, but each focuses on a different aspect of that process.

The STS approach assumes that allowing work groups greater control over their own activities—especially in linear, sequential tasks using stable technologies, such as those on the factory assembly line—will increase both worker productivity and satisfaction. STS thinking also applies to "white-collar factories," where the raw materials are forms or data rather than physical materials. The specific STS techniques are autonomous or semiautonomous work groups, job rotation, job enlargement, and group-based pay for productivity. There are new, as yet unevaluated attempts at applying STS thinking to other work settings such as health care, computer operations, and service organizations (Barko & Passmore, 1986).

Unlike Scientific Management (F. W. Taylor, 1911), which aimed at breaking down mass production jobs into their simplest components, STS aims at combining jobs into less specialized and less monotonous ones that add variety to work and facilitate communications within the work group. However, both the Scientific Management and STS approaches have the same goal: effective, productive workers. J. C. Taylor (1986) in reviewing the history of the use of autonomous work groups highlighted both their success and their longevity in a variety of work settings, including cotton-weaving mills, coal mines, and continuous-process petrochemical factories. Thus, STS represents yet another way to apply social psychological insights and technology to understanding and improving the workplace.

Quality circles (QCs). Yet another popular approach to improving organizational effectiveness, especially in increasing productivity and quality, are quality circles (QCs). Although QCs are not based specifically on social psychological theory, they clearly represent changes in the social psychology of the workplace and need to be examined from that perspective.

In the United States, QCs are small voluntary groups of workers (3 to 15 in number) that meet regularly to identify and solve job-related problems, especially those that affect productivity or quality. Although QCs are seen largely as a Japanese management tool, they are in fact the invention of an American, Edward Deming, who was unable to interest his employer, the Ford Motor Company, in his innovation but was quite successful in this enterprise in post-World War II Japan. The QC concept was reimported to the U.S. in the early 1970s. By 1980, more than 500 large American corporations had adopted QCs as a management strategy (Ferris & Wagner, 1985). More recently, however, there has been some disillusionment with QCs and their effectiveness as well as an awareness of some intrinsic issues in their usage in American organizations. Some observers of American organizations believe that QCs are yet another management fad whose time has come and gone.

QCs involve three major psychological assumptions: (a) Participation enhances productivity in and of itself, (b) workers desire such participation, and (c) groups outperform individuals in identifying and solving problems. Ferris and Wagner (1985) seriously questioned each of these assumptions. Their review of the QC research literature led them to conclude that participation affects productivity only when there are clear-cut implementation processes in place. American workers often resist participation because their inputs have been rejected regularly in the past. There are also many situations in which individuals do better at identifying and solving problems than groups do. Ferris and Wagner go on to point out that Japanese QCs are both mandatory and part of the Japanese collective management practices (and society in general). In contrast, American QCs operate under more individually focused American management and society. I would add that although QCs empower workers, they reduce the status and power of first-level supervisors who believe their jobs are at risk through QCs and may therefore tend to sabotage the QCs' work. Until these issues are addressed in both the design and implementation of QCs, their utility as instruments to improve organizational effectiveness will remain limited.

Quality of work life (QWL). Although increasingly popular in the management literature, quality of work life (QWL) remains a somewhat diffuse, fuzzy concept. Nadler & Lawler (1983) highlighted six different meanings of QWL that have evolved over time:

(1) QWL was first used for organization change research as a *dependent variable,* primarily based on some measure(s) of worker satisfaction;

(2) QWL was next used as an *approach* to improving labor-management relationships through collaboration on working conditions;

(3) QWL then became an umbrella concept for all organizational improvement *methods,* including OD, QCs, and STS-based interventions;

(4) later, QWL signified a *social movement* (Faucheux, Amado, & Laurent, 1982) based on humanistic values such as industrial democracy, full employment, participative management, individual personal growth, and intrinsic ennobling characteristics of work;

(5) QWL then became so general a concept that it encompassed *everything;* and

(6) finally, QWL became so diffuse a concept that it meant *nothing.*

Nadler and Lawler (1983) went on to suggest that QWL is best seen as a "way of thinking about people, work, and organizations. Its distinctive elements are (1) a concern about the impact of work on people as well as on organizational effectiveness, and (2) the idea of participation in organizational problem solving and decision making" (p. 26). The four specific organization-wide activities they include under their definition are (a) participative problem solving (rather than "participative management"); (b) work restructuring, including job enrichment, autonomous work groups, and other STS-based changes; (c) innovative reward systems, such as the Scanlon Plan and other gain-sharing plans that distribute some of the financial benefits of change among workers; and (d) work environment improvements, including such programs as flextime and improvement of the work site.

The definitional confusion surrounding QWL has helped to highlight the two independent values that underlie most organizational change efforts: organizational effectiveness (the "bottom line") and worker satisfaction (humanism). As noted above, these are largely independent outcomes and one does not necessarily lead to the other. An organization needs to choose the desired outcome and to be certain that the intervention chosen is most likely to lead to that result, although both affect the organizational culture.

Organizational Culture

The enormous growth of interest over the past few years in organizational culture on the part of both line managers and organizational theorists is a heartening sign of the growing acceptance of social psychological approaches to understanding (and changing) the workplace. The best-selling *In Search of Excellence* (Peters & Waterman, 1982) has provided a new and widely accepted way of understanding, managing, leading, and changing the culture of organizations, despite its limitations as a research study (Carroll, 1983).

Definitional Issues

If we are to understand this subject fully, however, there are two kinds of definitions of organizational culture that need to be identified and clarified. The first defines an organization's culture in terms of what is directly observable—the pattern of behaviors and artifacts prevalent in the organization, or "the way we do things around here" (Deal & Kennedy, 1982). The second definition is the ideational or embedded one that defines an organization's culture in terms of the basic assumptions and beliefs widely held by its members regarding human nature, the way of the world, and so on (Schein, 1985). According to Schein, these assumptions manifest themselves as values on the observable level—values about the way things "ought to be." These values in turn lead to behavioral patterns and artifacts that may or may not be interpretable. Regardless of which definition we use, the observable behaviors must be interpreted if they are to be understood and ordinarily do call for speculation about basic, underlying assumptions and beliefs. These speculations can be risky and

the future of "culture" as a useful organizational concept is yet unclear.

To illustrate how such basic assumptions can affect organizational culture, let us consider the basic assumption about the natural competitiveness of human nature. An assumption that competition is inherent in human nature will produce values about the positive consequences of direct confrontation ("We don't pull our punches around here") and the negative consequences of cooperation ("Nice guys come in last"). Such values, in turn, will lead to a combative interpersonal style, a macho corporate image, and a self-protective posture. Sathe (1983) developed a helpful manager's guide to understanding and managing the corporate culture; Schall (1983) applied a communications-rule strategy for analyzing organizational culture; and Martin, Feldman, Hatch, and Sitkin (1983) provided a schema for script and content analysis of the stories organizations tell about themselves. The use of such structured processes can go a long way to reduce the inherent unreliability of speculations about basic underlying assumptions.

Exercise 3. Rites and Rituals

Objective. To apply the concept of the functions of rites in organizational life to the students' experience.

Procedures

1. The instructor reviews the Beyer and Trice (1987) typology of organizational rites.
2. Each student is then asked to identify one campus rite illustrative of each of Beyer and Trice's types.
3. These illustrations are then shared by students in small groups, who then select the most notable example for each type.
4. The instructor surveys the small groups; posts the various illustrations; and offers some additional ones, perhaps from faculty life.

Beyer and Trice (1987) developed a useful typology for understanding an organization through its rites. They identify six major types of rites:

(1) *passage,* to facilitate people in transitioning into new roles, such as going through boot camp;

(2) *degradation,* to dissolve social identities and their power, such as "drumming out" a disgraced military officer;

(3) *enhancement,* to heighten the status of social identities and their power, such as university commencement ceremonies;

(4) *renewal,* to refurbish social structures and improve their functioning, such as off-site management meetings;

(5) *conflict reduction,* to manage conflict and aggression, such as collective bargaining to manage union-management differences; and

(6) *integration,* to increase bonding among organizational members and commit them to the system, such as the annual office picnic or Christmas party.

These six widespread rites in organizations have both their intended and accidental consequences and provide a convenient access point for understanding and managing organizational cultures.

Variations in Cultures

The strength of organizational cultures refers to how strongly the members of an organization hold certain basic assumptions. The changeability of an organization's culture appears to be a function of its strength, and this needs to be assessed before mounting any change effort (Wilkins & Ouchi, 1983). Furthermore, large, complex organizations frequently have several subcultures, even if there is a dominant overall culture. Marketing, production, research and development (R & D) are likely to differ from each other and from finance and corporate headquarters. R & D and finance units may both hold the dominant organization's basic assumptions about some subjects, but R & D will value innovation whereas finance will value "doing it by the numbers." Martin and Siehl (1983) provided a fascinating analysis of several of the subcultures (including a counter-culture) that exist in an organization with a dominant overall culture—General Motors.

Organizational cultures differ in function over the life cycle of the organization (Schein, 1985). For a young organization, the culture is something to be nurtured, especially if it can be made into a competitive advantage. Schein (1983) provided an interesting analysis of the role of the entrepreneurial founder in creating an organization's culture. For a mature organization, its culture can be a barrier to change and innovation; and for a declining organization, its culture may prevent a humane demise. The change strategies for each of these stages will differ. For instance, to change a mature organization that needs to innovate to survive in a more competitive environment, multiple leverage points for change are required (see the case illustration below).

Each organizational culture also needs to be regarded as a subculture of the industry in which it operates and of the total national culture. Much has been made in the recent past of the need for American industry to adopt Japanese management practices. However, Marsland and Beer (1983) pointed out that Japan's superior performance is a result of the match between its management concepts and its traditional culture. They recommended instead that

American management adopt practices that match our societal culture, which is more open and egalitarian, less hierarchical, and more consultative. Thus, as I noted above, quality circles, if they are to succeed, need to take into account the greater individualism, the lesser commitment to consensus building, and the changed role of first-line supervisors—circumstances that are typically American.

Exercise 4. Collegiate Subcultures

Objective. To understand and apply the concept of collegiate subcultures.

Procedures

1. Assume that there are four undergraduate collegiate subcultures:
   (a) *Academic,* marked by an interest in ideas and concepts, a concern for scholarship, and a commitment to the traditional academic values;
   (b) *Vocational,* marked by an interest in the "real world," pragmatism, and concern about how collegiate learning leads to success after graduation;
   (c) *Collegiate,* marked by participating in the social scene, engaging fully in collegiate extracurricular activities, and using college as an opportunity to "grow up"; and
   (d) *Nonconformist,* marked by an interest in political and social radicalism and a rejection of most conventional wisdom and traditional values.
2. The instructor initially presents a brief lecture on these four subcultures and asks the students to rank order the four in terms of the degree to which each dominates their campus. Then the students identify which subculture(s) they belong to.
3. The instructor then polls the class and creates an overall ranking. The faculty subculture and how it overlaps with the academic subculture is worthy of comment.

National cultures differ in their basic assumptions about the role of work itself in human life, and naturally these assumptions influence the workplace. All cultures recognize, at least implicitly, that a balance needs to be struck between work and nonwork life in terms of time, energy, and commitment. This balance is dramatically different in the three societies in which I have work experience—Japan, Great Britain, and the United States. The balance in Japan is very much in favor of work, especially for men of the managerial class. These men leave the house early in the morning, often 6 days a week, usually returning late in the evening after their families have had dinner. For Japanese men the dominant reference group is the company and the family is a distant second (Marsland & Beer, 1983). In Great Britain, the balance is different, with the family typically winning by a narrow margin. Having tea breaks, being home in time for dinner, taking holidays with the family, and not allowing work to intrude into family life are characteristic of the British, even of managers and executives. And the United States is somewhere in between, as our norms vary depending upon the industry and the geographical location. There are important lessons here for both adopting the management practices of other cultures and for exporting ours.

The American culture continues to be a fluid one. Over a dozen years ago, Yankelovich (1974) pointed out that American culture was changing with regard to the work ethic. Among the changes noted were a definition of success that includes self-realization and fulfillment; a reduced fear of economic insecurity; a less rigid division of labor between the sexes; and a growing psychology of "entitlement" to a variety of rights, such as full employment and job security. These changes in the American culture, together with (or perhaps because of) such demographic changes as a more native-born, better educated work force with a longer life span, are factors underlying the need for organizational change and have given rise to the concerns of today's organizational leaders with the organizational change process.

Culture and Climate

In this context, it is worthwhile to differentiate organizational culture from organizational climate. As we have seen, culture is a deep construct, always involving an attempt to understand what lies below the observable pattern of behaviors. Climate, on the other hand, refers to the more transient interpersonal or social "weather." Climate encompasses both the formal policies and informal norms that characterize peer and subordinate-superior relationships in an organization and how these relationships are experienced by organizational members—that is, how these relationships make them feel about the organization. Measuring climate typically involves asking organizational members to evaluate their work group along such dimensions as openness, trust, and respect. Climate is most often subsumed as an element of culture, although it has been used as a synonym for this as well. I find it useful to differentiate the two concepts.

The concept of organizational culture should prove to be a useful as well as a popular one for I/O psychologists as they attempt to understand and change the social psychology of the workplace. But this concept has other implications as well.

Applying the Concept of Culture

The widespread and growing acceptance of the concept of organizational culture will have significant effects on how I/O psychologists fulfill their roles, including their more traditional aspects. There will be an expansion and redefinition of the most common I/O roles of selection and training. In addition, some new roles—facilitating the management of mergers and acquisitions, creating programs of career development and pathing, examining succession planning, and facilitating strategic planning—will be created or enhanced.

Selection

The most traditional and best-understood role of I/O psychology has been in the organizational-entry process. The I/O psychologist has been largely a personnel selection specialist, selecting new employees based on careful job analyses and valid psychometric candidate appraisals and thus assuring that only the most skilled candidates are selected.

The traditional personnel function, however, has been broadened and renamed human resources management. This enhanced function is responsible for much of the monitoring and management of the organizational culture. The selection function has been broadened as well and is now seen as one aspect of a process of organizational entry where more than skills need to be considered; how well the person "fits" the organization becomes an important consideration.

The notion of "fit" raises several difficulties. It is not entirely clear what fit entails: Ability? Skill? Potential? Shared values with present members of the organization? In what degree and in what combination? If an organization only hires people who fit, it may find itself locked into today's reality rather than staffed for tomorrow's needs. Although the argument that matching the person to the organization is an attractive one, it is also not without its dangers.

Line managers are becoming increasingly aware that a competent, motivated work force can provide their organization with a competitive advantage, a major plus in today's economic environment. As a recent *Fortune* article (Dumaine, 1987) put it, "Hire smart, [that is] . . . make sure the candidate's style fits with your corporate culture" (p. 80), among other things. While the prescription is a sensible one, it is a difficult one to fill given our current technology for assessing both the culture and the candidates. Although Dumaine suggests that the quality of the fit can be assessed through the interview process (particularly if there is a series of independent interviews with different people), the research on the reliability and the validity of interviews would leave most I/O psychologists skeptical (Dunnette & Borman, 1979; Tenopyr & Oeltjen, 1982).

Another new aspect of selection is human resource planning, which involves developing the processes through which an organization can meet future human resources requirements based on both the strategic plan of the organization and changes in the external environment (Zedeck & Cascio, 1984). This means that the I/O psychologist must be actively involved in developing both the strategic plan and its consequent action programs if these human resources requirements are to be understood and met. Pfeiffer, Goodstein, and Nolan (1986) provided a potentially useful guide for such involvement. Nevertheless, the demands of human resource planning pose important practical questions, and much development in this regard still needs to be done.

Human resource planning will frequently require finding a work force that differs in significant ways from an organization's present work force. A rather unmotivated, bureaucratic group of employees may require a sizable infusion of hard-driving risk takers if the organization's new and ambitious goals are to be achieved. Producing such a change in the work force is often difficult given the attraction-selection-attrition cycle (Schneider, 1985) of most personnel selection processes, whereby certain kinds of people are attracted to and selected by an organization and leave if they do not fit in. Developing selection procedures for this new breed of employees does not easily accommodate the traditional selection model.

Nevertheless, candidates will be screened and some will be selected for employment. Then comes the induction phase of the transition—"breaking in" from being an outsider to being an insider.

Socialization

As new members enter organizations, several processes occur. The recruitment process itself is part of the socialization process because it provides individuals with their first glimpse of the organization. As both the individual and the organization move from the "mutual selling" phase of recruiting and selection to the individual's actually beginning the job, a new employee may experience "reality shock" (Jones, 1983) as many of the ambiguities about the new job are resolved. The orientation process (both formal and informal); the initial job assignment, including the work unit to which the employee is assigned; and early on-the-job training are all socialization processes that influence how readily and well the new employee fits in and how he or she experiences the job choice after having joined up.

From his review of the research on occupational entry, Wanous (1977) concluded that the accuracy of information held by outsiders about the organization that they are joining tends to be low, and that the expectations of these outsiders are almost always inflated. As individuals learn more about the organization, their views of it become less favorable, with this drop in favorability continuing for over a year.

Newcomers to organizations regularly confront discrepancies between their expectations and the realities of the situation (Wanous, 1977; Jones, 1983). Current members of the organization of course respond to the newcomers' efforts to make sense of the situation, which influences the newcomers' understanding of and integration into the organization as well as their commitment to it and their eventual success in it. Jones insisted, however, that this is an interactive process and that the newcomer is not simply molded by these socialization pressures.

One way to manage these discrepancies between expectations and realities is through Realistic Job Previews (RJPs). RJPs attempt to increase the amount and accuracy of the information typically given to job applicants, including providing films or videotapes of the workers engaged in the job as well as data about what current job incumbents like and dislike about it (Tenopyr & Oeltjen, 1982). RJPs remove discussions of the job requirements from the selection interview (where the mutual selling process often predominates) and provide more valid information about the job itself than the employment interviewer is likely to have. The use of RJPs appears to soften newcomers' "reality shock" and consistently lessens turnover among organizational newcomers (Tenopyr & Oeltjen, 1982; Wanous, 1977). A meta-analysis of 21 empirical studies of RJPs by Premack and Wanous (1985) concluded that RJPs

> appear to lower initial expectations about a job and an organization, to increase the number of candidates who drop out of further consideration for a job, to increase initial levels of organizational commitment and job satisfaction slightly, to increase job performance (for audiovisual RJPs), and to increase job survival. (p. 712)

These observations provide strong support for the use of RJPs as an integral part of job socialization.

Training

Traditionally, training in most organizations has meant cross-training in diverse areas such as sales, safety, management, and machine operations. Both Goldstein (1980) and Wexley (1984) highlighted the need to consider each and every specific training program (including skills training) as a process that occurs in an organizational context or culture. If the organizational culture is not taken into account in designing and delivering the training programs, employee or management suspicions and resistance are likely to interfere, which can lead to program failure.

Many business organizations have management training programs for new university graduates intended both to teach participants the many facets of the organization's operations by a rotation through a range of activities (a kind of internship) and to socialize them in the organization's management culture. In a study of the graduates from two such programs in Great Britain, Hebden (1986) found an increasing gap over time between the graduates' expectations and the realities that they were experiencing. This gap existed because the supervisors of these graduates did not share the values the training programs had attempted to develop or enhance. In another context, I have described the design of a highly successful management training program intended to hand down organizational cultural values—a "boot camp" for new managers (Goodstein, 1979). The success of this program, which is still operational today—almost 10 years later—and has itself become part of the organizational culture, is largely attributable to the involvement of senior managers of that organization in both the design and delivery of the program, a process that ensured that the program reflected an organizational context.

The process of organizational socialization through training is an important one, one probably better understood by Marine Corps drill sergeants, directors of monastic religious orders, and fraternity and sorority pledge masters than by most psychologists. As we view the entry process into organizations and the role of training in that process, we need to become both more sensitive to and more knowledgeable about these issues of socialization to an organizational culture.

Cross-Cultural Issues

Organizations often grow through mergers and acquisitions. Considerable attention to the financial strength, market position, management capability, and other tangible aspects of the other organization is always part of the merger or acquisition process. Rarely is any attention given to the culture of the other organization and how it will match that of the acquirer or merger partner. Yet a cultural mismatch is probably even a greater risk than that posed by any of the tangible factors. Given the differences among the cultures of various organizations, what happens when two organizations merge, or one acquires another and there is such a cultural mismatch? Lefko (1987) averred that more than half of these mergers and acquisitions fail primarily because of the clash between the two discrepant cultures and the inability of the management group to manage differences between the two.

For example, the acquisition of the Fireman's Fund Insurance Company by American Express failed largely on this basis. American Express, a financial services company, acquired Fireman's Fund, an old-line casualty liability company, in order to fill a gap in its product line. But American Express did not take into account that its aggressive, high-growth, short-term focus was incongruent with the traditional, conservative, long-term focus of the casualty insurance industry generally and Fireman's Fund in particular. Despite its best efforts to integrate Fireman's Fund into its operation, American Express divested itself of the other firm within a year after the acquisition.

As organizations look to mergers and acquisitions as a way of operating more efficiently and profitably in a highly competitive marketplace, they will need to become increasingly sensitive to the issues of differences in organizational cultures and how to manage them. The management of these differences has recently become a new venue for the practice of I/O psychology. For example, in the recent merger of two major computer companies—Burroughs and Sperry into Unisys—I/O psychologists were prominently involved in creating and facilitating transition task forces for various organizational functions, such as accounting and marketing. These task forces were made up of members of each function from both Burroughs and Sperry. Each task force served to develop a new organizational structure for its function and also to reduce the ambiguity and uncertainty that typically demoralizes organizations during a merger (Uttal, 1986). The large-scale involvement of a broad cross-section of both organizations was intended to increase understanding of and commitment to the merger. Although it is still too early to tell about the merger's success, the Unisys example reflects an increased awareness of these issues of organizational culture within organizational management.

There is also a growing tendency among business organizations, both American and foreign, to develop internationally through establishment of foreign subsidiaries. When organizations expand overseas, similar cross-cultural problems can arise. As I noted earlier, an organization's culture partially reflects the national culture in which it exists. R. H. Hall (1977) reviewed the literature in this area and concluded that "the culture of the system surrounding an organization has a major impact on the way the organization operates" (p. 310). Cross-cultural understanding is a necessity for organizations that operate transnationally.

Fortunately, there seems to be more awareness of the role of cross-cultural differences across national boundaries than within them, perhaps because of the clear language differences between many countries. Even so, in a survey of 105 American companies operating abroad, only one-third had any sort of formal training programs to prepare individuals for overseas work (Wexley, 1984). On the individual level, such training must go beyond language skills to include a clear awareness of how each of us (and our organizations) is culturally bound. On the organizational level, there are great difficulties in exporting management practices from one country to another; recall the earlier discussion about QCs, which need to be modified to fit the new soil into which they are to be implanted.

Exercise 5. Mergers

Objective. To apply the concept of subculture differences and the issues involved in organizational mergers to the students' own experience.

Procedures

1. The instructor explains that each of us carries with us expectations about how things are to be done. When we interact over an extended period with others who have different expectations about these same things, these differences in expectations must be managed.
2. Making new friends, entertaining a foreign visitor, moving in with a new roommate, and getting married are all common examples of individual "mergers" and are prototypical of the issues involved in organizational mergers. The individual differences may involve time management, eating preferences and schedules, holiday celebrations, and so on.
3. Each student should identify at least one such situation from his or her own experience and make notes on the specific differences that emerged and how these differences were managed over time.
4. Small groups of students share their experiences informally and the instructor elicits some especially noteworthy examples for additional discussion.

Torrence (1984) documented the issues involved in translating the Japanese concepts of lifetime employment and wages based on seniority to a new Kawasaki Motors plant operation in Nebraska. These concepts, which are functional in highly disciplined and culturally homogeneous Japan, simply were not directly exportable to nonconforming, heterogeneous American society. In order to avoid unionism, Kawasaki had to modify its management policies to include an equitable wage and salary system based on both seniority and merit. The company also had to increase job security through cross-training and community-relations activities and to establish a communications system that was more open than is typical in Japanese industrial units. Any such movement by an organization across national boundaries must consider the impact of the culture of the host country on the move, plan accordingly, and continue to carefully monitor what happens to the organization when crossing cultural boundaries.

Organizational Career Development

As the concept of organizational culture was accepted and human resource management systems became an integral part of organizational life, a concern with the career development process in organizations emerged. Preservation of the organizational culture requires a stable work force. Achieving this is facilitated by a career development process that allows individual needs for personally satisfying and productive work to be blended with the organization's needs for qualified people to meet present and future job requirements.

Career development thus involved *career planning* by individuals and *career management* by organizations (D. T. Hall, 1986). Years ago, psychologists (especially counseling psychologists) focused on the early stages of career planning, particularly the career exploration phase. Career issues throughout the life span have become integrated into counseling psychology fairly recently (Osipow, 1986). A burgeoning interface between counseling and I/O psychology has been fostered by the development of organizational career development programs in many companies (D. T. Hall & Associates, 1986).

Elements of career development programs. Organizational career development programs have involved employees at all levels of the organization, from hourly workers to top executives. Organizations have developed rather different career development programs, targeting specific employee groups and intending to address diverse organizational issues. In general, four different programmatic elements have been involved, singly and in every possible combination, in such efforts: (a) self-help programs, including career- and retirement-planning workshops and self-paced career workbooks; (b) individual counseling (either by internal or external staff) and outplacement; (c) internal career management systems, including internal posting of vacancies, assessment centers, and career and succession planning based on human resources forecasting; and (d) developmental programs, including job rotation, in-house courses for both skills and management development, educational reimbursement and tuition assistance, and formal mentoring.

Many of these program elements have been available in organizations for many years, including tuition assistance and management development programs. The new organizational career development process integrates career planning *and* career management in a complementary and supportive fashion to facilitate achievement of both individual and organizational goals. The development of these programs reflects a growing awareness by many organizations of the critical importance of their human resources. This alone often represents a massive change in the organization's culture.

Two of these programmatic elements are worthy of special attention: succession planning and formal mentoring. Both have important psychological aspects but have been relatively ignored by psychologists (House & Singh, 1987).

Succession planning. Succession planning involves the identification and grooming of successors for present job incumbents, typically for jobs at the top levels of the organization. This is an attempt by the organization to recognize the critical importance of certain key organizational members to the success of the organization and the continuity of its culture. Organizations thus develop plans for the orderly replacement of such persons when they retire and have a backup strategy in the case of an unplanned resignation, sudden illness, or death. This is especially important in view of the high degree of mobility of these key people.

Most organizations have some kind of succession plan, but it often is one of the most private issues in the organization and never discussed publicly. The open identification of a successor—the appointment of a "crown prince"—is rare, but there is much speculation within organizations about what is obvious: the grooming process. Such grooming may involve special appointments, titles, and schooling, as well as involvement in work that is ordinarily not part of that person's usual job. The secrecy surrounding such succession planning makes research in this area difficult.

In their summary of the available research on executive succession, House and Singh (1987) concluded that the match among the personal and professional characteristics of the successor, the organization, and the organization's environment is critical to the future success of that person. I would add that the relationship between the incumbent and the successor is equally important, particularly the degree to which there is mentoring.

Mentoring. Mentoring is the relationship between a junior and a senior colleague that contributes to the career development of the junior person. Although older people in organizations have taken younger people "under their wing" for generations, within the last few years mentoring has become a subject of strong interest among both managers and students of organizations (Kram, 1986).

In her research, Kram (1986) identified two important functions of mentoring: (a) career functions that enhance "learning the ropes" and preparing for advancement in the organization through coaching, sponsorship, and protection; and (2) psychosocial functions that provide a role model, informal counseling, acceptance and confirmation, and friendship. The psychosocial functions involve a mutually rewarding interpersonal bond, whereas the career functions are more organizationally based. In any primary mentoring relationship, both the career and the psychosocial functions must be present.

Using a variety of theories of adult and career development, most approaches to mentoring see the mentor as helping the protégé resolve the predictable development tasks of maturing both in and out of the organization. Mentoring relationships are not static ones, and most people have a variety of mentoring relationships, moving on to become mentors themselves.

Mentoring relationships are not without their problems. Individuals differ in how able they are to be intimate and supportive, how willing they are to seek or accept help and support, and how likely they are to take risks. Also, many people regard accepting help as a measure of weakness and thus pose obstacles to any potential mentors. Further, mentors often demand more loyalty from their juniors than is functional, and sometimes are reluctant to "let go" when the time comes to do so.

One perennial issue involves cross-gender mentoring, where there is often concern expressed over the increasing intimacy and sexual attraction that can develop as part of such mentoring. There also are issues of cross-gender stereotyping, problems of being female in a traditionally male-dominated work environment, and pressures from peer resentment that such cross-gender mentoring relationships produce. These added difficulties make cross-gender mentoring relationships even more fraught with problems than same-gender ones.

Despite these potential obstacles, there are now formal mentoring programs, and in some organizations with strong career development programs, managers are evaluated on their mentoring as part of the organization's formal performance appraisal system. Although we may question the wisdom of attempting to legislate what is essentially an interpersonal process, there is little doubt that the superior-subordinate relationship is one key ingredient in the dynamics of a career (Baird & Kram, 1983).

Managers at all levels in an organization have a responsibility for developing the employees they supervise (Orth, Wilkinson, & Benfari, 1987), whether or not a formal mentoring program exists. Managers *are* coaches and mentors. In these roles, they must use behavior modeling and prompt, behavior-based feedback to enhance the performance of their subordinates. Such coaching and mentoring must occur in a climate of trust and openness, one in which the supervisor is seen as committed to the subordinate and to the subordinate's development. Finally, both supervisor and subordinate should have realistic expectations about what each is expecting of the other (Baird & Kram, 1983).

Exercise 6. Mentoring

Objective. To apply the concept of mentoring to the students' own experience.

Procedures

1. Ask each student to identify someone "who took you under his or his wing." This could be a teacher, a boss, a minister, a scoutmaster, a relative, and so on.
2. Each student should then be asked to answer the following four questions about that relationship:
   (a) What specific function did your mentor perform for you?
   (b) What specific things did you provide for your mentor?
   (c) How did the relationship end, if it has?
   (d) What did you learn about yourself through this relationship?
3. The students share their responses to the questions in small groups and the instructor solicits noteworthy examples.

Organizational career development programs and other applications of the concept of organizational culture are all further evidence of the growing importance and usefulness of a social psychological approach to the workplace. To attempt to integrate many of these concepts and demonstrate their interrelationships, let us turn to a case illustration of a large-scale change effort based on this approach and its inherent technology.

Case Illustration

For the past half-dozen years I have been a consultant to British Airways (BA), a client system involved in a major organization-wide change effort—an undertaking described by Sir Colin Marshall, BA's Chief Executive, as one intended to change the organizational culture of BA. This cultural change was deemed necessary because of changes in the international airlines industry. Deregulation had heightened competition, and the Conservative Party leadership in Parliament had decided to "privatize" BA: to change BA from a governmental agency receiving a massive annual federal subsidy to a profit-making corporation with public ownership through the sale of shares on the London Stock Exchange. To sell shares at the desired price, BA first had to be made profitable.

The appointment of Sir Colin was itself a significant change in the BA culture. An outsider, he came with a marketing background and was atypical of his predecessors, all of whom were retired senior Royal Air Force officers. Sir Colin declared soon after his arrival that the strategy of BA was to become "the World's Favourite Airline." Shortly after the new strategy was announced, there was a massive reduction in the worldwide BA work force from 60,000 to 35,000. It is interesting to note that within a year after this staff reduction there was an improvement in virtually all BA performance indices—more on-time departures and arrivals, fewer out-of-service aircraft, less time "on hold" for telephone reservations, fewer lost bags, and so on.

A series of different training programs—Putting People First, Managing People First, and Leading a Service Business—was developed for BA executives and managers. The programs were all experiential and involved individual feedback to each participant about his or her behavior on the job. These training programs all had more or less the same general purpose: to identify the organization's dysfunctional management style and begin the process of developing a management style that would fit BA's new, competitive environment. In an earlier evaluation process, these managers themselves characterized BA's existing style as bureaucratic and militaristic with limited individual accountability. If the organization was to be market-driven, service-based, and profit-making, it would require an open, participative management style that would encourage employee commitment.

To support these changes, a number of internal systems at BA were changed. A new performance appraisal process was created that involved both customer service and subordinate development as key elements in fulfilling BA's new mission. The roles of the human resources staff were also changed from traditional bureaucratic personnel functions to that of internal OD consultants supporting and facilitating the change effort. A number of structural changes were also made, including the creation of many task forces with specific short-term change agendas, a reduction in the number of levels in the organizational hierarchy, and the introduction of some new computer technology for management information systems. Attention was paid to BA's symbols as well—new, upscale uniforms; refurbished aircraft; and a new corporate coat of arms.

The chaos and anger occasioned by all of this movement during the transitional phase of the change process now has largely abated and there are many signs of success. The first series of BA shares were quickly oversubscribed and appreciated over 70% during the first 6 months, bookings and revenues have significantly increased, and an effort is under way for BA to acquire its major British competitor, British Caledonia.

What should be apparent from this brief overview of a massive project is that the change process at BA was based on open-systems thinking. Both the design and implementation of this change effort relied on an understanding of the social psychology of the workplace in general and the BA workplace in particular. This was a multifaceted effort that used many leverage points to initiate and support the changes. The change process was intentionally managed with strong support from top management using transition teams with openness to feedback. There was an active management of the resistance to change using unfreezing strategies at all three levels—individual, structural and systems, and interpersonal. Virtually all the change processes that I have discussed were used in some measure, and the work continues.

Conclusion

The organizational aspect of I/O psychology differs from the industrial aspect in that its focus is on the system rather than on the individual. Working effectively at this level requires an in-depth understanding of group and organizational dynamics plus an understanding of and the skill to work on the individual level. The processes of data collection and data feedback involve many face-to-face interactions with individuals as well as with teams and groups. I have found that consulting with organizations on their planned change activities involves an integration of virtually all of the skills and knowledge of applied psychology—a process that is a continual "stretch" for me and for most of those colleagues with whom I have discussed these matters.

The organizational aspect of I/O psychology finds much of its empirical support in field studies and case reports. Few senior managers are initially interested in allowing the niceties of experimental design to be applied to a large-scale change effort in their organization. It is necessary to work hard and creatively to help such managers understand the benefits of involving an evaluation component in such organizational change programs.

I am delighted that the recent meta-analyses of much of this work have turned out to be so supportive of what we do. We need to use such reports to help convince managers that only through solid, field-based research can we determine both the direct impact of the change processes and their magnitude. Although these managers may initially believe that the best proof of the usefulness of an intervention strategy is found in their bottom line (that is, in the directly experienced positive consequences of the intervention), they can be persuaded that research and the real world are not necessarily incompatible. Their initial disinterest in research is often frustrating to those of us who were trained in this method of inquiry, but this should not prevent us from pushing for the inclusion of those research elements that do provide the basis for later data analyses.

On the other hand, to offset those frustrations, there is the delicious excitement of being involved in working with managers on issues that affect the lives and careers of large numbers of people and the success or failure of business enterprises, and actively participating in efforts to make the workplace a better place to be. For me that is a trade-off well worth making!

References

Argyris, C. (1970). *Intervention theory and method.* Reading, MA: Addison-Wesley.

Baird, L., & Kram, K. E. (1983). Career dynamics: Managing the superior/subordinate relationship. *Organizational Dynamics, 11*(4), 46–64.

Barko, W., & Passmore, W. (Eds.). (1986). Sociotechnical systems: Innovations in designing high performance systems [Special issue]. *Journal of Applied Behavioral Science, 22,* 193–360.

Beckhard, R. (1969). *Organization development: Strategies and models.* Reading, MA: Addison-Wesley.

Beckhard, R., & Harris, R. T. (1987). *Organization transitions: Managing complex change* (2nd ed.). Reading, MA: Addison-Wesley.

Beer, M., & Walton, A. E. (1987). Organization change and development. *Annual Review of Psychology, 38,* 339–367.

Benjamin, L. T., Jr., Hopkins, J. R., & Nation, J. R. (1986). *Psychology.* New York: Macmillan.

Bertalanffy, L. von (1956). General systems theory. *General systems (Yearbook of the Society for the Advancement of General Theory), 1,* 1–10.

Beyer, J. M., & Trice, H. M. (1987). How an organization's rites reveal its culture. *Organizational Dynamics, 16*(4), 5–24.

Bootzin, R. R., Bower, G. W., Zajonc, R. B., & Hall, E. (1986). *Psychology today* (6th ed.). New York: Random House.

Bramel, D., & Friend, R. (1981). Hawthorne, the myth of the docile worker, and class bias in psychology. *American Psychologist, 36,* 867–878.

Burke, W. W. (1982). *Organization development: Principles and practices.* Boston, MA: Little, Brown.

Burke, W. W. (1987). *Organization development: A normative view.* Reading, MA: Addison-Wesley.

Burke, W. W., Clark, L. P., & Koopman, C. (1984). Improving your OD project's chances of success. *Training and Development Journal, 38*(8), 62–68.

Carroll, D. T. (1983). A disappointing search for excellence. *Harvard Business Review, 61*(6), 78–88.

Coch, L., & French, J. R. P., Jr. (1948). Overcoming resistance to change. *Human Relations, 1,* 512–532.

Deal, T. E., and Kennedy, A. K. (1982). *Corporate cultures: The rites and rituals of corporate life.* Reading, MA: Addison-Wesley.

Dumaine, B. (1967, August 17). The new art of hiring smart. *Fortune,* pp. 78–81.

Dunnette, M. D., & Borman, W. C. (1979). Personnel selection and classification systems. *Annual Review of Psychology, 30,* 477–525.

Dyer, W. G. (1987). *Team building: Issues and alternatives* (2nd ed.). Reading, MA: Addison-Wesley.

Faucheux, C., Amedo, G., & Laurent, A. (1982). Organization development and change. *Annual Review of Psychology, 33,* 343–370.

Ferris, G. R., and Wagner, J. A. (1985). Quality circles in the United States: A conceptual reevaluation. *Journal of Applied Behavioral Science, 21*(2), 155–185.

Goldstein, I. L. (1980). Training in work organizations. *Annual Review of Psychology, 31,* 229–272.

Goodstein, L. D. (1979). Maintaining the organizational culture: An experiential strategy for socializing new managers. *Group & Organizational Studies, 4*(3), 287–293.

Guzzo, R. A., Jette, R. D., & Katzell, R. A. (1985). The effects of psychologically based intervention programs on worker productivity: A meta-analysis. *Personnel Psychology, 38,* 275–291.

Hackman, J. R. (1986). The psychology of self-management in organization. In M. S. Pallak & R. O. Perloff (Eds.), *Psychology and work: Productivity, change, and employment* (pp. 85–136). Washington, DC: American Psychological Association.

Hall, D. T. (1986). Introduction: An overview of current career development theory, research and practice. In D. T. Hall & Associates (Eds.), *Career development in organizations* (pp. 1–20). San Francisco: Jossey-Bass.

Hall, D. T., & Associates. (1986). *Career development in organizations.* San Francisco: Jossey-Bass.

Hall, R. H. (1977). *Organizations: Structure and process* (2nd ed.). Englewood Cliffs, NJ: Prentice-Hall.

Hebden, J. E. (1986). Adopting an organization's culture: The socialization of graduate trainees. *Organizational Dynamics, 15*(1), 46–64.

House, R. J., & Singh, J. V. (1987). Organizational behavior: Some new directions for I/O psychology. *Annual Review of Psychology, 38,* 669–718.

Jones, G. R. (1983). Psychological orientation and the process of organizational socialization: An interactionist perspective. *Academy of Management Review, 8,* 464–474.

Katz, D., & Kahn, R. L. (1978). *Social psychology of organizations* (2nd ed.). New York: Wiley.

Katzell, R. A., & Guzzo, R. A. (1983). Psychological approaches to productivity improvement. *American Psychologist, 38,* 468–472.

Kram, K. E. (1986). Mentoring in the workplace. In D. T. Hall & Associates (Eds.), *Career development in organizations* (pp. 160–201). San Francisco: Jossey-Bass.

Lefko, M. (1987, July 20). Why so many mergers fail. *Fortune,* pp. 113–114.

Lewin, K. (1958). Group decisions and social change. In E. E. Maccoby,

T. M. Newcomb, & E. L. Hartley (Eds.), *Readings in social psychology* (pp. 97–211). New York: Holt, Rinehart & Winston.

Macy, B. A., Izumi, H., Hurts, C. C. M., & Norton, L. W. (1986, October). *Meta-analysis of United States empirical change and work innovation field experiments.* Paper presented at the meeting of the Academy of Management, Chicago.

March, J. G., & Simon, H. A. (1958). *Organizations.* New York: Wiley.

Marsland, S., & Beer, M. (1983). The evolution of Japanese management: Lessons for U.S. managers. *Organizational Dynamics, 11*(3), 49–67.

Martin, J., Feldman, M. S., Hatch, M. J., & Sitkin, S. B. (1983). The uniqueness paradox in organizational stories. *Administrative Science Quarterly, 28*, 438–453.

Martin, J., & Siehl, S. (1983). Organization culture and counter-culture: An uneasy symbiosis. *Organizational Dynamics, 11*(3), 52–64.

Meyer, J. W., & Rowan, B. (1977). Institutional organization: Formal structure as myth and ceremony. *American Journal of Sociology, 83*, 340–363.

Moch, M. K. (1980). Job involvement, internal motivation, and employee integration into networks of work relationships. *Organizational Behavior and Human Performance, 25*, 15–31.

Nadler, D., & Lawler, E. E., III. (1983). Quality of work life: Perceptions and directions. *Organizational Dynamics, 11*, 20–30.

Nicholas, J. M. (1982). The comparative impact of organization development interventions on hard criteria measures. *Academy of Management Review, 9*, 531–543.

Nicholas, J. M., & Katz, M. (1985). Research methods and reporting practices in organization development. *Academy of Management Review, 10*, 737–749.

Olsen, K. H. (1987, July 19). Learning the dangers of success: The education of an entrepreneur. *The New York Times*, p. F 2.

Orth, C. D., Wilkinson, H. E., & Benfari, R. C. (1987). The manager's role as coach and mentor. *Organizational Dynamics, 15*(4), 66–75.

Osipow, S. H. (1986). Career issues through the life span. In M. S. Pallak & R. Perloff (Eds.), *Psychology and work: Productivity, change, and employment* (pp. 137–168). Washington, DC: American Psychological Association.

Peters, T., & Waterman, R. H., Jr. (1982) *In search of excellence: Lessons from America's best-run companies.* New York: Harper & Row.

Pfeiffer, J. W., Goodstein, L. D., & Nolan, T. M. (1986). *Applied strategic planning: A how to do it guide.* San Diego, CA: University Associates.

Porter, L. W., Lawler, E. E. III, & Hackman, J. R. (1975). *Behavior in organizations.* New York: McGraw-Hill.

Premack, S. L., & Wanous, J. P. (1985). A meta-analysis of realistic job previews. *Journal of Applied Psychology, 70*, 706–719.

Ransom, S., Hinings, B., & Greenwood, R. (1980). The structuring of organizational structures. *Administrative Science Quarterly, 25*, 1–17.

Roethlisberger, F. J., & Dickson, W. J. (1939). *Management and the worker.* Cambridge, MA: Harvard University Press.

Sashkin, M., & Burke, W. W. (1987). Organization development in the 1980's. *Journal of Management, 13*, 205–229.

Sathe, V. (1983). Some action implications of the corporate culture: A manager's guide to action. *Organizational Dynamics, 12*(2), 4–23.

Schall, M. S. (1983). A communications-rule approach to organizational culture. *Administrative Science Quarterly, 28,* 557–581.

Schein, E. G. (1969). *Process consultation: Its role in organization development.* Reading, MA: Addison-Wesley.

Schein, E. H. (1983). The role of the founder in creating an organizational culture. *Organizational Dynamics, 12*(1), 13–28.

Schein, E. H. (1985). *Organizational culture and leadership.* San Francisco: Jossey-Bass.

Schneider, B. (1985). Organizational behavior. *Annual Review of Psychology, 36,* 573–611.

Schrank, R. (1978). *Ten thousand working days.* Cambridge, MA: MIT Press.

Taylor, F. W. (1911). *The principles of scientific management.* New York: Harper.

Taylor, J. C. (1986). Long-term sociotechnical change in a computer operations department. *Journal of Applied Behavioral Science, 22,* 303–314.

Tenopyr, M. L., & Oeltjen, P. D. (1982). Personnel selection and classification. *Annual Review of Psychology, 33,* 581–618.

Terkel, S. (1972). *Working.* New York: Random House.

Thayer, P. (1982). Industrial/organizational psychology: Science and application. In C. J. Scheirer & A. M. Rogers (Eds.), *The G. Stanley Hall lecture series, Vol. 3* (pp. 5–30). Washington, DC: American Psychological Association.

Torrence, W. D. (1984). Blending East and West: With difficulties along the way. *Organizational Dynamics, 13*(2), 23–34.

Trist, E. L., & Bamforth, K. W. (1951). Some social and psychological consequences of the long-wall method of coal getting. *Human Relations, 4,* 1–38.

Turnage, J. J. (1987). Coverage of I/O psychology in introductory textbooks. *The Industrial Psychologist, 25*(2), 45–51.

Uttal, B. (1986, Nov. 24). A surprisingly sexy computer marriage. *Fortune,* pp. 46–52.

Waldbaum, P. (1987, July 24). Motivate or alienate? Firms hire gurus to change their "cultures." *The Wall Street Journal,* p. 19.

Wanous, J. P. (1977). Organizational entry: Newcomers moving from outside to inside. *Psychological Bulletin, 84,* 601–618.

Weber, M. (1947). *The theory of social and economic organization* (A. M. Henderson & T. Parsons, Trans.). New York: Oxford University Press.

Wexley, K. N. (1984). Personnel training. *Annual Review of Psychology, 35,* 519–551.

Wilkins, A. T., & Ouchi, W. G. (1983). Efficient cultures: Exploring the relationship between culture and organizational performance. *Administrative Science Quarterly, 28,* 468–481.

Yankelovich, D. (1974, December). Turbulence in the working world: Angry workers, happy grads. *Psychology Today,* pp. 80–89.

Zedeck, S., & Cascio, W. F. (1984). Psychological issues in personnel decisions. *Annual Review of Psychology, 35,* 461–518.

COMPARATIVE PSYCHOLOGY: CONTEMPORARY VIGOR CONTINUES A PROUD TRADITION

D onald A. Dewsbury is a professor of psychology at the University of Florida, where he has been on the faculty since 1966. He received his AB from Bucknell University and his PhD from the University of Michigan in 1965 and was a postdoctoral fellow at the University of California, Berkeley in 1965–1966.

His research is aimed at understanding the evolution and adaptive significance of behavior with a focus on reproductive behavior in rodents. He has published over 170 scientific papers and 7 books, including *Comparative Animal Behavior* (1978), *Comparative Psychology in the Twentieth Century* (1984), and *Leaders in the Study of Animal Behavior* (1985).

Dewsbury is a past president of the Animal Behavior Society and a fellow of the Animal Behavior Society, the American Psychological Association, and the American Association for the Advancement of Science. He serves as a consulting editor for *Contemporary Psychology*, the *Journal of Comparative Psychology*, *Behavioral Ecology and Sociobiology*, and *Behavior Research Methods, Instrumentation, and Computers*.

COMPARATIVE PSYCHOLOGY: CONTEMPORARY VIGOR CONTINUES A PROUD TRADITION

I must have been almost hypnotized by the word "evolution," which was music to my ear and seemed to fit my mouth better than any other. (Hall, 1927, p. 357)

. . . many . . . studies are made under artificial and highly specialized aspects, with too little reference to the life history and habits of the species in the state of nature. (Hall, 1909, p. 253)

Although G. Stanley Hall was not a true comparative psychologist, in these two passages he laid down what were to become two of the dominant themes in comparative psychology in the 20th century: an interest in the evolution of behavior and a concern for behavior in the natural lives of animals. Beginning in 1893 at Clark

I thank George Collier and two anonymous reviewers for comments on an earlier draft of this manuscript. Original research was supported by grant BNS-8520318 from the National Science Foundation.

University, Hall annually taught a course in "Psychogenesis," in which he dealt with the origins of life, paleontological findings, animal instinct, gregariousness, and human evolution.

Although some people believe that historically comparative psychology has been confined to the study of rats in mazes, interest in evolution and the natural lives of animals has existed in this field throughout the century. I shall try to sharpen the focus of what is meant by comparative psychology, discuss some of its historical roots, and elaborate on one prevalent contemporary approach to animal behavior that has emerged within comparative psychology. I shall then discuss the broad relevance of this field and some methods of instruction in it. A dominant theme will be that as a result of concern with evolution and the natural lives of animals, a view has emerged of animals as sensitive organisms shaped by natural selection to be in tune with constraints of their environments and to behave in ways that are adaptive in those environments. Animals behave as if they were sensitive economists, shading their behavior in response to shifting costs and benefits of alternative courses of action. The ultimate currency with which these economically tuned strategy systems seem to work is the differential production of viable, fertile offspring. I believe that understanding the effects of natural selection in shaping behavior that is effective in coping with different costs and benefits is critical to a comprehensive understanding of behavior.

Concern with the natural lives of animals and with evolutionary questions has altered the way in which we think about many behavioral patterns. To consider feeding in this way leads to a new view of the costs and benefits of different foraging patterns. Different patterns of mating and parenting can be analyzed as individual males and females act to maximize levels of inclusive fitness, often in diverse social contexts. Contemporary studies are revealing that animals have capacities to make social discriminations that were not anticipated. New perspectives on the processes of development, learning, and cognition arise from analyses in relation to selective forces in the natural lives of animals. These recent developments have profoundly altered the way in which we approach many long-standing questions in animal psychology.

The material in this chapter is presented in a logical order. However, some readers may be less interested in the logical and historical basis for comparative psychology than in its dynamic present status. They may wish to skip to the material concerned with the comparative psychology of today and then return to the foundation material.

The Nature of Comparative Psychology

Comparative psychologists study the behavioral patterns of a variety of animal species, emphasizing (though not exclusively) nonhuman animals. I shall use the term *animal psychology* to encompass all studies in psychology in which nonhuman animals provide the focus. Within animal psychology, one can delineate three different, though overlapping, emphases. Each is served by a different American Psychological Association (APA) journal. Some animal psychologists emphasize the psychological correlates of behavior and are served by *Behavioral Neuroscience.* Others focus on the processes mediating behavioral plasticity and are served by the *Journal of Experimental Psychology: Animal Behavior Processes.* To quote from its inside front cover, the *Journal of Comparative Psychology* publishes "laboratory and field studies of the behavioral patterns of various species as they relate to evolution, development, ecology, control, and functional significance." Fortunately, all three of these areas in animal psychology overlap, and there is much interaction among them.

Comparative psychology lies at the interface between psychology and biology and thus can be treated as part of psychobiology. Biology is a broad discipline that includes such "whole-animal" emphases as ecology, ethology, and evolution. Not all biology is physiological. Comparative psychologists often find their closest ties to the areas of whole-animal biology.

Like ethologists, comparative psychologists tend to emphasize four classes of questions in the study of behavior (see Tinbergen, 1963). The strategy is to begin analysis with careful observation and description of the behavior of the species under study and then to deal with the four classes or sets of questions. The first set concerns immediate causation—the relatively short-term determinants of behavior, such as stimuli, schedules of reinforcement, social environment, and so on. The second set concerns development and deals with longer-term events in the lives of individual organisms, from conception through maturity to aging. These two classes may be grouped as entailing *proximate causation.* The third and fourth classes concern *ultimate causation;* analysis transcends the lives of individual organisms. Questions of evolutionary history, or phylogeny, concern the evolutionary progression leading to the behavioral pattern in question. Questions of adaptive significance or function relate to the role that behavioral patterns play in survival and reproduction. In the latter case, there is no implication that the organism needs to be cognizant of the long-term consequences of its acts; its behavior may have been shaped by the action of natural selection on past generations. A comprehensive understanding of behavior requires that all four of these classes of questions be addressed.

Comparative psychology is dynamic, diverse, and active. It would be difficult to deal with the whole field in a single chapter. Fortunately, Rumbaugh (1985) has already provided a fine G. Stanley Hall lecture with an emphasis on cognition. I shall emphasize patterns that are more instinctive and refer the reader to Rumbaugh's paper for those which are more cognitive. Further, I shall stress the analysis of the adaptive significance of behavior. This approach leads to the view of the organism as a fine-tuned economic being adapted to use effective strategies in its environment.

Historical Bases for the Contemporary View

The view that I am delineating rests on the foundation of a broad biological understanding of evolution and behavior. Many of the fundamental tenets were developed outside of psychology. However, basic principles have been applied to behavior by comparative psychologists throughout the 20th century (Dewsbury, 1984a). Material prerequisite to the development of an understanding of the organism as an adapted and economically cognizant individual includes information on the evolution of behavior, the role of genes in behavior, concern for the natural lives of animals, and the comparative method. The foundations for this modern view have been part of comparative psychology for decades. This view differs sharply from portrayals of comparative psychology as having atrophied from a lack of attention to such considerations.

The Evolution of Behavior

Darwin's theory of evolution had profound implications for psychology, for it established the likelihood of mental continuity between human and nonhuman animals. Darwin believed that psychology would become "securely based on the foundation of an evolutionary perspective" (1859, p. 373). The theory of evolution was to have the most profound impact on comparative psychology. Darwin's protege, G. J. Romanes, pioneered the field in his *Animal Intelligence* (1882) and subsequent works, with the objective "of considering the facts of animal intelligence in their relation to the theory of Descent" (p. vi). The young John B. Watson (1906) called for the establishment "of an experimental station for the study of the evolution of the mind" (p. 156). An early APA President, James Mark Baldwin (1896), proposed a mechanism that could produce revolutionary change that resembled the inheritance of acquired traits, but which was based on better-established evolutionary principles; this mechanism is still termed the "Baldwin effect."

Baldwin (1909), Hall (1909), and Angell (1909) marked the 50th anniversary of the publication of *The Origin of Species* by remarking on how profoundly the theory had affected psychology; Howard (1927) proposed that psychology be spoken of as pre-Darwinian and post-Darwinian. The tradition was carried on in C. P. Stone's (1943) APA Presidential address, in which he reviewed progress in the understanding of evolutionary principles and prophetically directed attention to the field of behavioral ecology.

Genes and Behavior

The view that behavior evolves necessarily implies that genes influence behavior; evolutionary change is the result of shifting gene frequencies. However, the notion that genes influence behavior has often been stiffly resisted in psychology. Some confuse the view that genes influence behavior with the view that genes determine behavior, as if genes could act in the absence of interaction in the environment. Others are concerned that accepting the notion of genetically based individual differences might lead to justifying differences in individual rights before the law and in society. Such should not be the case. Comparative psychologists have long been interested in behavior genetics and have provided convincing evidence that genes are one factor affecting behavior.

One of the earliest substantive contributions to this field was Robert Yerkes' *The Dancing Mouse* (1907). Yerkes studied the behavior of a line of mutant mice that displayed repeated whirling, referred to as "dancing." He analyzed many aspects of the behavior of these mice, including their sensory capacities and ability to learn, and demonstrated genetic inheritance of the trait. Stone's (1932) analysis of strain differences in savageness in rats and Calvin Hall's (1947) work on the inheritance of audiogenic seizures in house mice are early classics of behavior genetics. The best-known work is that of Tryon (1940), who conducted a long-term study of genetic selection for rats that performed well or poorly in learning to traverse a maze. After generations of selective breeding, the offspring of maze-bright rats performed much better than those of the maze-dull line. More recently, comparative psychologists analyzing genetic influences on behavior have studied such phenotypes as perceptual preferences and imprinting in Japanese quail (Kovach, 1986) and the heritability of taxes in fruit flies (Hirsch & Boudreau, 1958). As Skinner (1930) noted, "inheritance of behavioral traits is so patent that there would seem to be no necessity for an experimental demonstration of the fact" (p. 344).

The Natural Lives of Animals

Although comparative psychologists set out to analyze the minds and intelligence of animals, it soon became apparent that this could be done most effectively by understanding the behavioral patterns displayed naturally in the normal habitat of the species. Kline (1899) believed that "a careful study of the instincts, dominant traits and habits of an animal—in brief its natural history should precede as far as possible any experimental study" (p. 399). Throughout the century, studies of the natural lives of animals have held their place alongside those of learning and cognitive processes. Surely a classic is the work of the young John B. Watson, who spent three summers studying the behavior of sooty and noddy terns in the Dry Tortuga Islands off the coast of Florida. In his third summer there, Watson was joined by Karl Lashley, who would himself profoundly influence comparative and physiological psychology. Watson surveyed the status and population characteristics of the two species and studied a wide range of behavioral patterns, including eating and drinking, the nesting cycle, mating behavior, mate and egg recognition, development, orientation, and even maze learning (see Watson, 1908). It is notable that Watson, the great developer of behaviorism, was at this stage of his career doing comparative field studies of the instinctive behavior of two closely related species of birds. Work of this type would later characterize ethology, and I believe that Watson merits credit as an early proto-ethologist.

Another indication of the role of field research on the natural lives of animals in comparative psychology can be found in the development of field studies of the behavior of nonhuman primates. Yerkes initiated major activity in this endeavor by sending H. C. Bingham, Henry Nissen, and C. R. Carpenter to the field to conduct such studies. Carpenter studied howler monkeys in Panama and both orangutans and gibbons in southeast Asia; he established a permanent colony of rhesus monkeys on Cayo Santiago in Puerto Rico (see Carpenter, 1964). Carpenter is properly regarded as the father of the modern area of primate field research, an endeavor that originated in psychology.

Even the study of rats in mazes, initiated by Linus Kline and Willard Small, was begun not with the selection of an arbitrary task, but with laboratory tasks designed to resemble the runways built by feral rats (see Miles, 1930). The extent to which learning tasks ought to be designed to mimic characteristics of the natural habitat rather than to be left as arbitrary as possible has been debated throughout the century. It became a basis for disagreement between the great student of animals in puzzle boxes, E. L. Thorndike (e.g., 1899), and the founder of the first North American organization for comparative psychology, the Society for the Study of Comparative Psychology, T. Wesley Mills (e.g., 1899). Objecting to Thorndike's methods, Mills wrote, "As well enclose a living man in a coffin, lower him against his will, into the earth, and attempt to deduce normal psychology from his conduct" (p. 266).

The importance of naturalistic concerns in comparative psychology has been reiterated by modern comparative psychologists, such as D. B. Miller (1977) and B. J. LeBoeuf, who edited an entire volume dealing with the natural history of Año Nuevo Island in California (LeBoeuf & Kaza, 1981).

Species Comparisons

Although species comparisons are of obvious importance in comparative psychology, I would argue that many studies in which no such comparisons are made fall well within the tradition being delineated. Nevertheless, study of a wide range of species has been characteristic throughout the 20th century. The man generally credited with conducting the first psychological study with rats, Linus Kline, was a leading advocate of comparative study. In his recommendations for a laboratory course, Kline (1899) included amoebae, vorticellae, paramecia, hydras, earthworms, slugs, fish (including sticklebacks), chicks, white rats, and cats. The tradition of studying invertebrates is strong. John F. Shepard (1911) compared the behavior of ants in mazes to that of rats, cats, and humans. However, his studies of ants were dwarfed by the long research program on ant behavior by his student, comparative psychologist T. C. Schneirla. The study of learning in invertebrates has been an active and controversial field for many years.

Other comparative psychologists have studied a bewildering array of vertebrate species, including fishes, amphibians, reptiles, birds, and mammals. Although studies do not have to be explicitly comparative to be part of comparative psychology, comparative psychology has been truly comparative throughout the century.

The Century in Perspective

Because my view of comparative psychology in the 20th century is somewhat controversial, it may help to clarify a few points and put the field in perspective. Comparative psychology is often portrayed historically as being extremely active during the early 1900s, but declining as the century progressed. This conclusion is generally based on an analysis of frequency counts of papers on various species and topics appearing in some psychological journals. I believe this analysis is flawed (Dewsbury, 1984a) and contend that the comparative tradition has continued throughout the century. The period generally targeted as a trough for comparative psychology lies roughly in the 1930s and 1940s. In my view, however, any field with the likes of Yerkes, Schneirla, Lashley, Carpenter, Nissen, Stone, Frank Beach, Leonard Carmichael, Harry Harlow, Daniel Lehrman, Norman Maier, and Carl Warden was in good shape.

However, profound changes did occur in animal psychology during the 1930s and 1940s. The study of the processes mediating learned behavior was in the ascent. The global theories of Hull, Tolman, Guthrie, Skinner, and others became dominant; comparative psychology, as I am using the term, justly was perceived as smaller in comparison. Although it may have been less dominant relative to learning theory, the tradition of comparative psychology continued undiminished and in some capable hands. It is this historical continuity that I want to emphasize.

Comparative psychology in America received a beneficial shot in the arm with the introduction of European ethology in the 1950s. Ethology was developed by zoologists, such as Konrad Lorenz and Niko Tinbergen, who stressed the study of behavioral evolution, a wide range of species, and careful observation and description. Am I not arguing that "comparative psychologists have really been doing ethological work all along" (Lorenz, 1985, p. xiii)? Yes and no. Comparative psychologists had displayed a strong tradition of interest in evolution, genetics, the natural lives of animals, and species comparison. What they lacked was the unity that comes from a comprehensive theory, a single-minded publicist, or a strong sense of a common bond. Ethologists developed a coherent theory and identity; comparative psychologists did not. The tragedy is that although all of the elements for a new behavioral synthesis were in place, the pieces and the field were fragmented, and some fine work had much less impact than it should have had. When ethology and modern evolutionary thought were developed, they were easily integrated into comparative psychology because the foundations had been solidly laid.

Early comparative psychologists exerted important influence within the broad field of psychology. Many were involved in the founding of APA. G. S. Hall, J. M. Baldwin, E. L. Thorndike, J. B. Watson, R. M. Yerkes, M. F. Washburn, W. Kohler, K. S. Lashley, L. Carmichael, C. P. Stone, D. O. Hebb, and H. F. Harlow all were APA presidents. Today's comparative psychologists have built an active and vigorous discipline on the foundation provided by their forebears.

Contemporary Comparative Psychology

Built on this solid foundation, the aspect of contemporary comparative psychology that I want to emphasize has developed especially in the last 15 years and in response to and conjunction with work in related disciplines concerned with the behavior of animals. I shall first summarize some of the basic principles that have been developed and then illustrate their application in comparative psychology in relation to the view of the organism as an adapted and economically sensitive creature.

Some Basic Principles of Contemporary Behavioral Evolution

Natural selection works through the differential transmission of copies of some genes, but not others, from the present generation to future ones. The shape of the structure and behavior of the organisms in future generations will depend on which organisms survive and reproduce, thus contributing to the gene pool of the next generation. To the extent that behavior is a reflection of genotype, the behavior of future populations is shaped in this way.

Genetic fitness. The term "genetic fitness" refers to the relative contribution to the next generation made by a particular organism, or more correctly genotype, relative to that of alternative genotypes. It entails a tautology, but a useful one as long as it is recognized as such. Genetic fitness represents the "bottom line" in the economic calculations, because by definition organisms must evolve in ways that maximize fitness. Fitness refers only to reproductive success, not to the judged effectiveness of the body or behavior of an organism except as it leads to successful reproduction. Much of the challenge in studying adaptation is to find methods to break the tautology; that is, to determine whether it appears likely that a particular behavioral pattern may relate to genetic fitness and, if so, the manner in which this might occur.

The level of action of natural selection. In principle, the differential reproductive success of different genotypes could occur at any of several levels: individual genes, individual organisms, small groups, or whole populations. Much writing in the early 1900s implied that selection worked at levels higher than the individual, as on groups. Although this may occur under some conditions, the notion that group selection is a major factor in evolution has been generally rejected. Consider two organisms, one of which sacrifices for the good of the group while the other concentrates on its own survival and reproduction. Which will have the higher fitness? In most cases, it will be the selfish individual. Genes related to behavioral patterns that yield net decreases in survival and reproduction must be selected against. Selection appears generally to work at the level of the individual. It is the individual that most effectively survives and reproduces that becomes the most effective progenitor of future generations.

Kin selection. Reproduction is not the only option for an organism shaped to ensure representation of its genes in future gene pools. An individual shares genes with its close relatives. It can help ensure the representation of those genes in future generations if it can aid in the survival and reproduction of those close relatives; this is kin selection. Fitness gained through one's own reproductive efforts may be treated as direct fitness. The additional component to fitness gained by increasing the representation of one's genes by aiding relatives other than one's own descendants may be said to constitute indirect

fitness (Brown & Brown, 1981). The value to an individual of reproductive success by relatives decreases as the relationship between individual and relatives becomes more distant and the proportion of
genes shared decreases. Perhaps the most remarkable example of a
pattern that may have evolved via kin selection is the existence of ster-
ile castes in insects. Individuals develop that are incapable of reproducing on their own but help instead in the rearing of their kin.

Caveats. The framework that has evolved stresses the individual
and its survival and reproduction. It is worth repeating that genes can
affect behavior only in interaction with each other and with the environment. The effects of genes on behavior can be subtle. For example,
a gene that altered an enzyme with the effect of improving the regurgi-
tation of food might aid a bird in caring for its young and thus relates
to parental care. Organisms are shaped by the interactions of many
such genes interacting with environmental factors in complex ways.

The competition among organisms is severe but often subtle
and indirect. The organism that wins may not be the most pugna-
cious but rather that which forages most effectively, avoids danger,
and cares for its young. As a result of natural selection, behavior becomes tuned to the environment, and organisms become economically in tune with the consequences of their acts, when the costs and
benefits relate to genetic fitness.

The application of these principles to humans has been controversial. Environmental factors appear more important and gene–
environment interaction much more complex in humans than in
nonhuman species. The consequences for differential reproduction
of alternative behavioral patterns are generally less clear. Later I shall
suggest that these principles provide an exciting source of hypotheses
for test and verification or rejection in humans. For the present, however, I would like to confine the application of these principles to the
behavior of nonhuman organisms.

When one says that an animal behaves as if following a certain
rule or adopting a certain strategy, one does not imply that this need
be a conscious process. Behavioral patterns are shaped to be adaptive
in given environments. Animals often behave according to "rules of
thumb," which appear as proximate guides to behavior that may be
proximate representations of effects of selection. To imply that animals necessarily understand these rules is to badly confuse proximate
with ultimate causation and to verge on teleology.

One also must guard in this endeavor against risking a Panglossian approach, in which we can generally find some way to match almost any behavioral pattern to some environmental constraint and
thus conclude that all animals live in the best of all possible worlds
(see Gould & Lewontin, 1979). These "just-so stories," like Kipling's
stories of "how the elephant got his trunk" or "how the leopard got
his spots," are scenarios that represent plausible functional explana-

tions of behavior, but which are post hoc and often untested. Such efforts are useful as sources of new ideas and interesting hypotheses. However, we must always remember that they are just that and in need of the most rigorous empirical testing possible. Some behavior may not be shaped by natural selection (see Snowdon, 1983). Some of our just-so stories may be oversimplifications. As long as one maintains the characteristic methodological rigor and the skepticism of the psychologist, these inconsistencies should eventually become apparent. A unique role for psychologists in the overall endeavor may be to examine important principles with the solid methodological foundation that has been the hallmark of the discipline; one can thus guard against becoming a Panglossian.

We generally analyze the adaptive significance of just a few related behavioral patterns (e.g., reproduction or feeding) at a time. We must always remember, however, that natural selection works on whole organisms. At some point it will be necessary for us to "reconstruct" the animal and view the interaction of different adaptations.

Finally, in delineating how selection has acted, we are not specifying how organisms *should* act; we are not delineating values. Because environmental factors can alter developmental pathways, behavioral patterns for which there may be some genetic predisposition often can be altered. The decision to modify such behavior requires an expression of values outside of the present system. However, in effecting modification, it is helpful to understand fully the system one is attempting to modify.

I believe that the set of principles about behavioral evolution of which these are the core has provided one of the most productive and exciting periods in the history of comparative psychology. Whatever the ultimate value of the principles, they have provided the impetus for us to ask new questions and to see aspects of animal behavior that may not have been seen without them.

Adapted Animals

I shall now describe some research by comparative psychologists that appears generally consistent with, and often stimulated by, the principles just delineated and that builds on the foundation developed throughout the century. Throughout their lives, organisms must apportion their efforts and energies according to many constraints. The effectiveness with which they do so affects their success in surviving and reproducing.

Optimal foraging. Optimal foraging theory was developed in the 1960s by ecologists (e.g., Emlen, 1966; MacArthur & Pianka, 1966) on the basic assumption that animals that foraged for food most efficiently would ultimately be the most fit (see Kamil & Roitblat, 1985).

If animals could maximize the amount of food gained per unit of time, or perhaps some other similar function, they would be acting more efficiently in their environment and ultimately should leave more offspring. There are many kinds of food, and this food is located in patches of different food density. Animals need to decide what kinds of food to eat, in which patch to search, how long to persist, and in what pattern to move. Because there are many competing demands, compromise may be necessary, as when an animal may need to reduce the gain per unit time to avoid exposure to a predator. The fundamental principle of optimality is essentially untestable. However, one can analyze what, if anything, animals appear selected to maximize and what decision rules appear to guide their behavior. The usefulness of this approach is that it leads one to view behavior in new ways and ask questions that might not have been asked without it.

Collier (e.g., Collier & Rovee-Collier, 1981), as well as many others, adapted operant conditioning procedures to simulate and analyze foraging in the laboratory. In the typical operant situation, an animal is deprived of food for a period of time and then placed into a test chamber for a test in which it may perform an operant response, such as pressing a lever, which has the effect of producing a small pellet of food. In Collier's test situation, by contrast, animals live continuously in the test environment, oversized cages, and are never deprived of food. However, all food is obtained as a consequence of operant responses. As an analog to the foraging pattern, Collier is interested not in the momentary responses that characterize the consumption phase of a feeding sequence, but in the meal patterns that are analogous to foraging. Thus, when an animal completes the operant requirement, it can eat for as long as it chooses. A meal is treated as terminated when the animal leaves the feeder for 10 minutes. The animal must then again complete the operant requirement in order to feed.

In general, Collier's animals performed in ways consistent with the notion of optimization. He divided the foraging process into stages of searching, identification, procurement, and handling. Consumption costs were manipulated in a one-lever situation, in which the number of lever presses required for food was manipulated. When the response requirement was high, animals ate less frequent, larger meals than when it was low. This finding was true of guinea pigs, chickens, ferrets, rats, and cats. In these, and many other, experiments animals behave in ways that appear to optimize the efficiency with which they feed.

The cost of both searching and procurement can be simulated and manipulated in a two-component situation by requiring a variable number (e.g., 5 or 100) of lever presses in each component. Completing a response requirement on the first component (i.e., the "search lever") produces a visual signal indicating that "prey" of either a high- or a low-procurement cost (100 or 5 lever presses) has been encountered. The animal can either feed or pass. Both search and procurement costs affect behavior. Animals almost always feed when presented with the low-cost alternative. The probability of feeding with the high-cost alternative varies with cost. Animals feed more when the search-lever press requirement is increased. Handling costs were manipulated when hulled or unhulled sunflower seeds were provided; the necessity of the animal's husking the seed increases handling cost.

Is this not just another instance of a Panglossian view, or worse, an indication that animals do pretty much what one expected them to do before the study was conducted? No. This approach leads to new insights in several respects. For example, much work done on feeding is done with food-deprived animals and is based on a "homeostatic-depletion-repletion" model of behavior (see Collier, 1986). In this model, animals feed in response to physiological changes indicating departure from homeostasis. The foraging literature suggests that superimposed on such processes is a buffering system that is more sensitive to the cost-benefit ratios of food patches in the environment. This sytem may normally control foraging and feeding under natural conditions. Feeding patterns are thus viewed as determined by the prevailing economics in the environment, not by the degree of depletion in the organism. When foraging and feeding strategies work effectively, depletion-repletion cycles may rarely occur. The economics prevailing in the environment will vary in different niches, and feeding patterns must be understood in relation to them.

In much classical work, the rate of operant responding is taken as a measure of response strength, which in turn varies as a direct function of the magnitude of reinforcement. In other words, the larger the reinforcement, the higher the response rate. However, with free-feeding, nondeprived animals that are allowed to regulate their meal patterns, this is not the case (Collier & Rovee-Collier, 1983). In one study, the duration of access to the food hopper was limited and manipulated. Under these conditions, response rate was a decreasing function of reinforcement magnitude. In essence, under conditions that decrease the rate of food intake, animals compensate by responding faster. This is a counterintuitive result, counter to the law of effect, and illustrates the value of this approach in generating new perspectives. As Collier and Rovee-Collier (1983) conclude, "Feeding patterns are strategies deployed in the service of fitness" (p. 438).

One benefit of this approach has been to facilitate communication between comparative psychologists and behavioral ecologists on the one hand and process-oriented operant conditioners on the other. Many foraging situations can be simulated with operant techniques. A schedule of reinforcement is essentially a set of environmental contingencies expressive of the pattern of payoffs for responses. If an animal is asked to choose between two schedules, as by pressing either of two levers, the situation resembles that faced by a forager asked to forage in one of two patches with differing densities and patterns of prey availability. The situation also resembles classical problems in probability learning (see Kamil, 1983; Kamil & Roitblat, 1985). If one wished to simulate travel time between patches, one could build in a delay between the possibility of responding to each of the alternatives. Many such studies have been done. Not all are consistent with theory, but the approach has been instructive.

Copulation and pregnancy. Mere survival represents but one aspect of fitness; the animal that must sacrifice reproduction to survive will have a low fitness indeed. Reproductive behavior is a critical aspect of all life forms.

The copulatory patterns of different mammalian species are remarkably diverse (Dewsbury, 1975b). The most studied copulatory pattern is that of male rats. Males pursue females and mount from the rear; receptive females display a pattern of lordosis, thus facilitating vaginal insertion. If the male fails to gain insertion, the event is scored as a *mount.* On many occasions the male gains vaginal insertion, lasting approximately ¼ to ⅓ seconds, and then displays a ballistic dismount without transferring any semen; these are termed *intromissions.* On other occasions the insertion is longer, the dismount pattern is distinctive, and sperm are transferred; these are called *ejaculations.* These events occur in organized *series,* each of which begins with an intromission, ends with an ejaculation, and is followed by a postejaculatory refractory period. Rested males display means of about 10 intromissions before ejaculation and about 7 ejaculations before reaching a criterion of satiation. What might be the functions of these patterns? Why do males display multiple intromissions before ejaculating instead of transferring semen as soon as possible? Why do they attain multiple ejaculations?

To begin to answer these questions, we need first to discuss female estrous cycles. Females of most species of muroid rodents have cycles that are completed only if they receive appropriate vaginal stimulation. Some species, reflex ovulators, only ovulate if they mate or receive comparable stimulation. Others, like rats, ovulate but the neuroendocrine changes that prepare the uterus for implantation of the fertilized ovum do not occur unless stimulation is received. In both, adequate supplies of sperm may be inadequate for successful pregnancy; it is male-produced vaginal stimulation that is necessary to trigger neuroendocrine reflexes necessary for pregnancy.

The functions of these patterns were understood first by Norman Adler and his associates (e.g., Adler, 1983). They showed that pregnancy in rats (i.e., the initiation of critical neuroendocrine responses) depended on the nonejaculatory intromissions the female receives. Females receiving a full supply of sperm but only a few intromissions failed to become pregnant. Further, the transport of sperm from the site of deposition to the site of fertilization depended on stimulation. That left the problem of multiple ejaculations. It turned out that most species were unlike Adler's rats, in that a single complete ejaculatory series was not enough to ensure maximal probabilities and levels of pregnancy; multiple ejaculations were required. Further, the stimulus requirements of the females of different species appear to be graded in rough correspondence to the amount of copulatory stimulation provided by the male (Dewsbury, 1978a). Thus, at least part of the reason for the multiple intromissions–multiple ejaculation pattern concerns the triggering of female responses critical for pregnancy.

At the time of ejaculation, males deposit materials that coagulate to form a copulatory plug. Adler's work revealed that the plug must be deposited tightly in the cervix for pregnancy to be successful. One additional function of the multiple intromissions may be to clean out the female's reproductive tract in preparation for the proper deposition of sperm and plug.

Copulation and competition. If natural selection works at the level of the individual, rather than that of the species, it would be critical for an animal to ensure that it is he or she, rather than a competitor, that is reproductively successful. To continue the economic analogy, reproductive effort can be treated as *parental investment,* of which an animal has only a limited supply (Trivers, 1972). It is critical that this investment be allocated effectively toward the animal's own offspring in ways that maximize reproductive success.

Females of many species copulate with more than one male during a single period of receptivity. It is first interesting to wonder what the benefits to the female of such multiple mating might be (see Schwagmeyer, 1984). From the perspective of the male, when a female mates with multiple partners, a situation of *sperm competition* exists (see Dewsbury, 1984b). One would expect the evolution of behavioral patterns that would help ensure that a female's offspring are sired by an individual male, rather than by a male mating before or after him. A variety of patterns of pre- and post-mating guarding and defense appear explicable in this context. It generally appears that the males that deliver the most sperm to a female sire the most young in that litter. Thus, another function of the multiple ejaculation pattern may be a kind of "sperm loading" that may function in outcompeting the sperm of other males.

Because the temporal patterning of sperm deposition is also important, the male–male competition can be quite complex. For example, females appear to require a period of quiescence, without vaginal stimulation, after each ejaculation if sperm transport is to be effected. The postejaculatory refractory period of each male seems to ensure that he does not disrupt his own sperm transport. However, if more than one male is present, a male may copulate soon after another ejaculates and may thus interfere with the sperm transport of the other, perhaps canceling out entirely any effectiveness of that ejaculation. If selection were for the good of the species rather than at the level of the individual, such interactions would be difficult to understand.

Parental behavior. Among the consequences of successful copulatory activity are pregnancy and the arrival of a litter of young. Parental care is extensive in many species of animals and all species of mammals. In many species of rodents, females maximize reproductive effort by breeding in a postpartum estrus that occurs within a day of parturition. Thus they carry one litter while nursing another. The allocation of time and effort to caring for themselves, caring for the new litter, and mating with an ardent male can be conceptualized as a time-sharing process, in which the distribution of time to different activities appears effectively allocated (Gilbert, Pelchat, & Adler, 1980).

The extent of male involvement in parental care varies greatly with the species and conditions. Thus involvement represents another compromise on the part of males. Time spent with a single female and caring for young is time that cannot be spent searching for additional mating partners and siring more young. However, nonhuman males are less philandering than has sometimes been proposed. It is emphatically not the case that nonhuman animals leave parental care exclusively to the female. Biparental care is common in most species of birds. Silver, Andrews, and Ball (1985) were able to correlate male parental involvement with a variety of ecological factors. Although paternal care is found in many species of rodents, its occurrence varies markedly with prevailing conditions (Dewsbury, 1985). Paternal care is far more common in nonhuman primates than was once thought and appears related to the energetics and economics of development (Snowdon & Suomi, 1982). Where energetic demands are considerable and predator pressure great, the incidence of male parental care is greatly increased.

Mating strategies, mating systems, and social organization. Males and females display behavioral patterns that can be treated as "strategies" (with no implication of conscious intent) to maximize individual fitness levels. The product of individuals acting to maximize reproductive success is a mating system. Such systems differ greatly among species and populations (see Lott, 1984).

In a long-term research program, Mason and his colleagues have contrasted the patterns of squirrel monkeys, *Saimiri sciureus,* and titi monkeys, *Callicebus moloch* (e.g., Mason, 1974). Field research by Mason and others revealed contrasting social systems in these species. Although squirrel monkeys live in variably sized, mixed-sex groups, titis are monogamous and territorial. Mason has uncovered a whole suite of traits that differentiate these two species and appear to drive their different mating systems. For example, in captive male–female pairs, titis generally stay closer together, are more often in contact, and groom each other more (Mason, 1974). In choice tests, titis show greater attraction to a cagemate than do squirrel monkeys (Mason, 1975). The basic psychophysiological response systems of the two species also are quite different and may underlie many of these behavioral differences (Cubicciotti, Mendoza, Mason, & Sassenrath, 1986).

Similarly, there is evidence that two species of microtine rodents, montane voles *(Microtus montanus)* and prairie voles *(M. ochrogaster)* differ in a parallel way, with the former being generally polygamous and the latter often monogamous. Again, a whole suite of traits differentiates the species and appears to underlie the differences in mating system. Prairie voles are much more contact-prone and huddle together readily. They are also quite selective of mates, choosing on the basis of such characteristics as familiarity, recency of mating, and social dominance. Montane voles do not huddle readily and mate less discriminately. Male prairie voles display more paternal care than do montane voles (see Dewsbury, in press).

Many species of vertebrates live in relatively stable groups in which dominance relationships and hierarchies provide the basis for organization (Bernstein, 1981). Although it is generally believed that dominant males copulate more and sire more offspring than subordinates, the literature is inconsistent (Dewsbury, 1982). For example, field studies by psychologists have revealed that higher ranking male American bison (Lott, 1979) and elephant seals (LeBoeuf, 1974) copulate more than subordinates, although the translation to production of offspring has yet to be demonstrated in these species. Females that mate with dominant males may be able to leave more viable offspring than those that mate with subordinates. Female elephant seals appear to incite male–male competition by protesting loudly when mounted. This signals surrounding males, with the effect that matings of subordinate males are interrupted while those of dominant males continue to completion (Cox & LeBoeuf, 1977).

Different species have different mating systems. These systems affect many behavioral processes. For example, dominance is a poor predictor of mating success in thirteen-lined ground squirrels, *Spermophilus tridecemlineatus.* Females are dispersed, and the premium for males is on the detection and location of receptive females in a pattern of "scramble competition" (Schwagmeyer & Woontner, 1986).

The flexibility of mating systems requires emphasis; the same species can show very different patterns in different areas (Lott, 1984). For example, in spiders of the species *Anselosimus eximius,* females may live either in colonies or alone. Christenson (1984) compared these alternative strategies and found both had advantages and disadvantages. Group living, for example, provided access to larger prey and protection from predators, whereas solitary living was quite risky but could lead to the founding of new colonies.

Individual discrimination and choice. These considerations suggest that animals could benefit in maximizing total (i.e., inclusive) fitness if they associated selectively with others of their species. For parents, it is critical that their limited parental care be directed at their young, not those others; selection works at the level of the individual. For the young, it is important to discriminate between their parents and other adults, which may be quite hostile to strange young. For kin selection to work, it must somehow be possible for an animal to selectively aid kin in preference to other animals more distantly related. At the time of mating, males and females may profit in several respects. They may produce the most fit offspring if they choose partners with "good" genes. These can be genes that lead to organisms better equipped for survival, better adapted to the local environment, or even that are more compatible with the genotype of the discriminator. Even with genotype constant, individuals could benefit if their partners were better able to deal with the environment and to provide resources for the young than are other animals. We would thus expect animals to make fine social discriminations. Such abilities have only recently been effectively demonstrated and are revealing that animals are much more sensitive to such characteristics than had been thought.

Richard Porter and his associates have studied kin associations in young spiny mice, *Acomys cahirinus,* which are murid rodents from the eastern Mediterranean region (Porter, in press). The testing procedure was simple: Four animals, two from each of two litters, were placed in a large cage and watched to determine who huddled with whom. Littermate siblings huddled together in preference to non-siblings. The effect was not found in mice under 2 weeks of age. The effect of retention of the cues of sibship was tested by isolating the animals for several days before testing. After 3 or 5 days of isolation, siblings still huddled selectively; however, the effect was lost in animals separated for 8 days. Littermate kin resemble each other in at least two ways, on the basis of similar genotypes and through familiarity resulting from being reared together. These can be dissociated with a cross-fostering design; that is, some pups from each litter are switched so that they grow up in association with nonkin littermates. When this was done, huddling appeared based on experience rather than genotype; littermates huddled, whether or not they were kin, and animals did not huddle selectively with nonlittermate kin.

Results of studies with two species of group squirrels, Arctic ground squirrels and Belding's ground squirrels, yielded related results that differed in some respects (Holmes & Sherman, 1982). When pups raised in different conditions were tested in an arena situation, those pups that had shared a natal nest were treated as siblings, whether or not they were true kin. However, among females reared apart, sister–sister pairs were less aggressive toward each other than were nonsister pairs. This suggests that females possess some mechanism permitting them to recognize kin even when they have not interacted with those individuals. It is interesting that the capacity is limited to females, because in the field female kin live near to and appear to aid each other, whereas males disperse widely from their birthsites. Equally interesting are differences within litters. The litters of the Belding's ground squirrels were conceived in the wild; multiple mating is common in this species, but paternity could be determined by an electrophoretic analysis of blood proteins. Holmes and Sherman found that full sisters were less agonistic and more cooperative toward each other than half-sisters, even though all had shared the same natal nest.

Parent–offspring recognition studies in four species of swallows reveal how greatly recognition processes can differ, even in closely related species (Beecher, Medvin, Stoddard, & Loesche, 1986). Bank swallows and barn swallows live in large, dense colonies where the possibility of losing contact with one's young is considerable. Cross-fostering and playback experiments revealed that parents of both species were able to recognize their young by voice alone. By contrast, this capacity was not found in either cliff swallows or rough-winged swallows, two species that live solitarily or in small groups. Individual differences among the calls of the young are greater in the colonial species and the parents can use these cues to identify their own young.

Rodents have generally been found to discriminate between individuals based on odors. For example, Porter (in press) found that anosmic spiny mice failed to huddle selectively with siblings. The source of such variability in odor is of great interest. One suggestion is that it may come from a string of genes known as the Major Histocompatibility Complex (MHC). These genes regulate the functioning of the immune systems of the body and are important in attacking or accepting tissue that is recognized as self or foreign. Beauchamp, Yamazaki, and Boyse (1985) studied congenic inbred strains of house mice, which differ genetically only in the MHC region. The researchers found that both male and female mice could discriminate on the basis of variation in this genetic complex, generally preferring to mate with individuals of a genotype different from their own. This would engender greater heterozygosity in the offspring and, presumably, allow them to deal with a broader spectrum of antigens. The preference is based on odor. Mice can be trained to distinguish between the odors of two animals differing in MHC genotype. Thus, the MHC system, which may be primordial in the evolution of individuality, appears to provide individual mice with a unique odor that can allow for adaptive mate choice.

Behavioral development. Psychologists, perhaps more than most other scientists, have been especially concerned with the ways in which behavior develops throughout the life of the individual organism. This concern has been characteristic of comparative psychology, as exemplified especially in the work of Wesley Mills and T. C. Schneirla. In some developmental analyses, the behavior of the young animal is viewed primarily as it relates to the ontogeny of adult behavior. The model is that the occurrence of complex adult behavior requires a series of graded steps to achieve a full expression. This view is correct and is one function of behavioral development. However, recent interest has focused on simultaneously occurring and parallel processes. Many behavioral patterns in the developing organism are better understood as adaptations to the current environment of the developing animal than as a preparation for adult life (Alberts, 1986; Hall & Oppenheim, 1987; Oppenheim, 1981). To reproduce, the developing organism must survive into adulthood. As it matures from embryo to neonate and through successive stages, it faces different situations and challenges. Many behavioral patterns are best understood as effective adaptations for meeting these challenges rather than as prophetic of the distant future. With a more ecologically oriented framework, psychologists have studied animals in more ecologically valid situations and have revealed processes and capacities previously unanticipated.

A representative example can be found in ingestive behavior. Infant rats display suckling; adults eat and drink. One can examine the relationship between these functionally similar activities. In doing so, Hall and Williams (1983) found differences in the response topography, stimulus control, internal control, and the neural substrates of suckling and eating. For example, although suckling depends on olfaction and is little affected by deprivation, eating is generally less affected by olfaction and is greatly affected by deprivation. However, it has been found that 3-day-old rat pups that are milk-deprived and placed in a warm, moist environment will display regulated ingestion from milk puddles on the floor, a capacity not previously recognized. This finding gives rise to the view of the infant as a "dual organism," in which a functional, adaptive infant mode and a developing adult mode are simultaneously present (see Alberts, 1986).

A parallel situation prevails regarding thermoregulation. When an infant rat is isolated in a cold environment, it is unable to regulate its body temperature effectively, although the adult can do so. However, this environment is not the normal one to which the infant is adapted; it normally lives in a nest with a parent and other pups.

When such groups of pups are studied, it is clear that they display adaptive group regulatory behavior in which individuals move through the huddle in ways that affect surface area and heat flow and that appear adaptive (Alberts, 1986).

The infants of altricial species have recently been found to possess learning abilities previously unsuspected (see Hall & Oppenheim, 1987). This research has been successful, in part, because the infant has been conceived in relation to its environment and the demands of that environment. The infant has a natural response repertoire that is effective in coping in this environment, and the infant's environment is very different from that of the adult.

One implication of this "ontogenetic adaptation" approach is that behavioral patterns that are adaptive at one developmental stage may not be so at other stages. This insight greatly complicates the study of adaptive significance. One way in which the problem can be approached is illustrated by Henderson's (1986) work on activity patterns in house mice. Henderson studied the genetic influences on different patterns of activity at different ages. He used the diallel-cross method, which entails breeding F_1 crosses among a series of inbred strains and comparing the behavior of the crosses to that of the parental genotypes. In theory, if the behavioral pattern under study is adaptive, the F_1 animals ought to score higher, on average, than the parents. Thus, if it is adaptive to learn, the F_1 mice should learn better, on average, than the parental genotypes. Henderson found significant genetic influences on activity at all ages. However, the pattern of effects changed with age. The young mouse pup has poorly developed sensory and motor capacities. If placed outside of the nest, its behavior is ineffective at getting back to the nest. The optimal behavior is to stay in one place and call to the parents. Henderson found a pattern of genetic dominance favoring low activity in young mouse pups. When 11-day-old pups were tested, there was genetic dominance favoring the rapid return to the nest, an ecologically relevant situation and response to it. At the same time, there was no suggestion of genetic dominance in an open field, an ecologically meaningless situation. At 15 days of age there is dominance favoring an explosive jumping pattern that appears adaptive in predator avoidance. The important points are that the genetic evidence is consistent with just-so stories about adaptation and that these patterns change with age, as the developing animal faces new situations, each of which must be dealt with if it is to survive, mature, and reproduce.

Even the developing fetus has been found to have some capacity to cope with its environment. Among the capacities of mammalian fetuses are the perception of tactile, acoustic, and chemical stimuli in utero; olfactory discrimination, sensitization, and habituation to previously neutral stimuli; orientation to novel stimuli; aversive conditioning; and behavioral adaptation to variations in conditions in the uterine environment (Smotherman & Robinson, in press).

The influences of environmental factors on the development of adult behavior can be subtle. An example can be found in the study of the development of birdsong, one of the most active research areas today. Much classical research was done with isolated young birds that were studied in relation to their capacity to learn from taped songs of various species of birds. However, in more recent work much more plasticity has been found than in the earlier work. This is because birds have been permitted to learn from live tutors rather than "tape" tutors (see Petrinovich, in press). The live bird provides a more potent stimulus to which the nestling is less likely to habituate, and the live bird thus appears to be more effective in these learning situations than a taped song. The more ecologically relevant situation again reveals greater capacity.

There is much research to show that adult patterns of sexual behavior are dependent on the perinatal hormonal environment (e.g., Adkins-Regan, 1985; Ward & Ward, 1985). An additional factor, however, is that mothers appear to recognize males and females and to groom males significantly more than females. These differences appear functional in facilitating adult sexual behavior (Moore, 1986).

With this dual-organism picture of the young animal, the individual is seen both coping with the present and developing mechanisms that will be used by it in the future.

Learning. The study of learning has been a prominent part of comparative psychology from its inception; comparative studies of learning are today being vigorously pursued in a variety of species. Process-oriented psychologists have generally preferred to study learning in tasks that appear arbitrary in relation to the life history of the species being studied. However, the more comparative-ecological approach, in which learning is studied in relation to the animal's adaptation to its environment, has shown a resurgence in recent years. This approach was greatly stimulated by Garcia's work on taste-aversion learning in rats (e.g., Garcia & Koelling, 1966). Rats drank water that was associated with a unique taste, saccharine, as well as flashing lights and noise. They were then made sick with X-irradiation. The rats associated the water's taste with illness, avoiding saccharine-flavored water in the future, but did not associate the visual-auditory stimulus with illness. The rats associated the visual-auditory stimulus with foot shock more readily than the taste. What was especially remarkable was that the delay between the behavior of ingesting and the reinforcement, illness, could be quite long—over an hour. The data suggested a predisposition in rats to associate internal malaise with taste and external pain with stimuli in other modalities. This behavior would appear adaptive because rats that ingest a novel substance, such as poison, and become ill some time later would profit by avoiding the unique taste, not the location where they afterwards became ill. This suggested that animals are "prepared" to make certain associations and "contraprepared" to make others, as the result of natural selection (Seligman, 1970).

At first, the results of these studies appeared to represent a challenge to general process learning theory. However, recent work has indicated that a synthesis of the adaptationist and general process approaches is feasible (Domjan, 1983; Garcia & Holder, 1985).

Consideration of learning as an adaptation appropriate for study employing the methods used with other adaptations has led to significant discoveries concerning the capacities of a variety of animal species. Olton (1977) studied rats in 8- or 17-arm radial mazes. A pellet of food was placed at the end of each arm, and the rat's task was to forage for the food without revisiting arms from which it had already depleted the resource. Rats do this effectively, avoiding revisits to previously visited arms and not relying on general response patterns, general algorithms, or intramaze marking; rather, the rats appear to remember and avoid where they have been. Shettleworth (1983) demonstrated remarkable memory capacity in birds that normally hoard food in scattered locations and retrieve it at later times. When marsh tits were permitted to store food in a laboratory simulation of the natural environment, they later visited the cache sites efficiently, going selectively to locations where they had stored food and avoiding revisits. Marmosets normally forage by moving about their environment in groups; Menzel and Juno (1985) developed a seminatural testing situation in which the marmosets could be tested as foraging groups. They found an efficient type of one-trial, learning-set learning under these conditions. In each case the learning and memory capacities were revealed to be appreciable when tests were designed to be compatible with the animals' natural behavior and environment.

Hollis (1984) has reinterpreted Pavlovian conditioning in relation to adaptive considerations. She studied the effectiveness of blue gouramis in defending their territories as a function of whether or not territorial intrusion was signaled and thus learned in a Pavlovian paradigm. Conditioned fish were better able to defend the territories than were animals not so conditioned. Hollis suggested that the biological function of classical conditioning is as preparation for the forthcoming unconditional stimulus—"anticipatory conditional responses function to optimize interactions with predators, rivals, mates, and food" (Hollis, 1984, p. 414), a function she labels *prefiguring*.

The contributions of an adaptation-optimization approach to learning are impressive. Several caveats are in order, however. First, it must be remembered that there are costs and benefits to the evolution of a learning-oriented developmental pattern (see Johnston, 1982). For example, development is generally slower, juveniles are more vulnerable, and developmental fallibility is increased. Many species retain developmental patterns that are well buffered against significant environmental variation. Such patterns generally appear adaptive for those species. As a learning-oriented species, we humans must remember that plasticity is not the only path to effective adaptation. Further, there are surely constraints on adaptation; situations arise in which it would appear adaptive for animals to be able to learn a particular response but in which they fail to do so. Animals lack infinite plasticity, and evolutionary processes can only modify that which already exists. Further, many of the adaptations that do exist may not be adaptations of the learning process itself, but of the uses to which existing processes are put (Beecher, 1988). The underlying learning mechanism(s) may be rather conservative over time.

The comparative-ecological approach is not the only valid approach to the study of animal learning. However, by viewing the animal in its ecological context as adapted to optimal behavioral patterns relevant to that context, significant insight has been gained into the function of learning processes in general. Application of the comparative methods used in the study of other adaptations should continue to yield significant insight into the processes of learning (Beecher, 1988; Domjan & Galef, 1983).

Cognition. One of the most dramatic trends in recent psychological research has been the growth of cognitive approaches in human and nonhuman psychology. The comparative approach has been quite prevalent in this endeavor, and animal cognition has become a major topic in comparative psychology (e.g., Mason, 1986; Roitblat, 1987). The cognitive achievements, especially in the area of language-related research, of animals such as dolphins (Herman, Richards, & Wolz, 1984), sea lions (Schusterman & Krieger, 1984), pygmy chimpanzees (Savage-Rumbaugh, McDonald, Sevcik, Hopkins, & Rubert, 1986), and especially chimpanzees (e.g., Gardner & Gardner, 1978; Premack, 1983; Savage-Rumbaugh, 1986) have become general knowledge. There is recent evidence that pigeons may display the cognitive process, or "chunking," in learning tasks in a manner similar in some respects to that of humans (Terrace, 1987). We may have even come full circle: The concept of mind can now again be introduced in scientifically respectable circles (e.g., Gallup, 1983) just as it was at the time that comparative psychology emerged.

A full treatment of comparative cognition is beyond the scope of this chapter; the reader is referred to Rumbaugh's (1985) G. Stanley Hall lecture. Cognitive abilities presumably evolved by permitting animals to solve real-world problems in real-world environments. The impressive performance of animals in tasks not directly related to their environments presumably evolved in the context of situations that were, but this hypothesis is essentially an article of faith that needs rigorous testing.

Current status. The view that animals have been adapted to maximize fitness in the environments in which they live has provided a foundation for integrating many diverse phenomena and a rich heuristic basis for generating new hypotheses. However, the approach must be used with caution (see Gould & Lewontin, 1979). Biological constraints prohibit animals from evolving many capacities that humans think might be adaptive for them, and many of the features that have evolved may not be adaptations at all. One should be cautious in accepting just-so stories. Despite these caveats, I believe that the principles of adaptation and optimization provide the most effective basis for integration and progress in comparative psychology.

Although it may be impossible to reach the level of experimental rigor when dealing with ultimate rather than proximate questions, rigorous research is nevertheless possible. One can use (a) the method of adaptive correlation, comparing the covariation of traits in different species; (b) the method of within-species correlation, relating traits to reproductive success within species; (c) experimental methods, designing experiments in which behavior is the independent variable and biologically important consequences are the dependent variable; and (d) the diallel-cross method, in which the genetic structure of a trait in a population provides the basis for inference regarding adaptive significance (see Dewsbury, 1978b). Thus adaptive significance can be studied empirically. By doing so, perspective on the study of behavior can be significantly increased.

Relevance

Clearly, I believe that comparative psychology deserves a prominent place in psychology. The primary reason, though least acceptable to many, is that it provides perspective. By examining the control, development, evolution, and adaptive significance of behavior in a variety of species, the behavior of our own can be seen in a new light and insight can thus be gained into our origins. This approach requires the removal of humans from the central place in analysis and entails parallel analyses rather than extrapolation from nonhumans to humans. As Beach put it,

> If we remove man from the central point in a comparative science of behavior, this may, in the long run, prove to be the very best way of reaching a better understanding of his place in nature and the behavioral characteristics which he shares with

other animals as well as those which he possesses alone or which are in him developed to a unique degree (1960, p. 17).

A related basis of relevance comes from the generation of hypotheses for consideration in research on humans. Much has been written in the last 15 years on the controversy concerning the relevance of sociobiological principles for humans. At one level, some of the basic principles must be true. Humans reproduce and do so differentially; gene pools must be changing in relation to this differential reproduction. However, the task of relating differential reproductive success to particular behavioral patterns is enormously more complex with humans than with nonhumans (e.g., Kitcher, 1985). Many scientists have become justly skeptical of simplistic extrapolations of sociobiological phenomena. However, the baby should not be thrown out with the bathwater. The literature on sociobiology can be an extremely rich source of interesting hypotheses and ideas for researchers and students alike. One can then design rigorous studies to consider the phenomenon in humans, remembering that the confirmation of the phenomenon does not necessarily confirm the existence of the principle. Other explanations must be considered.

An example of this approach can be found in the work of Daly and Wilson (1985) on child abuse. Reasoning from notions related to selection at the level of the individual and to kin selection, they compared the risk of child abuse for children that live with or apart from both biological parents. Both abuse and police apprehension were found to occur less often for children living with both biological parents. The research must be evaluated on its own as a study of human behavior. However, its genesis lies in the present framework and its implications are important.

The data from animal studies can also help in preventing simplistic extrapolations. For example, many data show that vertebrate social systems can be enormously variable within a species under different conditions (Lott, 1984). Such data should make one skeptical when told of "biological determinants" of social phenomena in humans.

In some cases the phenomena found in nonhumans, rather than the principles generated, can be generalized to humans. For example, just as female laboratory rats kept in close contact have been found to have synchronous estrous cycles (e.g., McClintock, 1983), human females living in close proximity have been found to have synchronous menstrual cycles (Graham & McGrew, 1980; McClintock, 1971). The principles underlying assortative mating in humans resemble those in nonhumans (Thiessen & Gregg, 1980). Interesting parallels also have been found between mother–young recognition patterns in humans and nonhumans (e.g., Porter, in press). Human mothers can distinguish photographs of their own babies from others after just a few hours of contact. They generally attribute this recognition to resemblance to relatives, especially the father, as would be suggested from sociobiological principles (e.g., Daly & Wilson, 1982). Within two days postpartum, a mother can distinguish a shirt soiled by her baby, as opposed to another, on the basis of olfactory cues alone. Similarly, fathers, grandmothers, and aunts can reliably identify garments worn by their neonatal relatives based on olfactory cues, and breast-fed babies can distinguish their mothers' axillary odors from those of other lactating females (Cernoch & Porter, 1985; Porter, Balogh, Cernoch, & Franchi, 1986).

Animal research can directly benefit humans (see N. E. Miller, 1985). An example from comparative research comes from the language-learning literature. Some of the methods developed for training chimpanzees in language research have been used successfully with severely retarded humans for whom other language intervention programs had proven ineffective (Savage-Rumbaugh, 1986). Direct economic benefits need not accrue only from applications to humans. For example, it is possible that learned taste aversions, like those described by Garcia and his colleagues, may be applicable in controlling coyote predation on sheep (Forthman Quick, Gustavson, & Rusiniak, 1985) and crow predation on eggs (Nicolaus, Cassel, Carlson, & Gustavson, 1983). If successful, these methods may help decrease predation without destroying the predator.

There are other ways in which knowledge from comparative psychology can be applied to nonhuman animals. An important instance lies in applying knowledge on reproductive behavior to captive breeding programs. With greater destruction of habitat, increasing numbers of species are becoming endangered and are unable to breed in nature. The most direct solution to this problem is to decrease habitat destruction. Where political considerations make this impossible, it is possible to breed animals in captivity so that reintroduction can later be effected. For example, Snowdon, Savage, and McConnell (1985) describe an effective breeding program for the endangered cotton-topped tamarins, *Saguinus oedipus,* that can substantially increase both birth and infant survival rates. Because most comparative psychologists are also animal lovers, application of comparative psychology for the betterment of nonhuman animals is important.

G. Stanley Hall believed in the multiple implications of comparative research, especially that done in zoos: "Besides their intrinsic and their practical value, such studies shed light on the nature, and often on the psychic genesis, of what is *a priori* and innate in man" (1885, p. 122).

Instruction in Comparative Psychology

Comparative psychology deserves a place in the curriculum of introductory courses in general psychology. Material from comparative psychology can provide a unique perspective on human behavior and its functions. The material discussed here and in the various textbooks in the field provides an ample basis for several lectures in the introductory course.

Undergraduate courses in comparative psychology taught at the entry level, just after the introductory general course, provide the opportunity for more sustained education in comparative psychology. Many good textbooks exist in the field of animal behavior; regrettably, however few texts have been written by psychologists (e.g., Dewsbury, 1978b).

One problem in organizing courses in comparative psychology, like those in many areas of psychology, lies in finding a unifying thread. Students like well-organized courses. By its very nature, comparative psychology deals with a broad spectrum of behavioral patterns in a wide range of species. It is justly perceived by students as being rather diffuse. Although the operant conditioner can base a course on a few fundamental principles, the comparative psychologist dealing with control, development, evolution, and function cannot be as focused. Focusing on the notions of adaptation and optimality can help organize the course, as long as appropriate caveats are fully developed.

Another problem is to avoid making the course dull. Animal behavior is intrinsically interesting; many people watch nature programs on television even though they will not have to take a final examination. Analyzing behavior necessarily deprives it of some of its mystery. A balance needs to be struck between conveying genuine fascination with animals and their behavior and the rigor of careful analysis and honest presentation of sophisticated research.

One way to enliven classes is with demonstrations. If students can see animal behavior, they gain an understanding that cannot be conveyed through even a long series of lectures. Some exposure to live animals can be a great motivator in learning.

Important ethical questions exist concerning the nature of the demonstrations to be used. I believe that there are today no effective alternatives to the use of animals in research in comparative psychology and animal behavior. However, the ethics concerning the use of animals in teaching are a different matter. Alternatives are available. Demonstrations should be used sparingly; demonstrations that cause pain or discomfort to the animal, though rarely used in comparative psychology, require extremely strong justification. Many procedures can be conducted once and filmed or videotaped for classroom presentation.

Humane, noninvasive demonstrations can expose students to real, living animals and perhaps to some discussion of the ethics of their use. Appropriate demonstrations will vary with available resources. At the University of Florida, we have used the contrast between montane voles and prairie voles (discussed earlier) in a demonstration. At the start of the lecture, the instructor introduces a male and female of each species, previously unfamiliar with each other, to adjacent cages. The lecturer then discusses the species and their social organization. By the end of the lecture, the prairie voles are generally huddled together, while the montane voles are at opposite ends of their cage. The students thus see major behavioral differences between these two remarkably similar-looking species.

The most effective way to bring animal behavior into the classroom is with films. Any effective course in comparative psychology ought to include at least a few films. There are many excellent films on animal behavior, and a list of these films is maintained by the Education Committee of the Animal Behaviour Society. Copies can be obtained from the Society secretary, whose address can be found in current issues of the journal *Animal Behaviour*. The Psychological Cinema Register at Pennsylvania State University is another excellent source.

Laboratory courses and projects can have great motivational impact. One means of minimizing the problems of ethics and expense is through computer simulations of experiments. At the University of Florida, for example, we have developed a series of computer simulations that are now generally available (Dewsbury, Bartness, Rogers, Sawrey, Durnin, & Levy, 1986). With these programs, we simulate laboratory projects on nest building in deer mice; artificial genetic selection for six behavioral traits; correlational analyses of rat copulatory behavior; the enforced interval effect in rat copulatory behavior; imprinting; and the effects of genotype, experience, and hormones on aggressive behavior in house mice. Although the programs are not state of the art, they are a useful alternative to hands-on research.

Computer simulations cannot completely replace hands-on experience with animals. An appreciation of animals and their complexity cannot be gotten from a cold computer. Humane laboratory projects can be conducted. We have used projects on spontaneous alternation in mealworms, tonic immobility in lizards, open-field behavior in rodents, play in young rodents, dominance and territoriality in crickets, and the behavior of local free-ranging dogs with general though varying degrees of success (see also Price & Stokes, 1975). Perhaps our most effective project is one in which each student makes a brief super-8 film or videotape of animal behavior outside of the laboratory (Dewsbury, 1975a). In each case, the student gains experience that cannot be duplicated without the use of animals.

Summary and Conclusions

Comparative psychology has been a part of psychology since its founding and has historical continuity throughout the 20th century. The foundation for contemporary comparative psychology can be found in older studies on such topics as the evolution of behavior, the link between genes and behavior, the natural lives of animals, and research on species comparisons. Contemporary studies can be organized around optimality and adaptation as they relate to the ways in which animals are adapted to the problems of survival and reproduction in different environments and to the maximization of fitness levels. Work in comparative psychology is a relevant part of the broader psychological endeavor and has an important place in psychology curricula.

The field of comparative psychology is dynamic and vigorous. It is intrinsically interdisciplinary, with strong ties to zoology, anthropology, animal science, and other disciplines. Psychologists working with scientists from other disciplines are making great strides in understanding animal behavior. However, we still await the great evolutionary synthesis envisaged by G. Stanley Hall:

> Only a pessimist can doubt that the need will, ere long, bring the man or the men to meet it in the only way it can be met, viz., by a comprehensive evolutionary synthesis in the psychological domain, which by every token seems at present to impend. (1909, p. 267)

References

Adkins-Regan, E. (1985). Nonmammalian psychosexual differentiation. In N. Adler, D. Pfaff, & R. W. Goy (Eds.), *Handbook of behavioral neurobiology: Vol. 7. Reproduction* (pp. 43–76). New York: Plenum.

Adler, N. T. (1983). The neuroethology of reproduction. In J. Ewert, R. Capranica, & D. Ingle (Eds.), *Advances in vertebrate neuroethology* (pp. 1033–1061). London: Plenum.

Alberts, J. R. (1986). New views of parent-offspring relationships. In W. T. Greenough & J. M. Juraska (Eds.), *Developmental neuropsychobiology* (pp. 449–478). New York: Academic Press.

Angell, J. R. (1909). The influence of Darwin on psychology. *Psychological Review, 16,* 152–169.

Baldwin, J. M. (1896). A new factor in evolution. *American Naturalist, 30,* 441–451, 536–553.

Baldwin, J. M. (1909). The influence of Darwin on theory of knowledge and philosophy. *Psychological Review, 16,* 207–218.

Beach, F. A. (1960). Experimental investigations of species-specific behavior. *American Psychologist, 15,* 1–18.

Beauchamp, G. K., Yamazaki, K., & Boyse, E. A. (1985). The chemosensory recognition of genetic individuality. *Scientific American, 253*(1), 86–92.

Beecher, M. D. (1988). Some comments on the adaptationist approach to learning. In R. C. Bolles & M. D. Beecher (Eds.), *Evolution and learning* (pp. 239–248). Hillsdale, NJ: Erlbaum.

Beecher, M. D., Medvin, M. B., Stoddard, P. K., & Loesche, P. (1986). Acoustic adaptations for parent-offspring recognition in swallows. *Experimental Biology, 45,* 179–193.

Bernstein, I. S. (1981). Dominance: The baby and the bathwater. *Behavioral and Brain Sciences, 4,* 419–457.

Brown, J. L., & Brown, E. R. (1981). Kin selection and individual selection in babblers. In R. D. Alexander & D. W. Tinkle (Eds.), *Natural selection and social behavior.* New York: Chiron.

Carpenter, C. R. (1964). *Naturalistic behavior of nonhuman primates.* University Park: Pennsylvania State University Press.

Cernoch, J. M., & Porter, R. H. (1985). Recognition of maternal axillary odors by infants. *Child Development, 56,* 1593–1598.

Christenson, T. E. (1984). Behaviour of colonial and solitary spiders of the theridiid species, *Anselosimus eximius. Animal Behaviour, 32,* 725–734.

Collier, G. (1986). The dialogue between the house economist and the resident physiologist. *Nutrition and Behavior, 3,* 9–26.

Collier, G. H., & Rovee-Collier, C. K. (1981). A comparative analysis of optimal foraging behavior: Laboratory simulations. In A. C. Kamil & T. D. Sargent (Eds.), *Foraging behavior: Ecological, ethological and psychological approaches* (pp. 39–76). New York: Garland.

Collier, G. H., & Rovee-Collier, C. K. (1983). An ecological perspective of reinforcement and motivation. In E. Satinoff & P. Teitelbaum (Eds.), *Handbook of behavioral neurobiology: Vol. 6* (pp. 427–441). New York: Plenum.

Cox, C. R., & LeBoeuf, B. J. (1977). Female incitation of male competition: A mechanism in sexual selection. *American Naturalist, 101,* 317–335.

Cubicciotti, D. D., Mendoza, S. P., Mason, W. A., & Sassenrath, E. N. (1986). Differences between *Saimiri sciureus* and *Callicebus moloch* in physiological responsiveness: Implications for behavior. *Journal of Comparative Psychology, 100,* 385–391.

Daly, M., & Wilson, M. (1982). Whom are newborn babies said to resemble? *Ethology and Sociobiology, 3,* 69–78.

Daly, M. & Wilson, M. (1985). Child abuse and other risks of not living with both parents. *Ethology and Sociobiology, 6,* 197–210.

Darwin, C. (1859). *On the origin of species by means of natural selection, or the preservation of favoured races in the struggle for life.* London: John Murray (Modern Library Edition, n.d.).

Dewsbury, D. A. (1975a). Filming animal behavior. In E. O. Price & A. W.

Stokes (Eds.), *Animal behavior in laboratory and field* (2nd ed.) (pp. 13–15). San Francisco: Freeman.

Dewsbury, D. A. (1975b). Diversity and adaptation in rodent copulatory behavior. *Science, 190,* 947–954.

Dewsbury, D. A. (1978a). The comparative method in studies of reproductive behavior. In T. E. McGill, D. A. Dewsbury, & B. D. Sachs (Eds.), *Sex and behavior: Status and prospectus* (pp. 83–112). New York: Plenum.

Dewsbury, D. A. (1978b). *Comparative animal behavior.* New York: McGraw-Hill.

Dewsbury, D. A. (1982). Dominance rank, copulatory behavior, and differential reproduction. *Quarterly Review of Biology, 57,* 135–159.

Dewsbury, D. A. (1984a). *Comparative psychology in the twentieth century.* Stroudsburg, PA: Hutchinson Ross.

Dewsbury, D. A. (1984b). Sperm competition in muroid rodents. In R. L. Smith (Ed.), *Sperm competition and the evolution of animal mating systems* (pp. 547–571). New York: Academic Press.

Dewsbury, D. A. (1985). Paternal behavior in rodents. *American Zoologist, 25,* 841–852.

Dewsbury, D. A. (in press). The comparative psychology of monogamy. In D. W. Leger (Ed.), *Nebraska symposium on motivation, 1987.* Lincoln, NE: University of Nebraska Press.

Dewsbury, D. A., Bartness, T. J., Rogers, C. J., Sawrey, D. K., Durnin, M. W., & Levy, C. M. (1986). *FIRM: Florida interactive modeler. Vol. III: Comparative animal behavior.* Iowa City, IA: Conduit.

Domjan, M. (1983). Biological constraints on instrumental and classical conditioning: Implications for general process theory. In G. H. Bower (Ed.), *The psychology of learning and motivation. Vol. 17* (pp. 215–276). New York: Academic Press.

Domjan, M., & Galef, B. G. (1983). Biological constraints on instrumental and classical conditioning: Retrospect and prospect. *Animal Learning & Behavior, 11,* 151–161.

Emlen, J. M. (1966). The role of time and energy in food preference. *American Naturalist, 100,* 611–617.

Forthman Quick, D. L., Gustavson, C. R., & Rusiniak, K. W. (1985). Coyote control and taste aversion. *Appetite, 6,* 253–264.

Gallup, G. G. (1983). Toward a comparative psychology of mind. In R. L. Mellgren (Ed.), *Animal cognition and behavior* (pp. 473–510). New York: North Holland.

Garcia, J., & Holder, M. D. (1985). Time, space and value. *Human Neurobiology, 4,* 81–89.

Garcia, J., & Koelling, R. A. (1966). The reaction of cue to consequence in avoidance learning. *Psychonomic Science, 5,* 123–124.

Gardner, R. A., & Gardner, B. T. (1978). Comparative psychology and language acquisition. *Annals of the New York Academy of Sciences, 309,* 37–76.

Gilbert, A. N., Pelchat, R. J., & Adler, N. T. (1980). Postpartum copulatory and maternal behaviour in Norway rats under seminatural conditions. *Animal Behaviour, 28,* 989–995.

Gould, S. J., & Lewontin, R. C. (1979). The spandrels of San Marco and the Panglossian paradigm: A critique of the adaptationist programme. *Proceedings of the Royal Society of London, Series B, 205,* 581–598.

Graham, C. A., & McGrew, W. C. (1980). Menstrual synchrony in female undergraduates living on a coeducational campus. *Psychoneuroendocrinology, 5,* 245–252.

Hall, C. S. (1947). Genetic differences in fatal audiogenic seizures between two inbred strains of house mice. *Journal of Heredity, 38,* 2–6.

Hall, G. S. (1885). The new psychology. *Andover Review, 3 (Feb., Mar.),* 120–135, 239–248.

Hall, G. S. (1909). Evolution and psychology. In T. C. Chamberlin (Ed.), *Fifty years of Darwinism* (pp. 251–267). New York: Holt.

Hall, G. S. (1927). *Life and confessions of a psychologist.* New York: Appleton.

Hall, W. G., & Oppenheim, R. W. (1987). Developmental psychobiology: Prenatal, perinatal, and early postnatal aspects of behavioral development. *Annual Review of Psychology, 38,* 91–128.

Hall, W. G., & Williams, C. L. (1983). Suckling isn't feeding, or is it? A search for developmental continuities. *Advances in the Study of Behavior, 13,* 219–254.

Henderson, N. D. (1986). Predicting relationships between psychological constructs and genetic characters: An analysis of changing genetic influences on activity in mice. *Behavior Genetics, 16,* 201–220.

Herman, L. M., Richards, D. G., & Wolz, J. P. (1984). Comprehension of sentences by bottlenosed dolphins. *Cognition, 16,* 129–219.

Hirsch, J., & Boudreau, J. C. (1958). Studies in experimental behavior genetics: I. The heritability of phototaxis in a population of *Drosophila melanogaster. Journal of Comparative and Physiological Psychology, 51,* 647–651.

Hollis, K. L. (1984). The biological function of Pavlovian conditioning: The best defense is a good offense. *Journal of Experimental Psychology: Animal Behavior Processes, 10,* 413–425.

Holmes, W. G., & Sherman, P. W. (1982). The ontogeny of kin recognition in two species of ground squirrels. *American Zoologist, 22,* 491–517.

Howard, D. T. (1927). The influence of evolutionary doctrine on psychology. *Psychological Review, 34,* 305–312.

Johnston, T. D. (1982). Selective costs and benefits in the evolution of learning. *Advances in the Study of Behavior, 12,* 65–106.

Kamil, A. C. (1983). Optimal foraging theory and the psychology of learning. *American Zoologist, 23,* 291–302.

Kamil, A. C., & Roitblat, H. L. (1985). The ecology of foraging behavior: Implications for animal learning and memory. *Annual Review of Psychology, 36,* 141–169.

Kitcher, P. (1985). *Vaunting ambition.* Cambridge, MA: MIT Press.

Kline, L. W. (1899). Suggestions toward a laboratory course in comparative psychology. *American Journal of Psychology, 10,* 399–430.

Kovach, J. K. (1986). Toward the genetics of an engram: The role of heredity in visual preferences and perceptual imprinting. In J. L. Fuller & E. C. Simmel (Eds.), *Perspectives in behavior genetics* (pp. 95–153). Hillsdale, NJ: Erlbaum.

LeBoeuf, B. J. (1974). Male–male competition and reproductive success in elephant seals. *American Zoologist, 14,* 163–176.

LeBoeuf, B. J., & Kaza, S. (Eds.). (1981). *The natural history of Año Nuevo.* Pacific Grove, CA: Boxwood.

Lorenz, K. Z. (1985). Foreword. In G. M. Burghardt (Ed.), *Foundations of comparative ethology* (pp. xiii–xiv). New York: Van Nostrand Reinhold.

Lott, D. F. (1979). Dominance relations and breeding rate in mature male American bison. *Zeitschrift fur Tierpsychologie, 49,* 418–432.

Lott, D. F. (1984). Intraspecific variation in the social systems of wild vertebrates. *Behaviour, 88,* 266–325.

MacArthur, R. H., and Pianka, E. R. (1966). On the optimal use of a patchy environment. *American Naturalist, 100,* 603–609.

Mason, W. A. (1974). Differential grouping patterns in two species of South American monkey. In N. F. White (Ed.), *Ethology and psychiatry* (pp. 153–168). Toronto: University of Toronto Press.

Mason, W. A. (1975). Comparative studies of social behavior in *Callicebus* and *Saimiri:* Strength and specificity of attraction between male-female cagemates. *Folia Primatologica, 23,* 113–123.

Mason, W. A. (1986). Behavior implies cognition. In W. Bechtel (Ed.), *Integrating scientific disciplines* (pp. 297–307). Dordrecht, Netherlands: Martinus Nijhoff.

McClintock, M. K. (1971). Menstrual synchrony and suppression. *Nature, 229,* 244–245.

McClintock, M. K. (1983). Synchronizing ovarian and birth cycles by female pheromones. In D. Muller-Schwarze & R. M. Silverstein (Eds.), *Chemical signals in vertebrates III* (pp. 159–178). New York: Plenum.

Menzel, E. W., & Juno, C. (1985). Social foraging in marmoset monkeys and the question of intelligence. *Philosophical transactions of the Royal Society of London, Series B, 308,* 145–158.

Miles, W. R. (1930). On the history of research with rats and mazes: A collection of notes. *Journal of General Psychology, 3,* 324–337.

Miller, D. B. (1977). Roles of naturalistic observation in comparative psychology. *American Psychologist, 32,* 211–219.

Miller, N. E. (1985). The value of behavioral research on animals. *American Psychologist, 40,* 423–440.

Mills, T. W. (1899). The nature of animal intelligence and the methods of investigating it. *Psychological Review, 6,* 262–274.

Moore, C. L. (1986). Interaction of species-typical environmental and hormonal factors in sexual differentiation of behavior. *Annals of the New York Academy of Sciences, 474,* 108–119.

Nicolaus, L. K., Cassel, J. F., Carlson, R. B., & Gustavson, C. R. (1983). Taste-aversion conditioning of crows to control predation on eggs. *Science, 220,* 212–214.

Olton, D. S. (1977). Spatial memory. *Scientific American, 236*(6), 82–98.

Oppenheim, R. W. (1981). Ontogenetic adaptations and retrogressive processes in the development of the nervous system and behaviour: A neuroembryological perspective. In K. J. Connolly & H. F. R. Prechtl (Eds.), *Maturation and development: Biological and psychological perspectives* (pp. 73–109). Philadelphia: Lippincott.

Petrinovich, L. (in press). The role of social factors in white-crowned sparrow song development. In T. Zentall & B. G. Galef (Eds.), *Social learning: A comparative approach.* Hillsdale, NJ: Erlbaum.

Porter, R. H. (in press). Kin recognition: Functions and mediating mechanisms. In C. B. Crawford, M. F. Smith, & D. L. Krebs (Eds.), *Sociobiology and psychology: Ideas, issues, and applications.* Hillsdale, NJ: Erlbaum.

Porter, R. H., Balogh, R. D., Cernoch, J. M., & Franchi, C. (1986). Recognition of kin through characteristic body odors. *Chemical Senses, 11,* 389–395.

Premack, D. (1983). The codes of man and beasts. *Behavioral and Brain Sciences, 6,* 125–167.

Price, E. O., & Stokes, A. W. (Eds.). (1975). *Animal behavior in laboratory and field* (2nd ed.). San Francisco: Freeman.

Roitblat, H. L. (1987). *Introduction to comparative cognition.* New York: Freeman.

Romanes, G. J. (1882). *Animal intelligence.* New York: Appleton.

Rumbaugh, D. M. (1985). Comparative psychology: Patterns in adaptation. In A. M. Rogers & C. J. Scheirer (Eds.), *The G. Stanley Hall lecture series, Vol. 5* (pp. 7–53). Washington, DC: American Psychological Association.

Savage-Rumbaugh, E. S. (1986). *Ape language: From conditioned response to symbol.* New York: Columbia University Press.

Savage-Rumbaugh, S., McDonald, K., Sevcik, R. A., Hopkins, W. D., & Rubert, E. (1986). Spontaneous symbol acquisition and communicative use by pygmy chimpanzees *(Pan paniscus). Journal of Experimental Psychology: General, 115,* 211–235.

Schusterman, R. J., & Krieger, K. (1984). California sea lions are capable of semantic comprehension. *Psychological Record, 34,* 3–23.

Schwagmeyer, P. L. (1984). Multiple mating and intersexual selection in thirteen-lined ground squirrels. In J. Murie & G. Michener (Eds.), *Biology of ground-dwelling squirrels* (pp. 275–293). Lincoln: University of Nebraska Press.

Schwagmeyer, P. L., & Woontner, S. J. (1986). Scramble competition polygyny in thirteen-lined ground squirrels: The relative contributions of overt conflict and competitive mate searching. *Behavioral Ecology and Sociobiology, 19,* 359–364.

Seligman, M. E. P. (1970). On the generality of the laws of learning. *Psychological Review, 77,* 406–418.

Shepard, J. F. (1911). Some results in comparative psychology. *Psychological Bulletin, 8,* 41–42.

Shettleworth, S. J. (1983). Memory in food-hoarding birds. *Scientific American, 248*(3), 102–110.

Silver, R., Andrews, H., & Ball, G. F. (1985). Paternal care in an ecological perspective: A quantitative analysis of avian subfamilies. *American Zoologist, 25,* 823–840.

Skinner, B. F. (1930). On the inheritance of maze behavior. *Journal of General Psychology, 4,* 342–346.

Smotherman, W. P., & Robinson, S. R. (in press). Psychobiology of fetal experience in the rat. In N. A. Krasnegor, E. M. Blass, M. A. Hofer, & W. P. Smotherman (Eds.), *Perinatal behavioral development: A psychological perspective.* New York: Academic Press.

Snowdon, C. T. (1983). Ethology, comparative psychology, and animal behavior. *Annual Review of Psychology, 34,* 63–94.

Snowdon, C. T., Savage, A., & McConnell, P. B. (1985). A breeding colony of cotton-top tamarins *(Saguinus oedipus). Laboratory Animal Science, 35,* 477–480.

Snowdon, C. T., & Suomi, S. J. (1982). Paternal behavior in primates. In

H. E. Fitzgerald, J. A. Mullins, & P. Gage (Eds.), *Child nurturance, Vol. 3* (pp. 63-108). New York: Plenum.

Stone, C. P. (1932). Wildness and savageness in rats of different strains. In C. P. Stone, C. W. Darrow, C. Landis, & L. A. Heath (Eds.), *Studies in the dynamics of behavior* (pp. 1-55). Chicago: University of Chicago Press.

Stone, C. P. (1943). Multiply, vary, let the strongest live and the weakest die—Charles Darwin. *Psychological Bulletin, 40,* 1-24.

Terrace, H. S. (1987). Chunking by a pigeon in a serial learning task. *Nature, 325,* 149-151.

Thiessen, D., & Gregg. B. (1980). Human assortative mating and genetic equilibrium: An evolutionary perspective. *Ethology and Sociobiology, 1,* 111-140.

Thorndike, E. (1899). A reply to "The nature of animal intelligence and the methods of investigating it." *Psychological Review, 6,* 412-420.

Tinbergen, N. (1963). On aims and methods of ethology. *Zeitschrift fur Tierpsychologie, 20,* 410-429.

Trivers, R. L. (1972). Parental investment and sexual selection. In B. Campbell (Ed.), *Sexual selection and the descent of man 1871-1971* (pp. 136-179). Chicago: Aldine.

Tryon, R. C. (1940). Genetic differences in maze-learning ability in rats. In G. M. Whipple (Ed.), *The thirty-ninth yearbook of the National Society for the Study of Education* (pp. 111-119). Bloomington, IL: Public School Publishing Co.

Ward, I. L., & Ward, O. B. (1985). Sexual behavior differentiation. Effects of prenatal manipulations in rats. In N. Adler, D. Pfaff, & R. W. Goy (Eds.), *Handbook of behavioral neurobiology, Vol. 7* (pp. 77-98). New York: Plenum.

Watson, J. B. (1906). The need of an experimental station for the study of certain problems in animal behavior. *Psychological Bulletin, 3,* 149-156.

Watson, J. B. (1908). The behavior of noddy terns and sooty terns. *Publications of the Carnegie Institution, 2*(103), 187-255.

Yerkes, R. M. (1907). *The dancing mouse.* New York: Macmillan.

ABNORMAL PSYCHOLOGY: NEW CHALLENGES AND BASIC FOUNDATIONS

Richard M. Suinn, professor and head of the Psychology Department at Colorado State, received his doctorate from Stanford in clinical psychology in 1959. He has taught in a college for undergraduates, a university with a graduate department, a medical school, and institutions in China and Mexico. Suinn has written a text in abnormal psychology and designed a behavior therapy for anxiety and two anxiety scales. For APA, he is chairperson of the Education and Training Board and former chairperson of the Board of Ethnic Minority Affairs, serves on the editorial board of two journals, and is on the executive committee of two Divisions. He was mayor of the city of Fort Collins, Colorado, and psychologist for three Olympic Teams.

ABNORMAL PSYCHOLOGY: NEW CHALLENGES AND BASIC FOUNDATIONS

The primary goals of the Hall Lectures are to illustrate a teaching style and to provide information of use in the classroom. To meet these goals, I've decided to do three things. First, each shift from one major topic to another will be made by calling your attention to a study that actually links the topics. With topics as diverse as genetics through culture, this should be no mean feat.

Second, I'm going to provide you with information that represents the best of what we know today about psychopathology, covering some new challenges that have been discovered within recent years as well as confirming some basic foundations.

Finally, I recognize that it is not possible to cover all of the instructional information that would be useful for your classroom. I have therefore appended some materials as resources that may be useful in your classes. They include discussion materials, references to sources, and tables and figures. The discussion materials are of three types. The first type consists of discussion questions with accompanying data from which to draw conclusions on topics such as "Does the season of the year influence your moods?", "Is a person's month of birth predictive of later likelihood of developing schizophrenia?", "Do angry, hostile cancer patients tend to die quicker or live longer?", and "What about multiple personalities today?". A second type of discussion material presents case histories that represent examples, such as a psychologist who hallucinated and later described his experience. I have also provided some additional information that should provoke lively discussion, such as the data that show a direct correlation between the salary of ministers and the price of beer!

As indicated previously, this chapter provides an update on the field of psychopathology today. Prior to writing this chapter, I began by surveying some of the nation's leading researchers on psychopathology, as well as sampling faculty who teach abnormal psychology. My primary purpose was to identify major modern developments in the field. I received replies from prominent psychologists such as Gottesman, Shneidman, Garmezy, Kazdin, and Spielberger and have organized my presentation around some of the materials they identified. In addition, I reviewed the major journals published in the last 8 years.

Although sometimes our field moves slowly and cautiously, occasionally some dramatic finding surfaces. I have identified some of these new challenges, but also wish to call your attention to the premise that the origins of psychopathology are not solely in psychological sources, but may also be discovered in other realms. This premise characterizes the organization of my undergraduate abnormal psychology textbook (Suinn, 1984), and I will illustrate the influence of these other realms in this chapter:

• *genetic factors,* including citing a major error in studies of twins that was recently discovered and one controversial study that has been said to usher in a new era of psychiatric research;

• *biological factors,* including a review of such important items as the dorsolateral prefrontal cortex, smooth pursuit eye movements (SPEM), and the dexamethasone suppression test;

• *familial factors,* which include what I believe to be *the* discovery of the decade in psychology; and

• *cultural factors,* including some exotic disorders and also what has been called the disease of the 1980s.

I will also discuss psychological theories of and treatment for depression; and I will conclude with a review of the status of therapies for psychopathology, an overview of trends in the field, and some speculation on future developments.

Genetic Factors in Psychopathology

The Case for Genetics

Let's start with the obvious: the recent confirmation of a genetic factor in Alzheimer's disease. According to Gottesman (1985), the "role of genetic contributors to [Alzheimer's disease] . . . is undisputed" (p. 4). One set of data compares the risk of Alzheimer's in the general population versus the risk when a family member is afflicted. In the general population, the risk is of 12 persons per 1,000 developing Alzheimer's. If a genetic factor is involved, then this risk should be higher among relatives of patients with Alzheimer's. And the data confirm this. If a sibling has shown Alzheimer's, then the risk factor increases from 12 per 1,000 to 77 per 1,000; and if both a sibling and one parent have Alzheimer's, then the risk escalates dramatically to 215 per 1,000 (Heston, Mastri, Anderson, & White, 1981; Kay, 1986)! Obviously there are causes of Alzheimer's other than genetic, but the genetic factor is now considered highly important.

I started with Alzheimer's because it seems reasonable to consider this disease process to be linked to heredity. On the other hand, some psychologists have found it difficult to accept the premise that schizophrenia may also be genetically caused. Yet the data are similar, and I'm sure you are aware of the prior data supporting the premise. It is not so much that there is new information, but rather that there is more sophisticated research, leading to revisions of prior data. (An excellent summary is available in Gottesman & Shields, 1982.) For instance, studies of mono- and dizygotic twins had identified 26 pairs in international studies from Denmark and Japan. However, it has now been discovered that the Japanese studies were mistranslated; instead the data should actually have been calculated on 12 pairs (Inouye, 1972; Mitsuda, 1967). Table 1 shows the current analyses of these data (Gottesman & Shields, 1982; Gottesman, McGuffin, et al., in press).

Table 1

Current Morbidity Risk Figures for Schizophrenia

	Current Revised Morbidity Risk Figures	Previous Estimates
General Population[a]	0.99	0.90
Half-siblings[a]	4.2	7.0
Full siblings[a]	9.6	14.3
Dizygotic twins[b]	12.1	17.6
Monozygotic twins [b]	44.3	77.6

Note. Based on [a]Gottesman and Shields (1982) and on [b]Gottesman et al. (in press) with permission.

In effect, although current analyses indicate lower risk figures, the fact still remains that the closer the relationship to a person who is schizophrenic, the higher the risk, as one might expect if genetics plays a role. The figures hold up in those adoption studies that control for environmental influences. In these studies children of schizophrenic patients were reared by nonschizophrenic parents, and results showed that these children still turn out to be at high risk. One such example of monozygotic twins reared apart is included as a discussion topic at the end of this chapter.

Current studies have also attempted to be more precise in estimating the contribution of heredity through the *hereditability index*. As a reference point, consider that diabetes mellitus, known to be genetically influenced, has an index of .71. In comparison the index for schizophrenia has been computed also to be .71, which is higher than that for other illnesses, such as hypertension (.58) or myocardial infarction (.33; see Kendler, 1983; Rao, Mortoin, Gottesman, & Lew, 1981). By this type of calculation, culture has been estimated to have an index of .20 with respect to schizophrenia.

Affective disorders (i.e., mood disturbances) also have been reconfirmed to have a genetic component. Typically, the bipolar disorder is considered more heavily influenced by heredity than other depressive disorders. For the general population, the risk of this disorder is 0.6. In comparison, the risk for relatives of a person with affective disorder is 1.8 for unipolar disorder, reaching a high of 5.2 for bipolar disorder (a risk five times higher than for relatives of patients with unipolar disorder; Rice et al., 1987). Prior twin data add further confirmation. For monozygotic twins, the concordance for bipolar disorder was 79% compared to 19% for dizygotic twins; for unipolar disorders, the concordance was 54% for monozygotic twins and 24% for dizygotic twins (Bertelsen, Harvald, & Hauge, 1977).

Two adoption studies also confirm the importance of genetics. An interesting study by Mendlewicz and Rainer (1977) took an innovative approach to studying adoptees. The researchers identified adoptees who became depressed as adults and then examined the presence of pathology in either their biological parents or their adoptive parents. The data for these depressed adults (index cases) were compared with adopted nondepressed adults. If depression is inherited, the biological parents would be expected to show a higher incidence of depression than would the adoptive parents. The results were that bipolar disorder appeared in 31% of the biological parents of the index patients as contrasted with only 12% of the patients' adoptive parents. In comparison, of the biological parents of adoptees who were themselves not depressed, 2% of these parents were diagnosed as bipolar; of the adoptive parents of these nondepressed adoptees, 10% were diagnosed as bipolar. Clearly genetic factors do seem to be important in bipolar depression.

Recently Wender et al. (1986) expanded on the Mendlewicz and Rainer research to include unipolar index patients and parents and other close relatives of adopted adults. In comparing the biological relatives with the adoptive relatives, the biological relatives showed an eightfold higher frequency of mood disorder. The study also examined similar data for neurotic depressives, because this type of depression is considered not genetically determined. The data, indeed, showed no significant differences.

Finally, results of a long-term study (Egeland & Hostetter, 1983) of a genetically and culturally isolated group, the Amish, have added more support to the case for the genetic factor. The Amish group studied was made up of 12,500 persons originally descended from 30 couples and considered a genetically and culturally homogeneous population.

The data from this study show not only affective disorder but also the incidence of other psychiatric disturbances in one family tree. The striking finding appears in the last generation, with 31% of the 51 grandchildren showing a mood disorder and 49%, or just under 1 in 2, showing some form of psychiatric disorder. These data are certainly similar to those reported earlier for an Alzheimer's family.

Egeland and Hostetter's (1983) study lasted over 5 years, and the researchers identified 112 Amish with psychiatric disorders. Of these, 71% involved an affective disorder. Egeland and Hostetter identified what appears to be a deviant gene near chromosome 11 in the bipolar patients, but not in the other people. Darrel Regier, a director of the National Institute of Mental Health, has called this finding "the first demonstration of a possible genetic basis for one of the major mental disorders. The study ushers in a new era of psychiatric research" (Hostetter, 1987, p. 16). Another salient point, given the hypothesized involvement of dopamine in psychopathology, is that the chromosome 11 region is also responsible for dopamine activity. Egeland and Hostetter are still careful to avoid the claim that this gene is the cause of bipolar disorder in all cases of this disorder or necessarily among non-Amish patients.

Interpretation of Genetic Factors

What does this all mean? Although genetic influences do appear to be confirmed, the actual nature of the gene structure or the roles in causing pathology are still open to interpretation (Faraone & Tsuang, 1985; Kendler & Eaves, 1986). Construction of possible models of genetic influences will stimulate future research that will clarify which models are more accurate. For example, Kendler and Eaves offer several ways of thinking about how the heredity factors can result in schizophrenia, such as through action independent from environment or through interaction with a predisposing environment.

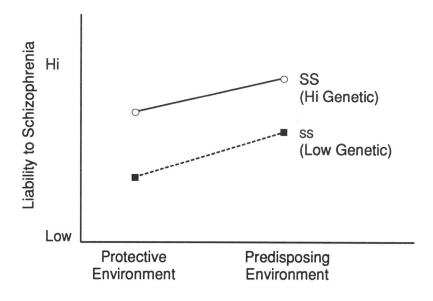

Figure 1. Independent model representing contributions of genetics and environment. Based on Kendler and Eaves (1986) with permission.

In the first type of model, both genetic and environmental factors can, independently or in combination, cause schizophrenia. Figure 1 illustrates this model, which suggests that a genetically prone (SS) person will always be at a higher risk for schizophrenia under either a protective or a schizophrenia-precipitating environment as compared with a person of low genetic risk (ss). This higher risk for an SS person, even in a protective environment, derives from the genetic hereditability index (.71), which is stronger than any influence from environment (estimated index of .20).

In the second type of model, genetic and environmental factors interact (Figure 2). The supposition here is that genetics predisposes a person to schizophrenia by increasing the person's sensitivity or responsiveness to environmental stresses. In other words, the genetically prone person (SS) is more reactive to a schizophrenia-precipitating environment (such as high stress from a hostile family). The model also proposes that the low genetic risk (ss) person actually possesses an insensitivity to the environment. Hence, even a seriously disturbing environment would not be predicted to precipitate schizophrenia in such a low-risk (environment-insensitive) person. Finally, according to the model, a genetically high-risk person would not become schizophrenic in a protective environment because the model requires that the environment be a stressful one.

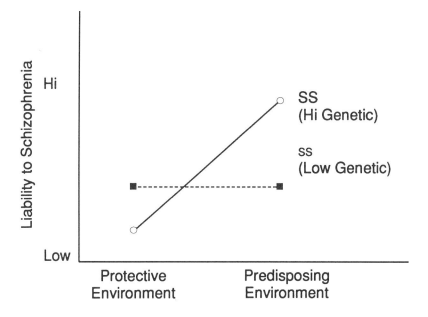

Figure 2. Interactive model representing contributions of genetics and environment. Based on Kendler and Eaves (1986) with permission.

One of the exciting aspects of research is that ideas stir up other ideas, which in turn lead to other fascinating results. The documentation on family morbidity risk has led to the genetic models just cited. In addition, family studies have also led to research on the influence of schizophrenic parents on their children. Children with one schizophrenic parent have been labelled as high-risk children. The important question is whether early signs, or "markers," of schizophrenia appear in these children. When biological factors such as attending behaviors are assessed, the answer seems to be yes. As part of the Minnesota High-Risk study, four groups of children had their attentional-vigilance processes tested. These groups were children of schizophrenic mothers, children whose mothers were psychiatrically disturbed but nonpsychotic, hyperactive children, and "normal" children. Results confirmed that significantly more children of schizophrenic parents showed deficits than did normal children or children with psychiatrically disturbed, nonpsychotic parents. Children of schizophrenic parents showed dysfunctions in attention involving signal-noise discrimination, while hyperactive children showed low scores reflecting caution in responding (Nuechterlein, 1984; personal communication, August 10, 1987). A major interpretation of such attentional deficits is that they reflect underlying neuropsychological dysfunctions. We thus have a research report that makes the link between genetics and basic biological processes, and serves as the transition to the next topic: biological factors in psychopathology.

Biological Factors in Psychopathology

The search for biological factors is not new; what is new are the gains made as a result of the development of new technologies—positron emission tomography (PET) scans, measures of hypofrontality, and SPEM. Such technologies have accelerated explorations of brain metabolism, frontal lobe functioning, and structural aspects of brain anatomy (see Barnes, 1987; Seidman, 1983; and Zahn, 1986, for excellent summaries of these technologies).

Neuropsychological Evidence and Pathology

The functioning of the frontal lobe of the brain has always been a prime suspect in schizophrenia. The prefrontal lobotomy was once used as a means for "curing" this disorder. Recently, the availability of PET scans has refocused attention on the frontal lobes. During a PET scan, a radioactive tracer substance, such as glucose, is introduced into the body, and the body's metabolism is recorded and analyzed by computer. Such analyses have revealed disturbances in cerebral blood flow and cerebral glucose metabolism; the term *hypofrontality* refers to such dysfunction. Such studies illustrate that the functioning of schizophrenics appears impaired, as shown by glucose metabolism differences in comparison with normal persons (Weinberger, Berman, & Zec, 1986). In addition, disturbed metabolism in the frontal regions appears associated with the presence of more severe schizophrenic symptoms, in that the patients are mute, highly withdrawn, inactive, and more disturbed by hallucinations (Ingvar, 1976).

A fascinating aspect of the glucose metabolism study is that research tasks were selected as measures of a specific part of the brain, the dorsolateral prefrontal cortex. The implication of this region as a possible location of some causes of schizophrenic symptoms is supported by other information, from which deductions have been made, as in a Sherlock Holmes plot. First, persons suffering from brain damage to this prefrontal cortex show symptoms very similar to schizophrenic symptoms: flat affect, withdrawal, apathy, inattention, poor concentration, poor insight, and restricted spontaneity—symptoms often labeled as the negative symptoms in schizophrenia. Second, primate studies (Alexander & Goldman, 1978) confirmed that symptoms from such damage are not exhibited until the animal reaches sexual maturity, which is consistent with observations that schizophrenia in people tends not to appear before adolescence. Finally, damage to this part of the brain may lead to dysfunction in dopamine metabolism, and dopamine (as I discuss later) seems involved in schizophrenia.

On the other hand, these data are still preliminary rather than conclusive. Some studies have failed to replicate the hypofrontality effect (Gur et al., 1987). Also, similar PET scan findings have been reported for other psychiatric disorders, such as depression, and hence may not be solely predictive of schizophrenia (Mathew et al., 1980). Therefore, if we're reading a detective story, we're obviously in the middle and not yet at the final chapter.

Another neuropsychological approach has been to seek indirect signs that may represent biological dysfunctions related to pathology. One set of research involves the findings of high-risk children and adolescents mentioned earlier. Erlenmeyer-Kimling, Kestenbaum, Bird, and Hilldoff (1984) and Nuechterlein (1984) confirmed that attentional defects appear to be early predictors of later schizophrenia. A simple but fascinating test of attentional competency is the assessment of a person's eye movements while his or her eyes are following a target. Among schizophrenics, smooth pursuit eye movements (SPEM) appear to be so reliably deviant that at least one expert has labeled it an important genetic marker, diagnostic of schizophrenia (Holzman & Solomon, 1984). The disturbance is described as *saccadic,* meaning that the movements are rapid, with jerks and jumps, rather than smooth. Figure 3 illustrates both normal and abnormal eye movement recordings. Of further interest is the fact that patients and their relatives show a high incidence of this deviance (70% of schizophrenics and 50% of relatives), with the rate being higher than found among nonschizophrenics (8%). Although this deviance is also sometimes found among other psychiatric patients, the degree to which the SPEM marker can be added to others to differentiate schizophrenia from other psychoses will be of interest. Significantly, the eye movement disorder appears at a much lower rate among relatives of nonschizophrenic patients (10%) than relatives of schizophrenic patients (50%).

Although the attentional studies assess indirectly the presence of underlying neurophysiological defects, an approach to gross anatomy has also been stimulated in recent years. Improved techniques have made possible rigorous examination through computerized axial tomography (CAT) scans or nuclear magnetic resonance imaging techniques. These data have identified anatomical abnormalities among schizophrenics. Among the most common abnormalities has been the presence of enlarged ventricles (Andreasen, Olsen, Dennert, & Smith, 1982). This abnormality appears in 20–35% of schizophrenics (Weinberger, DeLisi, Perman, Targum, & Wyatt, 1982). Further, the abnormality has not been restricted to chronic patients, but also has been identified in acute schizophrenics.

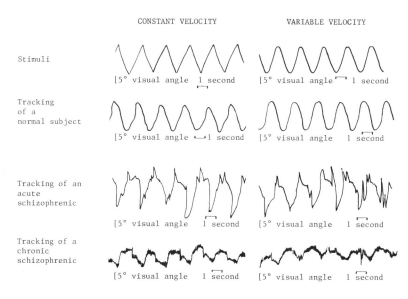

Figure 3. Examples of smooth pursuit tracking of normal, acute schizophrenic, and chronic schizophrenic subjects. From Cegalis and Sweeney (1979) with permission.

Such studies have reintroduced the concept of differing subtypes of schizophrenia, along the lines of earlier concepts of the chronic, poorer-prognosis, *process* (or nuclear) schizophrenia and the more acute, sudden onset, *reactive* schizophrenia. Certainly the hypothesis that process schizophrenia is associated with brain damage or dysfunction is consistent with findings regarding structural abnormalities (such as ventricular enlargements), attentional disturbances, and hypofrontality. It is also possible that schizophrenic symptoms might offer some clue of the possible locus of the neuropsychological pathology. For instance, symptoms have been subdivided as "negative" (apathy, socially inappropriate behaviors, blunting) and "positive" (active hallucinations, delusions, thought disorders). Seidman (1983), in a review of the literature, suggested that the negative symptoms are thought to be associated with frontal lobe abnormality, including hypoarousal of the cortex, and ventricular enlargement or cerebral atrophy. Positive symptoms may represent dysfunction in the limbic, midbrain, and upper brain stem regions. The patient is relatively intact in cortical structures and shows compensatory reactions to excessive subcortical arousal. One possible source of this arousal involves an excess of dopamine receptors. Following is a brief commentary on dopamine and on neurotransmitters and neurohormones.

Neuroendocrine Evidence

Neurotransmitters including dopamine have been suspected of playing major roles in psychopathology (McNeal & Cimbolic, 1986). The dopamine hypothesis regarding schizophrenia illustrates this logic, which uses facts to draw inferences:

• a drug (amphetamine) known to exacerbate the symptoms of schizophrenia is also known to increase dopamine;

• a medication (a neuroleptic drug such as Thorazine) known to eliminate the symptoms of schizophrenia is also known to block dopamine; and

• autopsies of brains of schizophrenics have discovered more dopamine receptors in these brains (Tsuang, 1982).

Neurohormones have also been considered major factors in psychopathology. In fact, Price, Charney, Rubin, and Henninger (1986) have concluded that the "most widely documented endocrine abnormality in major depression" (p. 849) involves the dysfunction of the hypothalamic-pituitary-adrenal system. Earlier suspicions about this neuroendocrine pathology and depression led to an especially creative piece of research. One outcome of the hypothalamic-pituitary-adrenal (HPT) disorder is its effect on cortisol secretion in the body. Normally, cortisol is secreted during the day, but automatically suppressed at night during sleep. If the cortisol level increases, a regulatory mechanism kicks in and cortisol secretion is suppressed. The compound, dexamethasone, is similar to cortisol; hence when it is administered, the suppression mechanism is triggered, and cortisol is reduced. If depression results from a dysfunction of the HPT system, then cortisol regulation might be the place such dysfunction shows most clearly. Thus, the dexamethasone suppression test (DST) was derived. In this test, dexamethasone is administered and cortisol suppression measured. For the nondepressed person, cortisol would be suppressed; but what happens in a depressed person? The highly interesting finding is that DST-depressed persons show different responses (Zimmerman, Coryel, & Pfohl, 1986). Figures 4, 5, and 6 show examples of such responses.

A nondepressed patient (personality disorder) without dexamethasone (Figure 4) exhibited the expected overnight suppression of cortisol, followed by a morning recovery. When dexamethasone is administered, cortisol is suppressed throughout the day. In a depressed patient during a depressed episode (Figure 5) there is failure of the normal suppression of cortisol. This figure also shows the return to the normal overnight suppression of cortisol once the patient recovered from the depression with lithium treatment. Figure 6 shows the results of the DST again with a depressed patient. As can be seen, the dexamethasone did not produce the expected suppression during this patient's depressive episode. On the other hand, after the patient recovered through the use of antidepressants, the DST led to the expected pattern of suppression of cortisol.

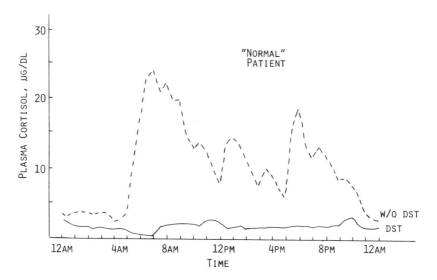

Figure 4. Response of "normal" patient to cortisol with and without dexamethasone. From Carroll et al. (1976) with permission.

A study by Schlesser, Winokur, and Sherman (1980) shows that the DST can make a differential diagnosis between depressed disorders and other psychiatric disorders. These researchers found that cortisol secretion remains high for the two depressed groups, but there was normal suppression for bipolar patients during their manic episodes and for schizophrenic patients. The measured cortisol levels were 7.9 for unipolar patients during their depressed episodes, 10.4 for bipolar patients during their depressed episodes, 5.2 for bipolar patients during their manic episodes, and 4.9 for schizophrenic patients.

These results seem to confirm a valuable modern diagnostic test for depressions. However, the DST is not foolproof, and false negatives do occur. Brown, Johnston, and Mayfield (1979) reported not only the numbers who were nonsuppressors but also those who were suppressors among the depressed sample. Thus, whereas 8 depressive patients were nonsuppressors, 12 other depressive patients were suppressors and would have been diagnosed as nondepressed had the DST been the sole diagnostic tool.

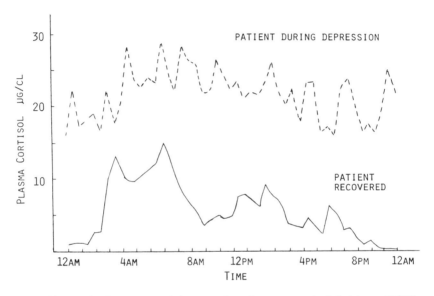

Figure 5. Response of depressed patient to cortisol (without DST). From Carroll et al. (1976) with permission.

There is an interesting follow-up to the DST research. Perhaps DST false negatives occur with patients whose depression has psychological rather than biological origins. Rehm (1977) developed a theory that one psychological cause of depression is a low level of self-reinforcement. Heiby, Campos, Remick, and Keller (1987) found that the false negative DST patients turned out to be depressives with low levels of self-reinforcement. Hence, some depression appears to have a biological component, whereas others may derive from psychological factors.

And if that is not enough to convince us that physiological factors are not the sole explanations for psychopathology, Bandura, Taylor, Williams, Mefford, and Barchas (1985) presented a study of self-efficacy and catecholamines. Working with spider phobics, they first demonstrated that neuroendocrine activity is directly influenced by level of self-efficacy beliefs. Subjects were asked to perform a task involving a spider, and where they possessed high self-efficacy for the task, low levels of catecholamine were maintained. Yet where the task was associated with lower self-efficacy, the catecholamine production went up. The effect of efficacy-raising training on catecholamines is significant. After each subject completed training to maximize self-efficacy belief, catecholamine levels for all tasks were equally low. In other words, although the prior data may suggest that physiological factors (such as neuroendocrines) seem causally related to psychopathology, Bandura et al.'s work also suggests that neuroendocrine levels themselves can be influenced by psychological variables.

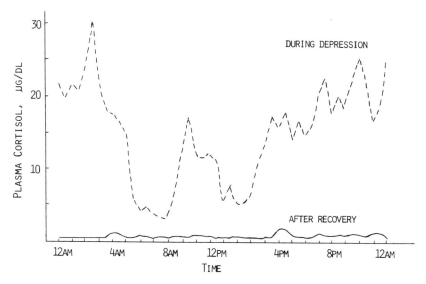

Figure 6. Response of depressed patient to cortisol (w/DST) during depression and after recovery. From Carroll et al. (1976) with permission.

Of final interest is an important study by Tarrier, Vaughn, Lader, and Leff (1979). The problem was to identify factors that precipitated high physiological reactions among schizophrenic patients during interviews. Tarrier et al. found that some schizophrenics under one condition showed very high autonomic reactivity, while other schizophrenics did not. The distinguishing condition was the presence of a family member and specifically the characteristic communication styles of that family member. Schizophrenics with relatives whose style involved high expressed emotion showed high reactivity. The following section on familial factors in psychopathology discusses expressed emotion and its definition and presents some significant findings.

Familial Factors in Psychopathology

The studies discussed here represent one of the most remarkable advances in the study of familial factors and what I consider to be one of *the* major findings of the decade (Koenigsberg & Handley, 1986; Leff & Vaughn, 1985). The work actually originated in England (Brown, Birley, & Wing, 1972) and shows how serendipity sometimes plays a role in new discoveries. As one example, Friedman and Rosenman (1974), the discoverers of Type A behavior, attribute their discovery to a patient's wife and an upholsterer. Believing that the common risk factors (e.g., diet, cholesterol) did not fully explain heart disease, Friedman and Rosenman were still puzzled about the key. However, matters fell neatly into place when a patient's wife called their attention to stress . . . and stress and impatience seemed to explain the observation of the upholsterer that the cardiologists' waiting room chairs were in need of repair only on the edges, which were worn down by impatient Type A patients sitting on the edge of their seats! In a similar way, Brown et al. began to study families when they noticed that male schizophrenic patients who relapsed tended to be those who went home to their wives. This led to the question of what it was about the presence of spouses that might be a factor, since one might assume that spouses would be good sources of support. As a result of Brown's interest, the first research on family communication styles known as "expressed emotionality" was published. The most impressive research on this topic is attributable to the now classic study of Vaughn and Leff (1976). Expressed emotion (EE) exists where family members show high levels of criticalness, hostility, and overinvolved emotionality when communicating with the person who later becomes schizophrenic. The Vaughn and Leff classic study is illustrated in Figure 7. The major conclusion is that schizophrenic patients from high EE families are much more subject to relapse and in greater need of medication than patients from low EE families.

The next logical question is whether relapse rates change if treatment is directly aimed at reducing the EE characteristics. Leff, Kuipers, and Berkowitz (1983) trained high-EE relatives in more healthy communication styles. The researchers then compared the relapse rates of those patients with relatives who had been trained versus those whose relatives had not received such training. The results were dramatic: After 2 years, the untrained group showed a relapse rate of 78% compared to only 20% of the trained group.

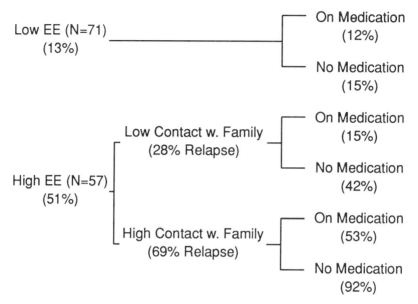

Figure 7. Total sample of patients: relapse rates. From Vaughn and Leff (1976) with permission.

But the final test of this concept is whether the presence of EE relatives is *predictive* of later breakdowns. Past research had been with patients who were already schizophrenic. A refinement of this approach was adopted in the UCLA Family Project (Rodnik, Goldstein, Lewis, & Doane, 1984) in which both communication and affective style were separated. Communications were rated as low or high deviance; affective style was rated as benign or poor (i.e., involving intrusiveness and guilt induction). Families were rated based on family discussions on emotionally sensitive topics. Although communication deviance and affective style separately did not predict later onset of schizophrenia, the combination of the two did (see Table 2). Low deviance with benign affective style was associated with nonpsychotic outcomes; high deviance with poorer affective style was associated with a higher likelihood of schizophrenic outcomes 5 years later.

The UCLA research actually used a revised version of the EE measure, but Vaughn, Snyder, Jones, Freeman, & Falloon (1984) did attempt an American replication with patients in California. They found the same trend of EE relating to relapse as in the UCLA sample. However, they also discovered that a much higher proportion of

American families showed high levels of EE than British subjects (67% versus 45%). This is an interesting case of cultural variables in action. To further clarify the role of such cultural differences a study by Moline, Singh, Morris, and Meltzer (1985) failed to replicate the EE results with Black patients in Illinois and with families with lower socioeconomic status. By adjusting the scoring system, however, Moline et al. were able to reproduce the results among the non-Black sample, but not with the Black sample.

Table 2
Communication Deviance (CD) and Affective Style (AS) as
Predictors of Schizophrenia Among Adolescents

	Low CD/ Benign AS	High CD/ Poorer AS
Normal or nonschizophrenic outcomes	100%	0%
Borderline, Character disorder outcomes	0%	36%
Schizophrenic outcomes	0%	64%

Note. Based on Rodnick et al. (1984) with permission.

Before leaving this issue, let us examine the question of cultural differences in what constitutes the normative level of EE behaviors. Thus far, it appears that levels of expressed emotion do differ, with families of American patients being highest, followed by families of patients of English, Mexican, and Indian (from India) origin at decreasing levels (Menon, Leff, Kuipers, et al., in press; Platman, 1983).

Cultural Factors in Psychopathology

The contribution of cultural factors to psychopathology continues to be seen in cross-cultural studies and has also become more evident from studies on American ethnic minorities (summarized in Pedersen, 1985; Pedersen, Draguns, Lonner, & Trimble, 1981; Westermeyer, 1985). It is also the topic reviewed by Richard Brislin elsewhere in this volume.

Ethnic Minorities and Psychopathology

The increase in numbers of ethnic minorities in the United States has finally brought attention to these groups, which already comprise over 20 percent of the nation's population. American Indians number over 1.3 million, Asians over 3.5 million, Blacks over 26.4 million, and Hispanics 14.6 million (U.S. Department of Commerce, 1981). Whereas cross-cultural studies from abroad have centered on the unique types of pathologies indigenous to other parts of the world, research on ethnic minorities in the United States has focused on improvement of psychotherapeutic models and mental health services (Suinn, 1987). Sue and Zane (1987) recently provided a reformulation of psychotherapy within a cultural context, and Sue (1987) spoke on this topic at the 1987 APA Convention. Therefore I will only highlight some of their observations:

• Therapists need to attend to their clients' cognitions. If a client's problems are conceptualized in ways incongruent with the client's cultural belief system, the credibility of the entire therapeutic process is jeopardized. For example, an Asian-American might be more mindful of family, whereas a Westerner might be more independent and self-reliant. It could therefore be a problem for the client when a therapist suggests that an Asian-American patient's goal should be to become more assertive and to confront his or her parents to resolve a conflict.

• Problem resolutions must be congruent with problem-solving behaviors that are acceptable and implementable within the clients' cultural environment. Costantino, Malgady, and Rogler (1986) have developed Cuento or folktale therapy that combines social learning modeling theory with Puerto Rican folktales for treating Puerto Rican children.

• The goals of therapy as defined by the client should be congruent with goals as defined by the therapist. Therapists with Western value systems should be aware of how their values affect the goals they establish for minority clients. Sue and Zane (1987) point out that Westerners tend to value being expressive, assertive, and self-disclosing. A therapist who *personally* holds these values could have difficulty working with a minority client from a culture with different values.

• Because of the high dropout rates of minority clients, therapists should be especially careful to identify early benefits of therapy that have value for these clients. Sue and Zane (1987) discuss this as a way to maintain client motivation. For example, if the client's culture defines a helping person as one who provides guidance or advice, then a therapist in an initial session might offer at least some minimal direction rather than using a completely nondirective style.

• Attention to fundamental steps in the therapeutic process, such as those cited above, is essential if more culturally specific intervention strategies, such as targeting of culturally relevant tactics, are to succeed (Rogler, Malgady, Costantino & Blumenthal, 1987; Sue, 1981). In the *American Psychologist,* Rogler et al. (1987) cite some examples for Hispanics, whereas special issues of *Psychotherapy* (Dudley & Rawlins, 1985) and *The Counseling Psychologist* (Smith & Vasquez, 1985) also touch on this topic as well as the general topic of work with minorities.

One current trend appears to be toward avoiding the broad sweep of the pendulum to the other extreme: from a prior claim that minority clients are no different in their treatment needs from nonminority clients, to the new claim that minorities must always receive culturally sensitive, specially-designed treatment. The first claim is an error of omission, the second claim an error of commission. The evolving position is to first treat the minority client as an individual and to seek to understand that individual's characteristics. If these characteristics include a strong cultural history and identity, then culturally sensitive approaches to treatment would be important. However, if the client shows little cultural determination in life issues, then ethnicity status may be less important. This approach recognizes that all clients, including nonminorities, possess cultural histories that must be considered in treatment planning. We Americans tend to forget that we too are products of a culture that has unique values, beliefs, and expectations, all of which shape our needs, problem-solving options, conflicts, goals, and attitudes. Therapists should therefore be sensitive to the relevance of such cultural factors in the early stages of intervention with minority *and* with nonminority clients.

Cross-cultural studies of other countries continue to identify disorders that appear distinctive to other societies. A brief summary offers some examples:

- Nicaragua: *grisi siknis* involves headaches, irrepressible anger toward nearby people, and aimless running and falling (Dennis, 1982).

- Korea: *hwa-byung* involves a violent fear of death from physical symptoms focused around the upper abdomen, e.g., sensations of fire and burning from the stomach up to the throat (Lin, 1983).

- Southeast Asia: *Koro* involves a delusion that genitals will retract into the body, panic with spasms and pain, and action to physically prevent the disappearance of the penis (Rubin, 1982).

- France: *bouffees delirantes* involves a transient psychotic condition involving trance states (Kroll, 1979).

- Japan: *shinkeitshitsu* involves fatigue, obsession and ambition toward perfection, and social withdrawal (Murase & Johnson, 1974).

More detailed case illustrations for abnormal psychology classes can be found in the articles cited above, as well as in Friedman and Faguet (1982).

Bulimia and Psychopathology

Remembering that the United States is also a country with a culture, I call your attention to one report that refers to 1981 in the United States as "the year of the binge purge syndrome" (Adler, 1982). Another considered "anorexia nervosa the disorder of the 1970s" and also cited "bulimia [as] the disorder of the 1980s" (Polivy & Herman, 1985, p. 200). Bulimia is characterized by episodes of binge eating, a feeling of loss of control over eating behaviors, preoccupation with body appearance, and attempts to prevent weight gain through a variety of methods such as self-induced vomiting (American Psychiatric Association, 1987; Russell, 1979).

Striegel-Moore, Silverstein, and Rodin (1986) explained bulimia as a response to American sociocultural norms. They first note that bulimia is primarily "a woman's problem" (p. 246). They then raise the questions: Why women? Which women in particular? And why now? And their answers all focus on the unique culture that women are exposed to in the 1980s. For instance, they point out that being thin is equated with being attractive in our society, and that women who internalize these standards are more subject to being bulimic. Garner, Garfinkel, Schwartz, and Thompson (1980) discovered that Miss America contestants and *Playboy* models have shown weights lower than the norms for American women. Further, the weights of these "ideal beauties" have declined over the last 20 years studied (1959–1978), and the finalists in Miss America contests since 1970 have weighed less than the other contestants.

Striegel-Moore et al. (1986) also provide evidence that subcultures responsive to such trends also have higher numbers of bulimic women. For instance, in schools where dating is emphasized (dating being associated with physical appearance), the prevalence of bulimia is high. Johnson, Lewis, Love, Stuckey, and Lewis (1984) found that about half of girls under age 14 already rated themselves as "overweight," even though they were actually within normal weight limits. More alarming was the fact that 50% of this young sample were already involved in use of diet pills, laxatives, or self-induced vomiting.

Finally, Striegel-Moore et al. (1986) also proposed that family values can exacerbate the problem, if the family also promotes thinness and emphasizes appearance. Further, they point out that women who are now bulimic are the daughters of the first Weight Watchers generation (Boskind-White & White, 1983).

Various interventions for bulimics are being designed and tested (Garner & Garfinkel, 1985) based on different theoretical analyses. For instance, one approach focuses on the notion that bulimia involves obsessive-compulsive features; hence Leitenberg, Gross, Peterson, and Rosen (1984) have used behavioral methods, such as exposure and response prevention therapy, that have proven successful with obsessive-compulsives. On the other hand, Fairburn (1981) assumed that the binging cycles would be reduced if the women acquired more appropriate eating habits. This habit control intervention therefore focused on normalizing the patient's eating pattern through scheduled and controlled meals. Another intervention focused on the premise that bulimics are subject to dichotomous thinking, that is, certain foods are "good" (diet) and others are"bad" (diet-breaking). For them, consumption of any amount of a "bad" food signals that the diet is broken anyway, and hence unrestrained eating might just as well take place, leading to binging (Polivy & Herman, 1985). With this in mind, Kirkley, Schneider, Agras, and Bachman (1985) included cognitive therapy in their program, aimed at breaking up the dichotomous thinking. Finally, pharmacotherapy has been attempted as a treatment (Pope, Hudson, Jonas, & Yurgelun-Todd, 1983). Based on follow-up success rates, the psychological approaches to treating bulimia appear to be more promising than the drug therapy.

Studies of bulimia have also examined the possibility that bulimia may be a form of depressive disorder. Although this is still open to question, research does confirm high prevalence of depressive symptoms among bulimic patients (Hinz & Williamson, 1987; Hsu, 1986; Walsh, Roose, Glassman, Gladis, & Sadik, 1985).In fact, the frequent appearance of depression with bulimia has led some to speculate that bulimia is actually a subform of depressive disorder (Yager & Strober, 1985)—which brings us to the next topic: depression and recent work regarding its effective treatment.

Depression

The modern history of depression has brought attention not only to genetic and biological factors of its origins, but also to purely psychological theories of the origins of certain depressions. In addition, developments regarding the theory of learned helplessness and research on treatment seem to be drawing serious attention to cognitive approaches in psychology.

Psychological Theories of Depression

There are three major psychological models of depression. Lewinsohn (1974) in one model views depression as a process of extinction. Depressed individuals initiate few reward-producing responses, which in turn leads to a lower amount of reinforcements from the environment. These events are then associated with the onset of dysphoria. This model acknowledges interaction between personal behaviors and environmental conditions. Specifically, susceptibility to depression is the end product of the range of the person's behaviors that can lead to reinforcement and the availability of reinforcing events in that person's environment. (One revision of this model is that of Rehm (1977), which emphasizes the role of self-administered reinforcement.)

Beck's model (Beck, Rush, Shaw, & Emery, 1979) offers a truly cognitive explanation, saying that depression derives from a person's distorted cognitions. The distortions are associated with what the model refers to as the negative triad of cognitive patterns: negative views of the world, negative views of the self, and negative views of the future. In addition, the thought processes of depressed persons are faulty, including tendencies to think in absolute terms, to overgeneralize, to draw conclusions without sufficient data, and to exaggerate the significance of undesirable outcomes.

Seligman's (1974) initial theory of learned helplessness proposed that depression was the consequence of loss of control. Specifically, depressive characteristics developed as a person experienced situations over which he or she had no control. In a later revision, a cognitive component was added involving attributions (Abramson, Seligman, & Teasdale, 1978). The first step remains the same in that the individual perceives that his or her behaviors are unrelated to outcomes. However, depression occurs depending upon the attributions made by the individual on three dimensions: internal-external, stable-unstable, and global-specific. Depression is likely where the person attributes failure to internal ("my own weakness"), stable ("this weakness is a long-standing and unchanging one"), and global ("this weakness is a hindrance in more than just this one setting") causes. I call attention to this revision partly because later I shall want to point to this trend of including cognitive elements in theories and practices. The next topic does relate to cognitive approaches but in terms of therapy for depression.

Cognitive Therapy for Depression

Perhaps the most significant development has been the continuing evidence in support of cognitively based therapy with depression, stimulated mainly by Beck's theory (Beck et al., 1979). Although other forms of psychotherapy have been developed for depression, cognitive behavior therapy has found support in the treatment of nonbipolar depressives, when compared with the use of drugs such as imipramine (see Table 3).

Table 3
Effects of Cognitive Therapy Compared With
Drug Therapy for Depressive Patients

	% Patients Recovering	
	Cognitive Therapy	Drug Therapy
Rush et al., 1977	79%	23%
Kovacs et al., 1981	83%	29%
Simons et al., 1986	53%	56%
Average of Studies	72%	36%

Note. Data from all three studies used with permission.

Cognitive therapy appears to have benefits for a wider number of patients than drug therapy. This is most noticeable in data that compare the numbers of patients who fail to improve from each treatment approach. In two such studies improvements were examined, finding an average of 13% did not benefit from cognitive therapy versus 19% from drug therapy (Murphy, Simons, Wetzel, & Lustman, 1984; Rush, Beck, Kovacs, & Hollon, 1977). Combining cognitive and drug therapy leads to some additional gains. Where patients received both therapies, 78% recovered and 11% showed no improvement (Murphy et al., 1984).

In sum, cognitive therapy appears to be gaining ground as a treatment of choice for unipolar depressions. But what about the status of other therapies? A brief overview of recent information from some selected studies is presented in the next section.

The Status of Therapies for Psychopathology

Review of Psychotherapies

Researchers have increasingly made use of the meta-analysis technique. In this approach, research findings from many studies are reviewed and outcomes statistically analyzed to provide a summary score referred to as "effect size." Smith, Glass, and Miller (1980) used journal abstracting services, major clinical journals in psychology, and dissertation abstracts to identify all controlled psychotherapy studies they could find. (Other useful reviews may be found in Howard, Kopta, Krause, & Orlinsky, 1986; Kazdin, 1986; Kendall, 1980; Miller & Berman, 1983; and Ursano & Hales, 1986). This produced 475 research reports. To put the effect sizes in perspective, keep in mind the following effect sizes, which will serve as reference points to interpret the meaning of other effect sizes for the various therapies:

    placebo effect size   = 0.56

    effect size after 9 months
        of classroom instruction
        on reading achievement
        (small class size)   = 0.82

With the above comparison points, some of the most interesting findings were as follows:

- all therapies versus placebo:
  - placebo   = 0.56
  - all therapies   = 0.93
- verbal psychotherapies versus behavioral therapies:
  - verbal   = 0.77
  - behavioral   = 0.96
- verbal versus behavioral for psychotics or depressives:
  - verbal   = 0.65 (psychotics); 0.95 (depressives)
  - behavioral   = 0.85 (psychotics); 1.27 (depressives)
- for psychoses:
  - humanistic Rx = 0.51
  - psychodynamic = 0.68
  - behavioral   = 0.85

A final set of trends, although not significant, involves identification of the strengths of various types of therapy. Strengths are defined in terms of the types of symptoms best addressed by the therapy approach. In brief, behavioral therapy worked best with fears and anxieties, emotional-somatic symptoms, global adjustment, and personal-vocational development; cognitive therapy was most effective with fears and anxieties and global adjustment; dynamic therapy worked best with emotional-somatic symptoms and work/school adjustment; and humanistic therapy was most effective with problems of self-esteem. On the other hand, behavioral and cognitive therapies had less impact on changing self-esteem, and dynamic therapy and humanistic therapy were less successful in achieving improvement in life adjustment goals.

Other Therapies

No summary of recent information can be complete without citing current reports in two other areas: the status of electroconvulsive therapy and the Vermont Longitudinal Study. Electroconvulsive therapy (ECT) has managed to remain viable despite public outcries and restrictions through state legislation (Fraser, 1982; Thompson & Blaine, 1987). There is an inclination to consider the approach barbaric and to dismiss its use; I recall that one reviewer criticized its inclusion in a standard textbook (Suinn, 1984). However, the research findings confirm that ECT does seem to have its place as an alternative, especially with depression (American Psychiatric Association, 1978; Scovern & Kilmann, 1980). One important gain has been the adoption of newer techniques, such as unilateral placement of electrodes and brief-pulse methods that permit shorter seizures and less memory interference (d'Elia, Ottasson, & Stromgren, 1983; Squire & Zouzounis, 1986). Even with these gains, ECT use has been declining, partly because there is still no reasonable understanding of why ECT works.

Finally, I would like to cite the Vermont Longitudinal Study (Harding, Brooks, Ashikaga, Straus, & Breier, 1987) because it offers some hope and some insights for severely disturbed schizophrenics. It is basically a follow-up study to see how patients have fared following discharge. These patients on the average had been ill for 16 years, totally unable to function for 10 years, and hospitalized for 6 consecutive years. The hospital relied upon a comprehensive approach, including chemotherapy, open ward status, graded privileges, vocational counseling, self-help groups, and use of halfway houses and support networks. The patients were chronic, backward, poorly educated, and lower class; in other words, those with the worst prognosis. Thirty-two years later, 68% had developed close friendships, 40% were employed, and 45% had no symptoms at all. Given the despairing prognosis of their hospitalization, these findings really deserve to be cited, if only to provide us all with a sense of hope regarding how to treat this serious disorder. The most interesting insight is that among the 40% employed, a number still had delusional or hallucinatory episodes—they had simply learned how to control these symptoms effectively. Recently, I have had contact with a woman who cannot distinguish her hallucinations from reality. However, her therapist has taught her to monitor her subjective experiences and to know when to be suspicious enough to call someone, such as her boyfriend, for some reality testing. The last I heard, she was making progress toward a successful professional career.

Overview: Trends and the Future

There are two major trends in abnormal psychology: the increased inclusion of cognitive variables and the broadening of developmental studies.

Cognitive Variables

I pointed out earlier that abnormal psychology has come to recognize cognitive variables. We have discussed Beck et al.'s (1979) theory of depression, Seligman's revision of his theory of learned helplessness (Abramson, Seligman, & Teasdale, 1978), and Bandura et al.'s (1985) research on self-efficacy, as well as the impact of cognitive therapy on depression. Current thinking about stress deserves mention as an additional example.

Various researchers (B. S. Dohrenwend & B. P. Dohrenwend, 1981; B. P. Dohrenwend & Shrout, 1985; Lazarus, DeLongis, Folkman, & Gruen, 1985; Lazarus & Folkman, 1984) have developed useful models of stress. They recognize life stressors, personal disposition, coping resources, and support systems. Lazarus (Lazarus & Folkman, 1984) has especially emphasized the importance of cognition by including "appraisal" as a key variable. The cognitive appraisal of stress is thus the key element that leads to stress, and similarly it is the appraisal of one's resources that influences the choice of coping responses.

As an important aside, the theories of stress have raised some promising ideas that may make it possible to make more precise predictions in psychopathology. Some examples of these ideas include the following:

• The concept of life stresses has led to the identification of types of stressors, which in turn has provided new information on possible predictor variables. For instance, life stress events now include a classification called "exit events." An exit event is a stressor involving some type of departure, such as death, divorce, separation, or a family member leaving. Exit events have been found to be predictive of suicide attempts (Slater & Depue, 1981).

• The concept of coping responses has led researchers to study the various types of possible coping strategies and to identify which ones appear to be unsuccessful in helping certain types of clients. The types of coping responses identified include problem focused, emotion focused, and appraisal focused (Billings, Cronkite, & Moos, 1983). Within the category of problem-focused coping responses, there are two subcategories: information seeking and problem solving. Depressives seem to rely more on information seeking, and this does not seem to help them. Within the category of emotion-focused coping responses there are the subcategories of emotional discharge and emotional regulation. Depressives seem to rely heavily on emotional discharge, again with little success in eliminating their depression. Thus, treatment of depressives might more effectively focus on replacing these less productive coping behaviors with more productive alternatives.

• The concept of matching coping responses to stressors can prove useful for therapists as they plan the direction of intervention. Emotion-focused interventions are more suited to high-stress situations where the client has little control over outcomes, such as traumatic situations (e.g., natural or environmental disaster, hostage captivity, or untreatable cancer). Problem-focused interventions would be more appropriate for transitory stressors where it is likely that a client will have a full return to normal life (Auerbach, 1986; Martelli, Auerbach, Alexander, & Mercuri, 1987).

In summary, the importance of cognitive variables in theory has become more prominent. The analysis of stress is a particularly good example of this trend.

Developmental Studies of Psychopathology

Prior research in psychopathology has tended to be cross-sectional, studying characteristics of existing patients. Longitudinal studies can provide added information, such as the validity of earlier predictor variables on later consequences. Certain developmental studies with children offer one such type of longitudinal data to enhance our knowledge in pathology, namely research on high-risk children and risk-resistant children (summarized in Garmezy, 1985; Watt, Anthony, Wynne, & Rolf, 1984).

The studies on high-risk children really began with genetic research, with "high-risk" defined as having one or both parents who were schizophrenic. A recent book edited by Watt, Anthony, Wynne, and Rolf (1984) provided a wide sampling of these studies including the Danish High Risk Project, the New York High Risk Project, the St. Louis High Risk Research Project, and the UCLA Family Project (Mednick, Cudeck, Griffith, Talovic, & Schulsinger, 1984; Worland, Janes, Anthony, McGinnis, & Cass, 1984). I noted earlier in this chapter that risk for schizophrenia can be identified early in life, as for example through signs of attentional dysfunctions (Erlenmeyer-Kimling et al., 1984; Nuechterlein, 1984). The UCLA project probed the link between family communication style and risk of pathology in the children (Rodnick et al., 1984). The New York research program uncovered the early signs associated with later development of schizophrenia, including childhood emotional volatility, abrasiveness in interpersonal relations, and deficiency in school motivation (Watt, Grubb, & Erlenmeyer-Kimling, 1982).

One approach that could extend the contributions of the high-risk projects would be to apply the path analysis approach. This could then more precisely identify the degree to which childhood symptoms directly predict adolescent or adult symptoms, as well as the degree to which family characteristics interact with such symptoms. Roff and Knight (1981) made an initial attempt at this involving maternal anxiety/neglect, childhood symptoms, and adult schizophrenia.

The studies of high risk have been very important in understanding early signs of psychopathology. However, Garmezy (1985) has argued that these high-risk studies are too one-sided. Garmezy sees the study of high-risk subjects as emphasizing failure, disability, and incompetence. In contrast, he has spearheaded work on "the invulnerable child" or the risk-resistant or ego-resilient child as focusing on "the language of children's successes, of their overcoming of adversity, of their potential for adaptation and self-sufficiency" (p. 225). Garmezy (1985; Masten & Garmezy, 1985) has identified what he considers the sine qua non of certain children's invulnerability to such stressors as parental psychopathology, poverty, or divorce. He proposes a protective triad of factors: (a) dispositional, (b) family cohesion and warmth, and (c) availability of an external support system. The dispositional (or temperamental) factors appear in the way infants respond to environmental changes, reachieve physiological equilibrium, respond to being comforted, and control sleep–wakefulness cycles (Block & Block, 1980). Family cohesion and warmth are self-explanatory and have been known to exist even after divorce between natural parents. Positive adaptation to divorce by children 5 years later is predicted from certain parental characteristics: the extent to which the parents resolved their conflict and anger; the resumption of good parenting in the home; and the maintenance of a positive relationship with the noncustodial parent (Wallerstein & Kelly, 1980). The third factor of the triad, the availability of an external support system, is congruent with all of the studies on stress management cited earlier. In the research on adult suicides, exit events and accumulation of recent stressors are predictive of suicide attempts; however, the availability of social support systems reduces suicidal risk (Slater and Depue, 1981). In research on risk-resistant children, a similar finding has emerged. Rutter (1979) found that an increased rate of psychiatric disorders among children was associated with the presence of maternal psychiatric disorders—a finding consistent with the initial definitions of high-risk children. Further, the prevalence increases dramatically as a child is forced to face other stresses in the environment such as overcrowding, marital discord, or low socioeconomic level. Interestingly, the presence of two or three stressors increased risk fourfold, while the presence of four factors produced a tenfold increase of risk. Once again regarding risk resistance, Rutter found temperament and parental warmth and affection to be protective factors. In addition, an external support system of teachers to whom the child could turn was a crucial risk reducer (Rutter, Maughan, Mortimore, & Ouston, 1979).

Summary

It seems clear to me that striking findings have appeared in the literature on abnormal psychology in a number of areas: genetic, biological, familial, cultural, and psychological. However, as I indicated earlier, it would be inaccurate to conclude that the origins of pathology can be said to belong in any one of these areas. Each appears to be a contributing factor, sometimes specific to a disorder (e.g., bipolar disorder seems the most likely candidate for a genetic factor). Some may provide significant explanations when our diagnostic classifications are more refined—for example, perhaps process schizophrenia and reactive schizophrenia need to be reconsidered as categories and the classification of "negative" and "positive" schizophrenic symptoms has value. We can certainly demonstrate that there are many interactions among these areas, with genetics influencing biological conditions, psychological conditions affecting neurochemical states, and cultural environments affecting familial characteristics. The fact that I could identify a research study that linked each of my major topics to the next demonstrates that interactions do exist. And this has been the major theme of this chapter: that the study of psychopathology is not a study of a single topic (genetic, biological, etc.) but rather a study of multiple origins and multiple interactions. Like good detectives, we must be wary of narrowing our list of suspects too quickly simply because an outstanding clue has surfaced. And, like readers of a good mystery story with a complex plot, we should realize that we are indeed still in the middle of our story and not yet on the last page where the solution is revealed!

Discussion Topic: Genetics

Questions: Does your birth month increase your risk of being schizophrenic?
If so, why would this be the case?
How would one design a study to find out?

The Data. Research has been conducted on schizophrenia and season of birth, with the first report being in 1929 but with the most recent being in 1984. Bradbury and Miller (1985) review the literature covering over 200,000 births and conclude "the seasonality effect can be regarded as firmly established" (p. 582). The data is summarized in Table 4.

Several hypotheses have been offered for this strange association:

Diathesis-stress hypothesis. Winter represents an environmental stress, possibly causing physical damage; there is some evidence for this in a reported relationship between winter birth and evidence of brain damage (Shur, 1982).

Genetic-fitness hypothesis. Surviving winter demands that the infant be more robust (only the fit survive); the hypothesis also states that the same genetic factor that insures robustness also produces schizophrenia; there is some evidence for this notion of robustness in that there was an excess of schizophrenic births during a decade of viral epidemics (1915–1924) in Australia (Jones & Frei, 1979).

Table 4
Season of Birth and Schizophrenia

Studies supporting winter births	69%
Studies with no results for winter	31%
Studies supporting summer births	0%

Note. Based on data calculated from Bradbury and Miller (1985) with permission.

Procreation-deviancy hypothesis. Parents of schizophrenics are said to be more prone to intercourse leading to conception during spring and summer (leading to winter deliveries); this hypothesis is difficult to test and has few supporters.

Discussion Topic: Biological

Questions: Is being left-handed a possible "marker" (symptom) of later schizophrenia?
What reasonable explanation might there be for such a relationship between handedness and psychopathology?

The Data. A number of studies have actually shown a trend for schizophrenics to either actually be left-handed, or at least to not be dominantly right-handed (instead being ambidextrous) (Nasrallah et al., 1982; Piran et al., 1982; Shan-Ming et al., 1985), with the most recent report being in the May 1987 issue of the *Journal of Abnormal Psychology* (Chapman & Chapman, 1987). Table 5 summarizes one set of findings, involving two types of measures of hemispheric dominance: percent persons who are left-hand dominant in writing, and percent who are left-eye dominant.

Table 5
Left-Handedness, Left-Eye Dominance, and Schizophrenia

	% Left-handed	% Left-eye dominant
Schizophrenic patients	23.1	73.0
Psychiatric patients who are not schizophrenic	6.3	12.5
Normal sample	11.1	27.8

Note. Based on Piran et al. (1982) with permission.

Why would this association be the case? One theoretical link is the fact that persons with temporal lobe epilepsy sometimes show symptoms similar to a schizophrenic psychosis, so there is speculation about brain involvement in schizophrenia. Further, schizophrenia involves symptoms such as thought and speech disturbances, and it is known that the left hemisphere of the brain tends to rule verbal and analytical functions; hence schizophrenia might be due to a disturbance of the left hemisphere. Finally, if there is a left-hemisphere disturbance, then the individual is not likely to be right-handed, since the left hemisphere controls the right hand. Therefore, schizophrenics are more likely to be either left-handed or ambidextrous (i.e., not dominantly right-handed).

Discussion Topic: Multiple Personality

Questions: Are multiple personalities real disorders, or are they artifacts created by therapists who seek publicity?
Are multiple personalities in the modern century still a rare phenomenon?
What causes multiple personalities to appear?

The Data. The appearance of multiple personalities in the literature seemed to suggest that these were rare disorders. The highly publicized case of Eve was brought to the public via a popular book and later a movie. Even more attention came from Eve herself, who revealed her identity to be that of Mrs. Chris Sizemore of Fairfax, Virginia. Her willingness to make public appearances included a presentation at the 1982 convention of the American Psychological Association (for an interview, see Suinn, *Fundamentals of abnormal psychology,* 1984, p. 180).

In actuality, there seems a resurgence of multiple personality disorders. Boor (1982) summarized the number of cases as follows: 1817–1944, 76 cases; 1944–1969, 14 cases; 1970–1979, 79 cases. Bliss (1983) believes that many cases of psychotics actually involve multiple personalities; specifically, patients with auditory hallucinations may actually be misdiagnosed. Bliss reported that 27 of 45 such patients (60%) were more accurately examples of multiple personality rather than patients suffering from hallucinations.

There is recognition that some investigators seem to "uncover" unusually higher numbers of multiple personality disorders in their caseload; one psychiatrist is cited who personally treated 50 cases (Greaves, 1980). One explanation is that patients are being subtly taught by their therapists to take on roles that simulate the multiple personality disorder, especially when the patient is susceptible while under hypnosis (Spanos, 1985).

Even with the possibility that some multiple personalities are created by therapists, there is still evidence that the disorder does exist. The etiology is said to involve the presence of an environment that fosters an attitude of extreme ambivalence towards others, along with a major trauma. Parents are generally perfectionistic and severe in their restrictions. There is family discord or rejection and ambivalence about the expression of anger and about sexuality.

Discussion Topic: Seasonal Affective Disorder

Questions: Are moods affected by the seasons? Winter seems gloomy . . . spring seems alive and cheerful.
Is it possible to brighten up a person by using bright lights?

The Data. A striking case of bipolar depression involved a 63-year-old man whose initial mood disorder started when he was 35 years old. Because he was a meticulous person, he had kept records of his mood states over 14 consecutive years, sharing this information with his therapists. Figure 8 shows the relationship that these records revealed. It appeared that his depressions would start during the summer months, whereas his manic states would begin during the winter (Lewy et al., 1982). On a larger group of patients, an association did seem to appear in some, but the typical pattern was for depression to be associated with fall or winter, and manic states to be precipitated by spring or summer (Wehr et al., 1986). One speculation involved the possibility that the seasons were influential because of the differences in the amount of light. Rosenthal et al.(1984) collected information on patients who were depressed mainly during the winter, and the average amount of daily light during these winter months. And there did indeed seem to be a relationship, with the highest numbers of patients experiencing depression during the months where there was the least amount of daily sunlight (Figure 9). Further, as the amount of sunlight increased, the numbers of depressed patients decreased. The correlation coefficient representing these data was found to be −.87. Moreover, when they allowed a 1-month lag between the light measurement and the depression measurement, the correlation went up to −.98! The possibility of a seasonal type of depression has now been accepted to the degree that DSM-III-R has included a classification of "seasonal pattern" for bipolar or recurrent major depressions.

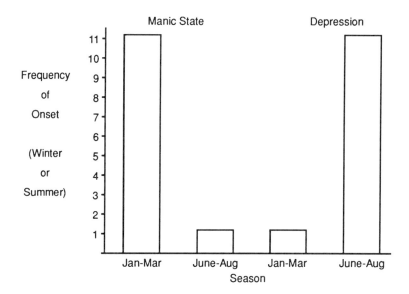

Figure 8. Frequency of onset of seasonal affective disorder by season. Based on Lewy et al. (1982) with permission.

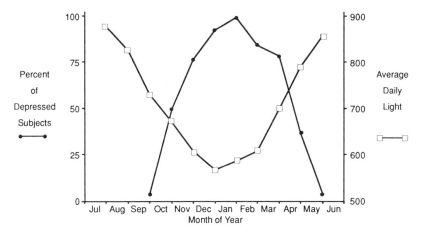

Figure 9. Illustration of inverse relationship of light to depression. Based on Rosenthal et al. (1983) with permission.

Discussion Topic: On Being Sane in Insane Places

Questions: What happened to the sane persons who allowed themselves to be hospitalized, and then tried to convince the staff that they were sane all the time?
What opinions do you have about the fact that errors were made by the hospital staff?
How does this experience relate to "Type I" and "Type II" errors?

The Data. The well-known study by Rosenhan (1973) had eight normal colleagues admitted to a psychiatric hospital. Each person complained of hearing voices that said "thud" or "hollow." In all other ways, these persons behaved normally. After admission, they sought to convince the hospital personnel that they were normal and not psychotic. It required anywhere from 7 to 52 days before these normal "patients" could convince the staff to discharge them . . . and even then, they were classified not as cured but as "in remission."

Typically, discussion of this study has pointed out the errors and biases to which hospital staff may be subject, or discussion may center around the problems of diagnostic techniques. Although these are useful topics, another approach can also be meaningful, and this focuses on the differences between Type I and Type II errors. Davis (1976) defends the diagnoses made by the hospital staff purely on base rates, since the most probable diagnosis of anyone reporting in to a psychiatric hospital is that of psychopathology rather than normalcy. However, the further point which Davis argues is to ask which type of error the public would prefer: a Type I or a Type II. The Type I error would involve failing to properly diagnose a person who is actually psychotic (diagnosing a psychotic person as normal; a false negative). The Type II error would involve failing to properly identify a healthy person as being healthy (diagnosing the healthy person as psychotic; a false positive). According to Davis, the two issues of the two errors pit the cost of turning a psychotic away from hospital care versus the outrage of the public that a sane person would be mistakenly called insane. For student discussions, which would the class prefer?

Discussion Topic: Case History, Hallucination (Psychosis)

Questions: What is it like to experience a hallucination?
            If I see things that aren't there or hear things that don't exist, am I crazy?

The Data. An interesting self-report has appeared in the *Journal of Abnormal Psychology* by a person who was otherwise normal (Goldstein, 1976). This personal account offers a unique experience about the intense reality of hallucinations. The writer is an experimental psychologist who had been hospitalized for surgery on his spine. He was extremely anxious and fearful of the surgery and had been sleep-deprived. Although he had been on some medication, he believes that the hallucination was stress-induced and not drug-induced:

> I saw a long, dark corridor, extending to the left of my door, which resembled the inside of a castle . . . with dark wood paneling . . . In this corridor single individuals, couples, groups of people, and children appeared to be moving toward my room . . . The images . . . *were* insistent, vivid, and remarkably varied in the colors and other details of clothing, in heights and ages of the individuals, and in their behavior.
>
> An hour or so after sunrise . . . my roommate, John, appeared to have company in bed with him. At the time, I immediately assumed that it was his wife . . . I did see that she had her arms around him, and I was quite positive that I saw [her] caressing him . . . notwithstanding the fact that at the time I was also aware . . . this just could not happen in a hospital (after a circumcision no less!) . . . While deciding what to do, I heard voices in the hallway . . . discussing the unusual situation I was seeing. The voices (nurses I assumed) remarked that "she had been there long enough," that "this sort of activity was not really allowed," and that "she should be asked to leave" . . . finally I . . . saw clearly that John was sleeping alone, [but] I was still partially convinced that his wife must have gone into the small bathroom adjoining the room. In spite of intense pain, I looked into the bathroom, and, of course, found no one. Just as I turned to return to my bed, I was astonished to hear, loud and very clearly, the voices of my two young children. Since they were in New York City (1,000 miles away), I knew that I was not hearing *their* voices. The voices were uncanny: perfect copies of my children's individual voice qualities and intonations. (p. 424)

Discussion Topic: Case Histories, Twins (Genetics)

Questions: How much control does genetics have in influencing our actions?

Wouldn't our environment and upbringing have more to do with shaping the kind of persons we become?

How do twin studies provide us with information on the role of genetics versus environment?

The Data. Identical twins share the exact same genetic origins, and therefore personality and other characteristics that they share could be attributed to genetics. However, because twins are raised in the same family environment, it is also difficult to rule out the influence of this environment. Therefore, we are interested in situations where the genetics are identical but the environments are different. This is the situation for identical twins reared apart. One pair of case histories illustrates some similarities even where the twins were raised in different households.

Herbert and Nick were identical twins; they were the bastard children of a half-Chinese 19-year-old girl "impregnated by a pinball machine repairman." Herbert was a bedwetter until age 12, a firesetter, and convicted of delinquency for theft. He was drafted in the Army and "served honorably, doing menial tasks" (Gottesman & Shields, 1982, p. 125). He was a delivery boy until age 22. On January 8, he was hospitalized, staring silently, believed he could read people's thoughts, and concerned about Communist aggression and war.

Nick was a bedwetter until age 14, a firesetter, and convicted of delinquency for theft. He was drafted in the Army and "served honorably, doing menial tasks" (p. 125). He was a delivery boy until age 22. On January 5 of the same week as his brother's admittance, he was admitted to a different hospital: His symptoms included being lost in thought, believing he had special powers, and being concerned about aggression by the devil. The twins have been hospitalized in different institutions for over 20 years and have not had contact with one another.

Discussion Topic: Avoiding Errors in Research

Questions: Are there dangers in interpreting tables that show associations between two factors, for instance, amount of light during a season and onset of depression?

What other explanations could there be when one factor seems highly correlated with another one?

The Data. Many studies measure changes in one factor, such as amount of daily light during winter months, and see if these changes seem to match up with changes in another factor, such as the number of patients reporting depression during that same time period. If the two seem to be associated, then sometimes it is concluded that one factor is the cause of the other. The association is referred to as a correlation. However, sometimes a correlation between two factors does not provide any proof of causality. Consider the study by Gibbons and Davis (1984) to prove just this point. They analyzed the association between the price of beer and the salaries of ministers, and showed that as the salaries of ministers increased, so did the price of beer (Figure 10). Now what does the price of beer have to do with the price of ministers? Absolutely nothing. Hence, one caution regarding such correlations is to understand that an association may be purely by chance. Or the association may be due to a third factor that causes simultaneous changes in the other two. For instance, the price of both beer and ministers might be climbing because of inflation. Consider the similarities between the associations shown in Figure 10 for beer and salaries, and those for Figure 11 for cortisol levels and depression. Figure 11 also suggests that there is a relationship between level of cortisol and the appearance of depression. The question is: Does this association prove a causal relationship? Let's discuss the issue in terms of the research on seasonal affective disorders.

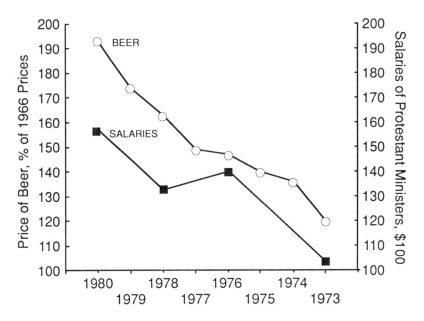

Figure 10. Association of beer and ministers' salaries. Based on Gibbons and Davis (1984) with permission.

In order for a causal connection to be proven, more than a simple correlation is needed. In the case of the seasonal affective disorders, the initial observation was that season seemed associated with onset of depression. The association in one patient was repeated with a larger group in order to insure that the correlation was not restricted to just the one case. The next step was to then influence a change in the one factor and to see if a change in that factor led to a change in the other. If such change did occur, then causality might be believed to be present. For instance, if we deliberately changed the price of beer and saw that the salaries of ministers also changed, then we might conclude a relationship. Exposing depressive patients suffering from seasonal affective disorder to light treatment that simulated a change in the season did seem to alleviate the depression for some patients.

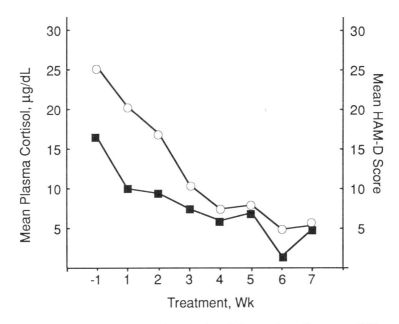

Figure 11. Association of cortisol and depression. Based on Gibbons and Davis (1984) with permission.

Discussion Topic: Psychological Factors and Cancer Survival

Questions: Cancer is an entirely medical problem; what would the psychological study contribute anyway?
Can one's personality really influence the chances for beating death from cancer?

The Data. Cancer does in fact appear to be a biological and medical issue. Although the actual mechanism for cancer is not known, certain origins are identifiable, such as smoking or radiation. Initially, attempts to uncover a "cancer personality"—that is, a personality that could be predicted as being susceptible to cancer—have been unsuccessful. However, other studies appear to have some potential in the examination of characteristics of patients that may influence survival, once cancer appears (Derogatis, 1986). One such study was reported by Geer et al. (1979). Women who had been diagnosed as having breast cancer were followed up 5 years after surgery.

Their progress was classified as follows: alive but with recurrence of cancer; alive with no recurrence; dead. "Favorable" outcomes were defined by such information as whether the cancer recurred and size or evidence of spread of the cancer. Patients were also classified in terms of their attitudes: "fighting spirit," denial, stoic, or helplessness. Results showed that 75% of the patients who were alive without recurrence of the cancer (favorable outcome) had been characterized as showing as "fighting spirit" or denial; 88% of those who had died had shown the stoic or helpless attitude. Those who were alive but with recurrences involved more patients with a stoic or helpless attitude than a fighting spirit or denial.

It is too early to determine the mechanisms whereby attitudes can influence such medical outcomes. There is speculation that psychoimmunology may be a legitimate concept: The body's immune system can be responsive to psychological states. Certainly this is consistent with knowledge that emotions or beliefs can influence physiological conditions, such as catecholamine secretion (Strickland, 1985). But the final answer is yet to come.

References

Abramson, L., Seligman, M., & Teasdale, J. (1978). Learned helplessness in humans: Critique and reformulation. *Journal of Abnormal Psychology, 87,* 49–74.

Adler, J. (1982, January 4). Looking back at '81. *Newsweek,* 26–52.

Alexander, G., & Goldman, P. (1978). Functional development of the dorsolateral prefrontal cortex: An analysis utilizing reversible cryogenic depression. *Brain Research, 143,* 233–249.

American Psychiatric Association. (1978). *Report No. 14 of the American Psychiatric Association Task Force on Convulsive Therapy.* Washington, DC: Author.

American Psychiatric Association. (1987). *Diagnostic and statistical manual of mental disorders (3rd ed., revised).* Washington, DC: Author.

Andreasen, N., Olsen, S., Dennert, J., & Smith, M. (1982). Ventricular enlargement in schizophrenia: Relationship to positive and negative symptoms. *American Journal of Psychiatry, 139,* 297–302.

Auerbach, S. (1986). Assumptions of crisis theory and a temporary model of crisis intervention. In S. Auerbach & A. Stolberg (Eds.), *Crisis intervention with children and families* (pp. 3–37). New York: Hemisphere/ McGraw-Hill.

Bandura, A., Taylor, C., Williams, S., Mefford, I., & Barchas, J. (1985). Catecholamine secretion as a function of perceived coping self-efficacy. *Journal of Consulting and Clinical Psychology, 54,* 406–414.

Barnes, D. (1987). Biological issues in schizophrenia. *Science, 235,* 430–433.

Beck, A., Rush, A., Shaw, B., & Emery, G. (1979). *Cognitive therapy of depression.* New York: Guilford Press.

Bertelsen, A., Harvald, B., & Hauge, M. (1977). A Danish twin study of manic-depressive disorders. *British Journal of Psychiatry, 130,* 330–351.

Billings, A., Cronkite, R., & Moos, R. (1983). Social-environmental factors in unipolar depression: Comparisons of depressed patients and nondepressed controls. *Journal of Abnormal Psychology, 92,* 119–133.

Bliss, E., Larson, E., & Nakashima, S. (1983). Auditory hallucinations and schizophrenia. *Journal of Nervous and Mental Disease, 171,* 30–33.

Block, J., & Block, J. (1980). The role of ego-control and ego-resiliency in the organization of behavior. In W. Collins (Ed.), *Development of cognition, affect, and social relations: The Minnesota Symposia on Child Psychology, 13,* 39–101. Hillsdale, NJ: Erlbaum Associates.

Boor, M. (1982). The multiple personality epidemic: Additional cases and inferences regarding diagnosis, etiology, dynamics and treatment. *Journal of Nervous and Mental Disease, 170,* 302–304.

Boskind-White, M., & White, W. (1983). *Bulimarexia: The binge/purge cycle.* New York: Norton.

Bradbury, T., & Miller, G. (1985). Season of birth in schizophrenia: A review of evidence, methodology, and etiology. *Psychological Bulletin, 98,* 569–594.

Brown, G., Birley, J., & Wing, J. (1972). Influence of family life on the course of schizophrenic disorders: A replication. *British Journal of Psychiatry, 121,* 241–258.

Brown, W., Johnston, R., & Mayfield, D. (1979). The 24-hour dexamethasone suppression test in a clinical setting: Relationship to diagnosis, symptoms and response to treatment. *American Journal of Psychiatry, 136,* 543–547.

Carroll, B., Curtis, G., & Mendels, J. (1976). Neuroendocrine regulation in depression. *Archives of General Psychiatry, 33,* 1039–1044.

Cegalis, J. A., & Sweeney, J. A. (1979). Eye movements in schizophrenia: A quantitative analysis. *Biological Psychiatry, 14,* 13–26.

Chapman, J., & Chapman, L. (1987). Handedness of hypothetically psychosis-prone subjects. *Journal of Abnormal Psychology, 96,* 89–93.

Costantino, G., Malgady, R., & Rogler, R. (1985). Cuento therapy: Folk tales as a culturally sensitive psychotherapy for Puerto Rican children. *Hispanic Research Center Monograph No. 12.* Maplewood, NJ: Waterfront Press.

Davis, D. (1976). On being *detectably* sane in insane places: Base rates and psychodiagnosis. *Journal of Abnormal Psychology, 85,* 416–422.

d'Elia, G., Ottasson, J., & Stromgren, L. (1983). Present practice of electroconvulsive therapy in Scandinavia. *Archives of General Psychiatry, 40,* 577–581.

Dennis, P. (1982). Grisi Siknis among the Miskito. *Medical Anthropology, 5,* 445–505.

Derogatis, L. (1986). Psychology in cancer medicine: A perspective and overview. *Journal of Consulting and Clinical Psychology, 54,* 632–638.

Dohrenwend, B. S., & Dohrenwend, B. P. (Eds.) (1981). *Stressful life events and their contexts.* New York: Prodist.

Dohrenwend, B. P., & Shrout, P. (1985). "Hassles" in the conceptualization and measurement of life stress variables. *American Psychologist, 40,* 780–785.

Dudley, G., & Rawlins, M. (Eds.). (1985). Psychotherapy with ethnic minorities. *Psychotherapy, 22,* 308–478.

Egeland, J., & Hostetter, A. (1983). An Amish Study I: Affective disorders among the Amish, 1976–1980. *American Journal of Psychiatry, 140,* 56–61.

Erlenmeyer-Kimling, L., Kestenbaum, C., Bird, H., & Hilldoff, U. (1984). Assessment of the New York High-Risk Project subjects in sample A who are now clinically deviant. In M. Watt, E. Anthony, L. Wynne, & J. Rolf, (Eds.), *Children at risk for schizophrenia: A longitudinal perspective* (pp. 227–239). New York: Cambridge University Press.

Fairburn, C. (1981). A cognitive behavioral approach to the treatment of bulimia. *Psychological Medicine, 11,* 707–711.

Faraone, S., & Tsuang, M. (1985). Quantitative models of the genetic transmission of schizophrenia. *Psychological Bulletin, 98,* 41–66.

Fraser, M. (1982). *ECT: A clinical guide.* New York: Wiley.

Friedman, C., & Faguet, R. (Eds.). (1982). *Extraordinary diseases of human behavior.* New York: Plenum Press.

Friedman, M., & Rosenman, R. (1974). *Type A behavior and your heart.* New York: Knopf.

Garmezy, N. (1985). Stress-resistant children: The search for protective factors. In J. Stevenson (Ed.), *Recent research in developmental psychopathology. Journal of Child Psychology and Psychiatry Book Supplement No. 4* (pp. 213–233). Oxford: Pergamon Press.

Garner, D., & Garfinkel, P. (Eds.) (1985). *Handbook of psychotherapy for anorexia nervosa and bulimia.* New York: Guilford Press.

Garner, D., Garfinkel, P., Schwartz, D., & Thompson, M. (1980). Cultural expectations of thinness of women. *Psychological Reports, 47,* 483, 491.

Geer, S., Morris, T., & Pettingale, K. (1979). Psychological response to breast cancer: Effect on outcome. *Lancet, ii,* 785–787.

Gibbons, R., & Davis, J. (1984). The price of beer and the salaries of priests: Analysis and display of longitudinal psychiatric data. *Archives of General Psychiatry, 41,* 1183–1184.

Goldstein, A. (1976). Hallucinatory experience: A personal account. *Journal of Abnormal Psychology, 85,* 423–429.

Gottesman, I. (1985). The contribution of genetic factors to the common psychopathologies. *Resource Paper to the Report of the National Mental Health Association Commission on the Prevention of Mental-Emotional Disabilities.* Arlington, VA: National Mental Health Association.

Gottesman, I., McGuffin, P., Farmer, A., McGue, M., Vogler, G., Bertelsen, A., & Rao, D. (in press). Genetics and schizophrenia—Current state of negotiations. In F. Vogler & K. Sperling (Eds.), *Human genetics.* New York: Springer-Verlag.

Gottesman, I., & Shields, J. (1982). *Schizophrenia: The epigenetic puzzle.* New York: Cambridge University Press.

Greaves, G. (1980). Multiple personality 165 years after Mary Reynolds. *Journal of Nervous and Mental Disease, 168,* 577–595.

Gur, R., Resnick, S., Alavi, A., Gur, R., Caroff, S., Dann, R., Silver, F., Saykin, A., Chawluk, J., Kushner, M., & Reivich, M. (1987). Regional brain function in schizophrenia: I. A Positron Emission Tomography study. *Archives of General Psychiatry, 44,* 119–125.

Harding, C., Brooks, G., Ashikaga, T., Straus, J., & Breier, A. (1987). The Vermont longitudinal study of persons with severe mental illness, II: Long-term outcome of subjects who retrospectively met DSM-III criteria for schizophrenia. *American Journal of Psychiatry, 144,* 727–735.

Heiby, E., Campos, P., Remick, R., & Keller, F. (1987). Dexamethasone suppression and self-reinforcement correlates of clinical depression. *Journal of Abnormal Psychology, 96,* 70–72.

Heston, L., Mastri, A., Anderson, E., & White, J. (1981). Dementia of the Alzheimer type. *Archives of General Psychiatry, 38,* 1085–1090.

Hinz, L., & Williamson, D. (1987). Bulimia and depression: A review of the affective variant hypothesis. *Psychological Bulletin, 102,* 150–158.

Holzman, P., & Solomon, C. (1984). Pursuit eye movement dysfunctions in schizophrenia. *Archives of General Psychiatry, 41,* 136–139.

Hostetter, A. (1987, May). Scientists warn role of biology miscast in wake of Amish study. *APA Monitor, 18,* 16–17.

Howard, K., Kopta, S., Krause, M., & Orlinsky, D. (1986). The dose-effect relationship in psychotherapy. *American Psychologist, 41,* 159–164.

Hsu, L. (1986). The treatment of anorexia nervosa. *American Journal of Psychiatry, 143,* 473–481.

Ingvar, D. (1976). Functional landscapes of the dominant hemisphere. *Brain Research, 107,* 181–197.

Inouye, E. (1972). Monozygotic twins with schizophrenia reared apart in infancy. *Japanese Journal of Human Genetics, 16,* 182–190.

Johnson, C., Lewis, C., Love, S., Stuckey, M., & Lewis, L. (1984). Incidence and correlates of bulimic behavior in a female high school population. *Journal of Youth and Adolescence, 13,* 6.

Jones, I., & Frei, D. (1979). Seasonal births in schizophrenia: A southern hemisphere study using matched pairs. *Acta Psychometrica Scandinavica, 59,* 164–172.

Kay, D. (1986). The epidemiology of Alzheimer's disease. *British Medical Bulletin, 42,* 19–23.

Kazdin, A. (Ed.). (1986). Psychotherapy research [Special issue]. *Journal of Consulting and Clinical Psychology, 54,* 3–118.

Kendall, P. (1985). Toward a cognitive-behavioral model of child psychopathology and a critique of related interventions. *Journal of Abnormal Child Psychology, 13,* 357–372.

Kendell, R. (1980).The present status of electroconvulsive therapy. *British Journal of Psychiatry, 139,* 265–283.

Kendler, K. (1983). Overview: A current perspective on twin studies of schizophrenia. *American Journal of Psychiatry, 140,* 1413–1425.

Kendler, K. & Eaves, L. (1986). Models for the joint effect of genotype and environment on liability to psychiatric illness. *American Journal of Psychiatry, 143,* 279–289.

Kirkley, B., Schneider, J. Agras, W., & Bachman, J. (1985). Comparison of two group treatments for bulimia. *Journal of Consulting and Clinical Psychology, 53,* 43–48.

Koenigsberg, H., & Handley, R. (1986). Expressed emotion: From predictive index to clinical construct. *American Journal of Psychiatry, 143,* 1361–1373.

Kovacs, M., Rush, A., Beck, A., & Hollon, S.(1981). Depressed outpatients treated with cognitive therapy of pharmocotherapy: A one year follow-up. *Archives of General Psychiatry, 38,* 33–39.

Kroll, J. (1979). Philosophical foundations of French and US nosology. *American Journal of Psychiatry, 136,* 1135–1138.

Lazarus, R., DeLongis, A., Folkman, S., & Gruen, R. (1985). Stress and adaptational outcomes: The problem of confounded measures. *American Psychologist, 40,* 770–779.

Lazarus, R., & Folkman, S. (1984). *Stress, appraisal, and coping.* New York: Springer.

Leff, J., Kuipers, L., & Berkowitz, R. (1983). Intervention in families of schizophrenics and its effects on relapse rate. In W. McFarlane (Ed.), *Family therapy in schizophrenia* (pp. 173–187). New York: Guilford Press.

Leff, J., & Vaughn, C. (1985). *Expressed emotion in families.* New York: Guilford Press.

Leitenberg, H., Gross, J., Peterson, J., & Rosen, J. (1984). Analysis of an anxiety model and the process of change during exposure plus response prevention treatment of bulimia nervosa. *Behavior Therapy, 15,* 3–20.

Lewinsohn, P. (1974). A behavioral approach to depression. In R. Friedman & M. Katz (Eds.), *The psychology of depression.* Washington, DC: Winston.

Lewy, A., Kern, H., Rosenthal, N., & Wehr, T. (1982). Bright artificial light treatment of a manic-depressive patient with a seasonal mood cycle. *American Journal of Psychiatry, 139,* 1496–1498.

Lin, K. (1983). Hwa-Byung: A Korean culture-bound syndrome? *American Journal of Psychiatry, 140,* 107.

Martelli, M., Auerbach, S., Alexander, J., & Mercuri, L. (1987). Stress management in the health care setting: Matching interventions with patient coping styles. *Journal of Consulting and Clinical Psychology, 55,* 201–207.

Masten, A., & Garmezy, N. (1985). Risk, vulnerability and protective factors in developmental psychopathology. In B. Lahey & A. Kazdin (Eds.), *Advances in clinical child psychology* (pp. 1–53). New York: Plenum.

Mathew, R., Meyer, J., Francis, D., Semchuk, K., Mortel, K., & Claghorn, J. (1980). Cerebral blood flow in depression. *American Journal of Psychiatry, 137,* 1449–1450.

McNeal, E., & Cimbolic, P. (1986). Antidepressants and biochemical theories of depression. *Psychological Bulletin, 99,* 361–374.

Mednick, S., Cudeck, R., Griffith, J., Talovic, S., & Schulsinger, F. (1984). The Danish High Risk Project: Recent methods and findings. In M. Watt, E. Anthony, L. Wynne, & J. Rolf (Eds.), *Children at risk for schizophrenia: A longitudinal perspective* (pp. 21–42). New York: Cambridge University Press.

Mendlewicz, J., & Rainer, J. (1977). Adoption study supporting genetic transmission in manic-depressive illness. *Nature, 268,* 327–329.

Menon, D., Leff, J., Kuipers, et al. (in press). The distribution of expressed emotion components among relatives of schizophrenic patients in Aarhus and Chandegarh. *British Journal of Psychiatry.*

Miller, R., & Berman, J. (1983). The efficacy of cognitive behavior therapies: A quantitative review of the research evidence. *Psychological Bulletin, 94,* 39–53.

Mitsuda, H. (1967). *Clinical genetics in psychiatry.* Tokyo: Igaku Shoin.

Moline, R., Singh, S., Morris, A., & Meltzer, H. (1985). Family expressed emotion and relapse in schizophrenia in 24 urban American patients. *American Journal of Psychiatry, 142,* 1078–1081.

Murase, T., & Johnson, F. (1974). Naikan, Morita, and Western psychotherapy. *Archives of General Psychiatry, 31,* 121–128.

Murphy, G., Simons, A., Wetzel, R., & Lustman, P. (1984). Cognitive therapy and pharmacotherapy. *Archives of General Psychiatry, 41,* 33–41.

Nasrallah, H., McCalley-Whitters, M., & Kuperman, S. (1982). Neurological differences between paranoid and nonparanoid schizophrenia: Part I. Sensory-motor lateralization. *Journal of Clinical Psychiatry, 43,* 305–306.

Nee, L., Polinsky, R., Eldridge, R., Weingartner, H., Smallberg, S., & Ebert, M. (1983). A family with histologically confirmed Alzheimer's disease. *Archives of Neurology, 40,* 203–208.

Norton, J. (1982). *Expressed emotion, affective style, voice tone and communication deviance as predictors of offspring schizophrenia spectrum disorders.* Unpublished doctoral dissertation, University of California, Los Angeles.

Nuechterlein, K. (1984). Sustained attention among schizophrenic children vulnerable to adult schizophrenia and among hyperactive children. In M. Watt, E. Anthony, L. Wynne, & J. Rolf, (Eds.), *Children at risk for schizophrenia: A longitudinal perspective* (pp. 304–311). New York: Cambridge University Press.

Pedersen, P. (Ed.). (1985). *Handbook of cross-cultural counseling and therapy.* Westport, CT: Greenwood Press.

Pedersen, P., Draguns, J., Lonner, W., & Trimble, J. (Eds.). (1981). *Counseling across cultures* (rev. ed.). Honolulu: East-West Center.

Piran, N., Bigler, E., & Cohen, D. (1982). Motoric laterality and eye dominance suggest unique pattern of cerebral organization in schizophrenia. *Archives of General Psychiatry, 39,* 1006–1010.

Platman, S. (1983). Family caretaking and expressed emotionality: An evaluation. *Hospital and Community Psychiatry, 34,* 921–925.

Polivy, J., & Herman, C. (1985). Dieting and binging: A causal analysis. *American Psychologist, 40,* 193–201.

Pope, H., Hudson, J., Jonas, J., & Yurgelun-Todd, D. (1983). Bulimia treated with Imiprimine: A placebo-controlled, double-blind study. *American Journal of Psychiatry, 140,* 554–558.

Price, L., Charney, D., Rubin, A., & Heninger, G. (1986). Alpha 2-adrenergic receptor function in depression. *Archives of General Psychiatry, 43,* 849–858.

Rao, D., Mortoin, N., Gottesman, I., & Lew, R. (1981). Path analysis of qualitative data on pairs of relatives: Application to schizophrenia. *Human Heredity, 31,* 325–333.

Rehm, L. (1977). A self-control model of depression. *Behavior Therapy, 8,* 787–804.

Rice, J., Reich, T., Andreasen, N., Endicott, J., Van Eerdewegh, M., Fishman, R., Hirshfeld, R., & Klerman, G. (1987). The familial transmission of bipolar illness. *Archives of General Psychiatry, 44,* 441–450.

Rodnick, E., Goldstein, M., Lewis, J., & Doane, J. (1984). Parental communication style, affect, and role as precursors of offspring schizophrenia spectrum disorders. In M. Watt, E. Anthony, L. Wynne, & J. Rolf, (Eds.), *Children at risk for schizophrenia: A longitudinal perspective* (pp. 81–101). New York: Cambridge University Press.

Roff, J., & Knight, R. (1981). Family characteristics, childhood symptoms, and adult outcome of schizophrenia. *Journal of Abnormal Psychology, 90,* 510–520.

Rogler, L., Malgady, R., Costantino, G., & Blumenthal, R. (1987). What do culturally sensitive mental health services mean? *American Psychologist, 42,* 565–570.

Rosenhan, D. (1973). On being sane in insane places. *Science, 179,* 250–258.

Rosenthal, N., Sack, D., & Wehr, T. (1983). Seasonal variation in affective disorders. In T. Wehr & F. Goodwin (Eds.), *Circadian rhythms in psychiatry* (pp. 185–200). Pacific Grove, CA: Boxwood Press.

Rubin, R. (1982). Koro (Shook Yang). In C. Friedmann & R. Faguet (Eds.), *Extraordinary disorders of human behavior* (pp. 155–172). New York: Plenum.

Rush, A., Beck, A., Kovacs, M., & Hollon, S. (1977). Comparative efficacy of cognitive therapy and pharmacotherapy in the treatment of depressive outpatients. *Cognitive Therapy and Research, 1,* 17–37.

Russell, G. (1979). Bulimia nervosa: An ominous variant of anorexia nervosa. *Psychological Medicine, 9,* 429–448.

Rutter, M. (1979). Protective factors in children's responses to stress and disadvantage. In M. Kent & J. K. Rolf (Eds.), *Aggression and antisocial behaviour in childhood and adolescence* (pp. 95–113). Oxford: Pergamon Press.

Rutter, M., Maughan, B., Mortimore, P., & Ouston, S. (1979). *Fifteen thousand hours: Secondary schools and their effects on children.* Cambridge, MA: Harvard University Press.

Schlesser, M., Winokur, G., & Sherman, B. (1980). Hypothalamic-pituitary-adrenal axis activity in depressive illness. *Archives of General Psychiatry, 37,* 737–743.

Scovern, A., & Kilmann, P. (1980). Status of electroconvulsive therapy: Review of the outcome literature. *Psychological Bulletin, 87,* 260–303.

Seidman, L. (1983). Schizophrenia and brain dysfunction: An integration of recent neurodiagnostic findings. *Psychological Bulletin, 94,* 195–238.

Seligman, M. (1974). Depression and learned helplessness. In R. Friedman & M. Katz (Eds.), *The psychology of depression: Contemporary theory and research.* New York: Winston-Wiley.

Shan-Ming, Y., Flor-Henry, P., Dayi, C., Tiangi, L., Shuguang, Q., & Zenxiang, M. (1985). Imbalance of hemispheric functions in the major psychoses: A study of handedness in the People's Republic of China. *Biological Psychiatry, 20,* 906–917.

Shur, E. (1982). Season of birth in high and low genetic risk schizophrenics. *British Journal of Psychiatry, 140,* 410–415.

Simons, A., Murphy, G., Levine, J., & Wetzel, R. (1986). Cognitive therapy and pharmacotherapy for depression. *Archives of General Psychiatry, 43,* 43–48.

Slater, J., & Depue, R. (1981). The contribution of environmental events and social support to serious suicide attempts in primary depressive disorders. *Journal of Abnormal Psychology, 90,* 275–285.

Smith, E., & Vasquez, M. (Eds.) (1985). Cross-cultural counseling. *The Counseling Psychologist, 13,* 531–709.

Smith, M., Glass, G., & Miller, T. (1980). *The benefits of psychotherapy.* Baltimore, MD: Johns Hopkins University Press.

Spanos, N., Weekes, J., & Betrand, L. (1985). Multiple personality: A social psychological perspective. *Journal of Abnormal Psychology, 94,* 362–376.

Squire, L., & Zouzounis, J. (1986). ECT and memory: Brief pulse versus sine wave. *American Journal of Psychiatry, 143,* 596–601.

Strickland, B. (1985, September). *The impact of behavioral responses on the immune system.* Paper presented at the Prevention Research Seminar Series, National Institute of Mental Health, Rockville, MD.

Striegel-Moore, R., Silverstein, L., & Rodin, J. (1986). Toward an understanding of risk factors for bulimia. *American Psychologist, 41,* 246–263.

Sue, D. (1981). *Counseling the culturally different.* New York: Wiley.

Sue, S. (1987, August). *Psychotherapeutic services for ethnic minorities: Two decades of research findings.* Address, 1986 Award for Distinguished Contributions of Psychology in the Public Interest, American Psychological Association Convention, New York.

Sue, S., & Zane, N. (1987). The role of culture and cultural techniques in psychotherapy: Critique and reformulation. *American Psychologist, 42,* 37–45.

Suinn, R. (1984). *Fundamentals of abnormal psychology.* Chicago: Nelson-Hall.

Suinn, R. (1987, February). *Proceedings. National Institute of Mental Health: Conference on Mental Health Service Delivery for Ethnic Minorities.* Rockville, MD: National Institute of Mental Health.

Tarrier, N., Vaughn, C., Lader, M., & Leff, J. (1979). Bodily reactions to people and events in schizophrenia. *Archives of General Psychiatry, 36,* 311–315.

Thompson, J., & Blaine, J. (1987). Use of ECT in the United States in 1975 and 1980. *American Journal of Psychiatry, 144,* 557–562.

Tsuang, M. (1982). *Schizophrenia: The facts.* New York: Oxford University Press.

U.S. Department of Commerce, Bureau of the Census. (1981). *1980 census of population—supplementary reports.* Washington, DC: U.S. Government Printing Office.

Ursano, R., & Hales, R. (1986). A review of brief individual psychotherapies. *American Journal of Psychiatry, 143,* 1507–1517.

Vaughn, C., & Leff, J. (1976). The influence of family and social factors on the course of psychiatric illness. *British Journal of Psychiatry, 129,* 125–137.

Vaughn, C., Snyder, K., Jones, S., Freeman, W., & Falloon, I. (1984). Family factors in schizophrenic relapse: A replication in California of British research in expressed emotion. *Archives of General Psychiatry, 41,* 1169–1177.

Wallerstein, J., & Kelly, J. (1980). *Surviving the breakup: How children and parents cope with divorce.* New York: Basic Books.

Walsh, B., Roose, S., Glassman, A., Gladis, M., & Sadik, C. (1985). Bulimia and depression. *Psychosomatic Medicine, 47,* 123–131.

Watt, M., Anthony, E., Wynne, L., & Rolf, J. (Eds.). (1984). *Children at risk for schizophrenia: A longitudinal perspective.* New York: Cambridge University Press.

Watt, N., Grubb, T., & Erlenmeyer-Kimling, L. (1982). Social, emotional, and intellectual barriers at school among children at high risk for schizophrenia. *Journal of Consulting and Clinical Psychology, 50,* 171–181.

Weinberger, D., Berman, K., & Zec, R. (1986). Physiologic dysfunction of dorsolateral prefrontal cortex in schizophrenia. I: Regional cerebral blood flow evidence. *Archives of General Psychiatry, 43,* 114–124.

Weinberger, D., DeLisi, L., Perman, G., Targum, S., & Wyatt, R. (1982). Computed tomography in schizophreniform disorder and other acute psychiatric disorders. *Archives of General Psychiatry, 39,* 778–783.

Wender, P., Kety, S., Rosenthal, D., Schulsinger, F., Ortmann, J., & Lunde, I. (1986). Psychiatric disorders in the biological and adoptive families of adopted individuals with affective disorders. *Archives of General Psychiatry, 43,* 923–929.

Westermeyer, J. (1985). Psychiatric diagnosis across cultural boundaries. *American Journal of Psychiatry, 142,* 798–805.

Worland, J., Janes, C., Anthony, E., McGinnis, M., & Cass, L. (1984). St. Louis High Risk Research Project: Comprehensive progress report of experimental studies. In M. Watt, E. Anthony, L. Wynne, & J. Rolf, (Eds.), *Children at risk for schizophrenia: A longitudinal perspective* (pp. 105–147). New York: Cambridge University Press.

Yager, J., & Strober, M. (1985). Family aspects of eating disorders. In A. Francis & R. Hales (Eds.), *Annual review of psychiatry, Vol. 4* (pp. 481–502). Washington, DC: American Psychiatric Press.

Zahn, T. (1986). Psychophysiological approaches to psychopathology. In M. Coles, E. Donchin, & S. Porges (Eds.), *Psychophysiology.* New York: Guilford Press.

Zimmerman, M., Coryel, W., & Pfohl, B. (1986). The validity of the dexamethasone suppression test as a marker for endogenous depression. *Archives of General Psychiatry, 43,* 347–355.

RICHARD W. BRISLIN

INCREASING AWARENESS OF CLASS, ETHNICITY, CULTURE, AND RACE BY EXPANDING ON STUDENTS' OWN EXPERIENCES

R ichard W. Brislin is a research associate at the Institute of Culture and Communication, East-West Center, in Honolulu, Hawaii. His first experiences with human diversity due to cultural influences were a result of his father's job assignments and occurred during his high school years in Anchorage, Alaska and during his college years in Agana, Guam. He attended the Pennsylvania State University and received a PhD degree in psychology in 1969. Since coming to the East-West Center in 1972, Brislin has directed programs for international educators, cross-cultural researchers, and various specialists involved in formal programs that encourage intercultural interaction. One of these programs overlapped with a conference to develop the *Handbook of Cross-Cultural Psychology* (1980; Harry Triandis, senior editor), of which Brislin is a co-editor. His other books include *Cross-Cultural Research Methods* (1973, with W. Lonner and R. Thorndike); *Cross-Cultural Orientation Programs* (1975, with P. Pedersen); *Cross-Cultural Encounters: Face to Face Interaction* (1981); the three-volume *Handbook of Intercultural Training* (1983, coedited with D. Landis); and *Intercultural Interactions: A Practical Guide* (1986). He has held positions as visiting professor at Georgetown University, the University of British Columbia, and the University of Iowa. His hobbies include collecting materials related to the American circus and playing banjo, Celtic harp, and pennywhistle in a string band devoted to the dissemination of American and Irish folk music.

INCREASING AWARENESS OF CLASS, ETHNICITY, CULTURE, AND RACE BY EXPANDING ON STUDENTS' OWN EXPERIENCES

To become more sophisticated in their study of psychology, students must become aware of the extreme diversity of human behavior and of a number of general concepts that summarize major factors that contribute to the reality of human diversity. These include (a) the social class into which they are born and in which they are exposed to some impactful socialization experiences; (b) the ethnic group membership they claim, or which others claim for them; (c) the culture in which they are raised, which exposes them to predictable cognitions, attitudes, values, and frequently performed behaviors; and (d) the racial group membership they have, which is a result of their genetic heritage. However, many students have had limited experience with the variability represented by these four concepts. Students frequently come from homogenous backgrounds giving them limited exposure to diverse races, cultures, social classes, and ethnic groups. The major purpose of this chapter is to expand students' awareness of these complex concepts through exercises and illustrative examples that begin with their existing knowledge. Further, as their knowledge increases, the importance of the four concepts is demonstrated by showing how they relate to such important topics as education, health, interpersonal relations, and child rearing practices.

Of course, social class, ethnicity, culture, and race do not exhaust the major concepts summarizing influences on human diversity. Others have been reviewed in previously published G. Stanley Hall collections: age (Kagan, 1985; Schlossberg, 1984); sex (Denmark, 1983); psychological abnormalities (Sarason, 1983); and the physical environment in which people find themselves (Saegert, 1986; Stokols, 1982). As with the four concepts examined in this chapter, many psychological phenomena can be understood only when viewed in the context of other factors. For instance, a person's age, sex, social class, cultural background, and current environment all affect obesity and a person's attitude toward and ease in losing weight (Brownell, 1982; Grunberg, 1982; Rodin, 1981). Yet there has to be a starting point for introducing these topics to students, and the best teaching method may be to treat them one at a time and later to cover combinations of and interactions among the four concepts.

This chapter has three major parts. In the first, the concepts of class, ethnicity, culture, and race will be explained. Further, research will be reviewed that points out important relations between and among these four concepts and such dependent variables as educational achievement, health, interpersonal relationships, and child rearing practices. For all four concepts, the point will be made that the general label (e.g., class) is almost always too broad for a helpful analysis of human behavior. Rather than accepting the general label as having explanatory use, a better practice is to ask what more specific independent variables (e.g., number of books in the home, which is partly affected by parental income) have an impact on dependent variables (e.g., progress in reading in school).

In a second section, research will be reviewed that requires understanding of two or more of the concepts. In addition, other research areas will be reviewed that have suffered because of faulty understanding of the four concepts. To preview one conclusion, many research findings have found a purported relationship between race (especially Black–White differences) and educational achievement (reviewed by Katz, 1973, who is sensitive to the dangers of facile conclusions concerning supposed racial differences). Such findings disappear or become much smaller in magnitude when the class background of students is assessed (e.g., Bardouille-Crema, Black, and Feldhusen, 1986). That is, the largest differences are often between middle-class and working-class Whites, or between middle- and working-class Blacks, rather than between students who happen to have different skin colors.

A third section will consider the four concepts as social categories individuals use to think about other people and how to behave toward them. Research in this area is based on the assumption that people are *placed* into categories based on their class, ethnicity, culture, and race. Moreover, people use these categories to think about themselves (e.g., "I don't have the social class standing to join that club") and others ("He's not our type—he wouldn't be comfortable in this club"). The facts corresponding to the four concepts are less important than how they are *used* by individuals in their social relations. The topics of prejudice and discrimination, with histories of extensive research and study (e.g., Allport, 1954), are central to social categorization research because people can be denied opportunities once the four concepts are used to place them into an unfavorably viewed outgroup.

Throughout this chapter, exercises will be suggested that can be used to involve and to interest students. All the exercises have been tried out in classes and all demand little or no specialized equipment. Most of the exercises take the form of asking students to examine their past experiences for insights related to a concept, to react to critical incidents (or specific accounts of behavior involving interpersonal relations) into which they place themselves, or to participate in small group interactions. I have tried to follow much of McKeachie's (1986) thoughtful advice concerning the development of undergraduate courses. Specifically, there are opportunities for students to talk, to write, and to challenge their own possible misconceptions while doing so. This participation demands student activity and contributions to class discussions rather than a more passive processing of lectures. One of the primary techniques used to introduce the key concepts—critical incidents—is suggested as a way to make students' thinking more precise. Thinking in terms of critical incidents is similar to thinking according to scripted behaviors (Abelson, 1981). It is suggested that a normal way of thinking (scripts) can be improved by making students' analyses more complex, multidimensional, and subject to change in the face of new evidence. Another of McKeachie's suggestions is to encourage peer teaching, and some of the exercises described provide opportunities for the development of cooperative learning groups. Throughout the chapter, concepts are introduced that students can use when they take courses in other disciplines, especially sociology, anthropology, biology, and education.

Social Class

Social class, sometimes referred to as socioeconomic status, has not been adequately studied by psychologists in the United States. Sociologists are more likely to study its nature and effects, and consequently much of this review draws from work in that discipline. Perhaps the reason for neglect is that American psychologists prefer to believe in a relatively classless society where individual effort can overcome the drawbacks of birth into a low-income household. Psychologists have also been more interested in differences that exist *within* individuals, such as variations in intelligence, personality, and motivation, than they have in the *collective* differences brought about by membership in a social category such as class. Class is more actively studied by psychologists in other countries. This was made clear to me recently when doing a literature search using the *Psychological Abstracts.* With few exceptions, when an abstract indicated that effects of social class on human behavior were being explicity investigated, the research had been done in Australia, Canada, or Western Europe. I am concerned with this neglect in the United States and will try to show the importance of social class membership in understanding a number of important psychological phenomena.

Social class has traditionally been defined as a position in a society's hierarchy of prestige, income, power, and influence. Markers include family income, prestige of neighborhood, prestige of occupation of head(s) of household, and educational level of those same household leaders. Most definitions include the presence of a wealthy upper class, a comfortable middle class, a struggling working class that experiences uncertainty with respect to job stability, and a frustrated underclass whose members are frequently if not constantly faced with unemployment and little hope for positive change. The latter two groupings are sometimes combined and are called the lower class. Although adequate for the United States, other factors are needed to understand social class in other countries. These include (in different countries) the status of a family's name and bloodline, the prestige of the caste into which a person is born, the names of one's patrons or protectors, the *infrequency* of any physical labor that might dirty one's hand, and the amount of time available for scholarly activities of one's own choosing. In a treatment from which I will draw heavily, Gilbert and Kahl (1982) suggest that individual or family income is the central variable in the United States and that others follow from the limitations or opportunites brought about by people's income. For instance, income is both a reflection of one's education and affects how much education parents can offer to their children. In turn, education influences the prestige level of various occupations: A person cannot become a medical doctor, lawyer, or psychologist without extensive formal education. Income also determines the amount of money people can spend on housing, which in turn affects the prestige level of neighborhoods in which they might live.

I recommend that professors begin with the analysis of social class. Students are more likely to have observed, and possibly to have experienced firsthand, variability in wealthy versus poor families in contrast to variability in ethnicity, culture, or race.

Exercise 1: Defining Social Class

Rather soon after introducing the nature of human diversity, ask students to either define social class in a short paragraph or to draw pictures that summarize their views. Have them write down their analyses and later compare across students by asking selected individuals to read their definitions or to come to the blackboard to draw their pictures. Essays or pictures will almost always contain the idea of a hierarchy and will have income as a major criterion. One student drew Figure 1, which captures a number of factors.

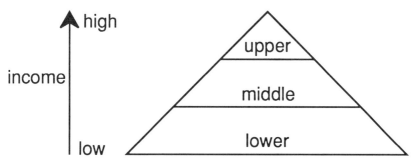

Figure 1. Graphic depiction of social class done by a student for Exercise 1.

Interestingly, given the broad base and smaller middle section, this student may have recognized a point made by Thurow (1987). The lower or working class is increasing in numbers and the middle class is shrinking in size. One reason is that good-paying jobs in industries such as steel, automobiles, and machine tools have decreased given greater international competition since the 1960s. These jobs have been replaced by lower-paying service jobs (e.g., restaurant personnel, tourism related salaried workers, repairmen and women). To reach a middle-class life-style, a family of four needs about $31,000 per year in 1987 (of course, this figure must be adjusted in future years). To reach this level, both husband and wife often must work, which creates the need for more low-wage service jobs (e.g., day care, domestic help). Only 25% of men and women reach this level if only one partner in the marriage brings in income:

And although the dominant pattern today is a full-time male worker and a part-time female worker, the pattern is rapidly shifting toward a way of life in which both husband and wife work full time. . . . As an increasing number of families have two full-time workers, the households that do not will fall farther and farther behind economically. (Thurow, 1987, p. 35)

The people left behind in the movement through social class levels include households headed by women, and these reached a staggering 31% of households in 1985. Dependence on one income, combined with the well-known fact of lower salaries earned by women, can result in poverty. Women and children constitute 77% of people living in poverty, and 50% of these poor people live in female-headed households with no husband present.

Exercise 2: Interpersonal Relations and Social Class

To analyze further the impact of income, ask students to think of a town or city they know well and in which they have lived. This will often be their hometown where they went to high school, or it could be the town in which their college or university is located. Ask them to list the relative status of neighborhoods, and encourage them to generate as many status levels as they can. Most students can generate six or seven levels if they give the task sufficient thought. With few exceptions, the various levels will be based on the amount of money homes cost. Then ask students to mark their own neighborhoods or to mark the entry on their list most like the neighborhood in which they live(d). For the next step, ask students to recall the ten closest friends from the town they are analyzing. The students will then be asked to indicate the neighborhoods these friends are from, again by either marking a listed entry or by marking a given friend's neighborhood, which is similar to a listed entry. Ask students to count the number of friends from neighborhoods at their own level, one level above, and from one level below their own. The majority, if not all ten friends, will be from the same or close levels. One interpretation could be that physical proximity affects friendship networks. This exercise should also suggest to students that class background, in this case indicated by the proxy variable of neighborhood, can have a significant effect (Kohn, 1977; Gilbert & Kahl, 1982).

One result of friendship networks is the person one chooses as a spouse. If people's friends are from a similar class background as themselves, then marital choices will reflect this fact. Thurow (1987) argues that this is the case:

> If high-income males marry high-income females and low-income males marry low-income females (tendencies that are borne out by the available statistics), the net result is wider gaps as potentially high-income women married to already high-income males enter the labor force. (p. 35)

An interesting image may help communicate the growing disparity between well-off and poor people. Discount stores such as K-Mart and upscale stores such as Bloomingdale's do well, while stores that have traditionally served the solid middle class (e.g., Gimbels, Montgomery Ward) do less well or go out of business. Sears Roebuck and Penney's have worked hard to change their images, partly through periodic face-lifts and partly through the addition of services such as insurance, stock brokerage, and even dentistry. These latter two stores are now seen as adequate places to shop for a wide variety of reasonably priced but fashionable goods and up-to-date help with money matters.

Social Skills and Careers

Kohn (1977) argues, based on his research with over 4,000 respondents, that parents from different class backgrounds emphasize different values when raising their children. Middle-class parents emphasize self-control, intellectual curiosity, and consideration for others. This leads to the adult characteristics of self-direction and empathetic understanding. On the other hand, working-class parents focus on obedience, neatness, and good manners, the latter often involving quietness and invisibility when adults are present (Gilbert and Kahl, 1982). These emphases lead to a concern with external standards, such as obedience to authority, acceptance of what other people think of as good manners, and difficulty in articulating one's wishes to authority figures. The middle class emphases lead to adolescents and adults who are comfortable with self-starting, self-instigated behaviors and ease in interacting with others outside the immediate kin or friendship network.

Kohn (1977) further concludes that middle-class children are raised to take on professional and managerial jobs that demand intellectual curiosity and good social skills. For instance, a key skill good managers have is the ability to understand subordinates' needs, even if the latter are unable to articulate them clearly. Note that this skill is a result of the empathetic understanding and consideration for others that middle-class parents encourage in their children. On the other hand, working-class children are raised to take wage labor jobs that involve physical effort and that are closely supervised. They take such jobs partly as a result of a lesser emphasis on intellectual curiosity and partly as a result of parental concern for external standards and obedience, in this case to the standards and desires of a visible supervisor.

Social skills (Argyle, 1980) are extraordinarily important, so important and so central to success in the professions that they take precedence over purely intellectual skills in many promotion decisions. Despite their importance, they are rarely discussed because many people think that they would be pointing out the obvious if they mention these qualities. Yet, to preview one of the points to be made later in the discussion of culture, many matters that are rarely discussed and are taken for granted are central to people's lives. But because everyone *thinks* that all people should have a certain set of skills or traits, those who do not possess the desired qualities are deprived of society's opportunities and rewards. And because such matters are rarely discussed, there is little opportunity to make corrections.

One of the basic sets of social skills is meeting previously unfamiliar people, quickly putting them at ease, engaging in pleasant and friendly small talk, making them feel welcome in a new setting, and encouraging them to talk about topics with which they are comfortable (remember the middle-class concern with empathetic understanding). As a result, the socially skilled person gains a reputation as someone who should be given time, attention, and opportunities, for instance in a job interview or with help in cutting through bureaucratic red tape when the need arises. Social skills are often developed by participation in various community activities where any one individual can learn to meet and interact comfortably with many different others (Lundberg, 1974). People can also learn to work through bureaucracies and to work with people who are unpleasant and yet cannot be ignored if individuals are to achieve their goals, whether those goals be a set of scholarship recommendations, the creation of a new club, or a plan for a fund-raiser. High school activities are one place for such experiences. High school, after all, is a complex bureaucracy with its share of unpleasant people. But students from the working class participate in far fewer extracurricular activities than do students from the middle class (Lindgren and Suter, 1985). One reason goes back to income: Working-class teenagers often have after-school jobs and must contribute to the family income. Yet those jobs involve the supervised tasks, defined by others rather than by the individual worker, which were discussed earlier. The after-school work does not encourage the self-starting movement of making one's way through a bureaucracy and the development of social skills leading to comfort while interacting with many different people.

A number of psychologists have developed training programs to encourage the development of social skills in people who did not have the opportunity to acquire them as a result of their socialization

(Armstrong, 1985; Trower, Bryant, and Argyle, 1978). Such training often involves the creation of role-play scenarios in which participants have the opportunity to practice skills such as communicating their qualifications and preferences in a job interview, meeting a number of new people at a party, returning damaged merchandise to a store without being abrasive to clerks, and finding out the exact person in an office who can help cut through the red tape blocking implementation of a plan.

Exercise 3: Socially Skilled Behaviors

Ask students to engage in socially skillful behaviors within an assigned period of time and to report back concerning what happened. The socially skilled behaviors would be ones that a person might not always perform in a given situation but which are within the realm of appropriateness. For instance, if a store's salesclerk is not busy, the student might engage him or her in a pleasant conversation that draws around to the salesclerk's unique interests. Or if requesting a book from the reference librarian, the student might smile, use a pleasant tone of voice, and express appreciation for the college library's services. One student at a large university reported back this experience. He enjoyed a guest lecture that a professor gave in a large class. Rather than keep his feelings to himself, he stopped by during the professor's office hours and told her. The professor then responded, "Thank you. And your name is?" The student and the professor had a 30-minute chat. The student now has a good relationship with one more professor. (The lack of such relations, of course, is a common student complaint at large universities.) The point of the exercise is to show students that positive outcomes come from the use of socially skilled behaviors, and that people with social skills are better able to benefit from a society's potential rewards. Professors might then relate telephone calls they surely have had concerning recommendation of students or colleagues for jobs. The person on the other end of the phone says, "It's clear that the applicant is qualified for the job in terms of intellectual skills. But is the applicant a pleasant person who will be a good colleague to others in the workplace?"

Educational Achievement

Students from the working class often do not do as well in school as their middle-class peers. There are many reasons for this (Lundgren and Suter, 1985). Working-class students *think* that their parents expect less of them in terms of future educational achievement, even when this is not the case. Children of parents without large amounts of formal education are less likely to aspire to college attendance for themselves, compared to children of middle-class parents. Of course, family income again plays a factor. Even when working-class adolescents might consider attending a low-cost community college, the amount of money they would lose by a 2- to 4-year absence from the work force makes college attendance difficult to consider. Furthermore, an additional significant factor is suggested by arguments that the cultural context of education is disadvantageous to lower income/ inner city children (Boykin, 1986).

Another reason is that success in high school and college demands verbal skills, and working-class students have either less exposure, less expertise, or less confidence with such skills. Gullo (1981) found that 3- to 5-year-old working-class children, when asked to talk about pictures, had more difficulty with various "wh—" questions than students from the middle class. Such questions start with what, who, when, where, why, and so forth. "What" questions were answered as competently by students from both class backgrounds, since there was a pictured object to which students could refer. But when asked questions starting with the other "wh—" words that did not have a clearly pictured referent, working-class students did not do as well. About half the language teachers use to address students consists of questions. If one group of students understands the questions less well than another, the first group will benefit less from the teacher's lesson.

The verbal differences continue past preschool. In a study of kindergarten children, Jones and McMillan (1973) asked students to tell others about an enjoyable experience and also to describe pictures. Working-class children used one-third fewer words and in general used shorter, less informative statements. In a study of 8-year-old Black and White children from different class backgrounds, Yando, Seitz, and Zigler (1979) found that racial differences meant little. Achievement differences were far more strongly related to social class.

> Advantaged children . . . chose harder problems both on their first attempt and across all attempts on the Reading task, findings which remained significant after covariance analysis [for both IQ and mental age]. The greater self-confidence of advantaged children on the Reading task is not surprising in light of the repeated findings that advantaged children are more proficient in reading than disadvantaged children. What is surprising was the consistency of the self-confidence difference even when MA and IQ were controlled. Indeed, it is striking that even the most capable disadvantaged children showed such low expectations in their abilities. (p. 88)

This self-limiting view of the working class may continue well into adulthood. Arbuckle, Gold, and Andres (1986) found that lower class older people rated themselves as poorer in memory adequacy than age peers from the middle class, even when such memory differences were nonexistent.

An important point made by Lindgren et al. (1985) is that class itself is not the best predictor of the results reviewed in their own work and in the research discussed here. There are some working-class students who do well in school and some who do less well. The results reviewed here are trends comparing large numbers of students from different class backgrounds. The most helpful research looks at the exact behaviors parents of students who perform well employ when interacting with their children. The total set of behaviors constitutes the children's home background, which prepares them for school and helps them progress through their formal educational experiences. Most of these happen to be correlated with class level. But individual working- and underclass parents can and do engage in these behaviors, sometimes at considerable sacrifice, and the behaviors are predictive of school success. This list of parental behaviors comes from a variety of sources: Dunn (1981); Graue, Weinstein, and Walberg (1983); Lindgren and Suter (1985); the United States Department of Education's publication "What works: Research about teaching and learning" (1986); and my own discussions with schoolteachers.

Parents of more successful students monitor the amount and type of television their children watch. They do not allow indiscriminate use of television, and they do not use it as a babysitter. They encourage children to read instead of watching the especially mindless shows. They discuss the content of news and documentary programs with their children. For younger children, these parents know about and encourage the watching of "Sesame Street" and "The Electric Company." They place watching these programs higher in their priorities than the game shows and soap operas that compete in the same time slots on other channels.

Parents of successful schoolchildren often talk with their sons and daughters. They engage children in meaningful conversations and listen to what their children have to say. They praise their children for verbal expression. When posing problems or introducing puzzles to their children that demand thought, parents use inquiry methods. Instead of demonstrating the solution themselves, which would make children dependent upon the presence of a teacher, the more successful parents encourage children to figure out the problem on their own. Parents then praise the children when the problem is solved. By using this approach, children are better prepared to solve a wide variety of intellectual problems encountered in school without the constant presence of a teacher at their side. Note these parental behaviors encourage the middle-class goal of self-direction discussed earlier.

Successful parents read to their children, read themselves during voluntary leisure time activity, have large amounts of reading matter around the house, and make frequent visits to public libraries. They encourage children to talk about what has just been read. This important activity encourages the development of reading comprehension, a skill central to virtually all subject matters a student will encounter. Parents also can ask questions about the stories, giving children practice with the "wh—"questions, as previously discussed. Parents of successful schoolchildren understand the work of specialists, such as special reading teachers, school psychologists, and speech-hearing therapists who might be called in to serve the needs of a given student. They provide a quiet place where children can do their homework and take an interest in the assignments their children bring home. They encourage their children to complete their assignments on time and occasionally can help with homework. They maintain a good relationship with the children's teachers. Although there may be an image in some communities that teachers do not want any meddling from parents, this has not been my experience and is not the recommendation of the "What works?" (1986) project. Teachers are happy to cooperate with interested parents, and the interaction benefits the children.

To summarize some key points about social class, the United States does have class barriers that are easier to transcend than those in many other countries. Yet because of an unwillingness to admit the continuing presence of a class hierarchy, Americans are ill equipped to discuss the major factors that make the transmission of class standing from parent to child more likely than not. Several factors have been reviewed here: friendship networks which lead to the selection of a specific marital partner; dual career marriages leading to a growing gap between high- and low-income households; types of adult jobs for which children are socialized; social skills; and readiness for and continual encouragement in school. None of these matters are easy to discuss. Americans seem better at discussing race, given the recent history of the civil rights movement, than they are at discussing class. Like most Americans, I am uncomfortable discussing class, and the material on social class was the hardest for me to prepare in the development of this chapter. Like Pettigrew (1986), I do not want to see class distinctions become the next major source of intergroup discrimination. Yet if social class and its effects are not discussed in detail, then there is little opportunity for intervention to increase the chances of happiness (Freedman, 1978) among people from different class backgrounds. Social class leads to more intervention opportunities than at least two of the other concepts under discussion in this chapter. It is easier to change the behaviors leading to the perpetuation of social class than it is to change people's race or ethnicity.

Ethnicity

All people have an identity consisting of every statement they can make that includes the words I, my, mine, or me. The simplest division of such statements places them into personal and collective identities (Hui and Triandis, 1986). Personal statements describe aspects of an individualized self, and many such statements given by respondents use adjectives much like those found in personality tests: "I am friendly, dominant, shy, quiet, a go-getter, ambitious," and so forth. Collective statements involve membership in a social category, sometimes a primary group whose members have face-to-face relationships with each other ("I am a wife and mother"; "I am on the varsity debate team"). Collective statements can also refer to a larger social category whose members might or might not ever interact ("I am a sophomore at the university"; "I am a psychologist"). A person's ethnicity can be part of that collective identity. A collective identity serves a necessary linking function between given individuals and their smooth functioning in the larger society.

Exercise 4: Who Am I?

Ask students to write 20 statements about themselves, each statement beginning with "I am. . . . " The instructions are as follows:

> Please write 20 different statements in response to the simple question (addressed to yourself), Who am I? Begin each statement with I am. . . . Respond as if you are giving the answers to yourself, not to someone else. Write your answers in the order that they occur to you. Do not worry about importance or logic. Go fairly fast.

There should be a number of interesting results. If the majority of students are Caucasian, people from minority groups, such as Blacks, Chicanos, American Indians, and foreign students, should be far more likely to mention ethnicity (McGuire, McGuire, Child, and Fujioka, 1978). As part of their search for an identity, people emphasize the distinctiveness in themselves. If they are from a minority group, then they are distinctive in comparison to the majority group in society. Even though the majority Caucasians could mention an ethnicity more specific than "American," since they know that their ancestors came from other countries, they most often do not. The exception will occur if a Caucasian is (or feels) visibly distinctive from other Caucasians, such as Americans of Swedish ancestry with fair skin, blond hair, and blue eyes. Other findings may emerge as a result of the quest for distinctiveness. If there is a large difference in the number of men versus women on a campus, for instance, the members of the less numerous group should be more likely to mention their gender. The fact that many Americans do not list their ethnicity is important since it demonstrates the large individual differences in the saliency of ethnic identity. The relative lack of concern many Americans have with ethnicity makes it difficult for them to understand conflict in many parts of the world where ethnic loyalties play a major role (e.g., the Mideast, India, Fiji, Philippines).

Exercise 5: What Does Ethnicity Do?

Ask how many students listed their ethnicity as one of the 20 entries. Such answers might be "Black," "Italian-American," "Vietnamese," "Jewish," or "Indonesian." If there are enough students who mentioned ethnicity to make them the central figures of 4–5 person groups (e.g., in a class of 60 students, if 12 mentioned ethnicity), then form such groups. If not, then ask a question such as "How many people feel that their ethnicity is important enough so that they would have mentioned it given 30 statements?" There should be enough people who can be central figures of groups at this point.

Each group has the task of answering the question, "What would happen if my ethnicity was removed and I had the identity of 'American?'" The people who did not mention ethnicity can either contribute to the list of what would be lost, or they can question the group's central figure to help him or her generate a list. Assume that the central figure is a Japanese-American. People in the group would prompt the central figure with questions like, "What would you miss if you *were not* Japanese-American?"

This is what I call a good tooth-pulling exercise. The tooth-pulling aspect is that answers to the questions will not come easily. The classroom will not be filled with the crackle of quick and constant verbalizations. But the good part is that students will think carefully and will take the task seriously. Groups may not formulate long lists, but each entry will be the product of productive effort. Collect the answers in a central place, perhaps by asking a spokesperson from each group to write the entries on the blackboard.

Responses might include the following. Students who value their ethnicity would lose a sense of distinctiveness from others; the feeling that "I'm not like everyone else" is important to them. They would lose a sense of a place in historical continuity. If they were "American," after all, then they would be part of a very young country, which dates to 1607 at the earliest. Those who value their British, Jewish, African, or Japanese heritage can trace their history back far further in time. People sensitive to a cultural tradition within their ethnic group, such as closeness within a nuclear or extended family, will list such traditions. Others would miss leisure time activities associated with their ethnic group: dance forms, music, literature, and membership in clubs. Occasionally, students will mention that they would miss participation in rituals which they enjoy, such as weddings, bull sessions at the neighborhood store that caters to ethnic food preferences, and celebration of certain holidays not given much attention by the larger society. Foreign students may have especially interesting entries focusing on aspects of culture that they find puzzling when they think of their own backgrounds. One foreign student said that if he were an American he would not want to ever think of putting his elderly parents in a nursing home, since such a separation from his parents and such an abdication of responsibilities would be abhorrent in his mind.

These contributions should provide a good introduction to coverage of more formal definitions. There is agreement among psychologists, sociologists, and anthropologists on some of the central aspects of ethnicity, although there is less agreement concerning how ethnicity should be best conceptualized with respect to related concepts such as race, culture, residence, religion, minority group, and so forth. The following list of ethnicity's central aspects comes from a variety of sources: Casino (1983); Cohen (1978); Henderson (1979); Wu and Foster (1982).

Ethnicity involves a sense of common descent, heritage, and the presence of traditions passed on by previous generations. Even though people might live in one country and claim it when asked about nationality, their ethnicity may be a result of their ancestors' presence in another. Ethnic groups are distinct from others in the same society through such distinguishing features as language or accent in a society's primary language, physical features, family names, and customs. Members of some ethnic groups are likely to share a common religion: Catholicism in the Republic of Ireland or the Philippines, or Islam in Iran. Members of the same ethnic group share a sense of common fate as well as an interest in and concern with what happens to fellow members.

Wu and Foster (1982) make a distinction between features that are unchangeable or very difficult to change and those that can be modified more readily. It is as difficult or impossible to change a major feature of one's physical appearance as it is for adults to learn a society's language of commerce without an accent. Likewise, it is very hard to change such central aspects of one's life as respect for the views of elders, religious beliefs, or regard for education. Other features sometimes associated with ethnicity are easier to change: dress, food consumption, hairstyle, and leisure time activities.

Similarly, distinctions are made between objective and subjective ethnic identity. Objective identity involves criteria for which there is visible proof and about which community members can agree. Physical features, language, and genealogy are examples. Subjective identity refers to a person's own cognitions, feelings, and behaviors. A person may not seem to have objective indices of a certain identity but may subjectively claim and value the identity nevertheless. Examples are light-skinned Blacks who could "pass" as Whites but who are quick to tell of their Black heritage when questioned. Difficulties can arise when there are clashes between objective and subjective indices. In Hawaii, people can claim certain benefits such as access to private schooling, land, and job training if they can objectively show that a certain percentage of their heritage is Hawaiian (e.g., one-eighth for schooling, one-half for land). Some people, then, may subjectively feel Hawaiian but will be frustrated if they cannot show objective proof of their claim. Occasionally, the clash can stem from the opposite direction of adequate objective but problematic subjective indices, as shown in the following dilemma that might be presented to students.

Exercise 6: The Functions of Ethnicity

My daughter, now 12 years old, is adopted. She is part Japanese (25%) but observers would have to strain to see any Japanese physical features. My wife and I are both Caucasian (Italian and Irish ancestry, respectively), and we have raised our daughter in a typically middle-class American home. Despite our urgings that she explore her ethnicity by, for instance, taking readily available Japanese language courses in her school, she shows no interest.

College scholarships are available to Americans of Japanese ancestry. These scholarships almost always have the purpose of encouraging students from a certain ethnic background to continue their studies through college. The scholarships are established with the belief that there may not be other funds available for a given student. My daughter's 25% Japanese heritage, which can be readily documented, is enough to enter competition for such scholarships. Should her parents encourage her to apply for them?

Students will have various opinions. One position will be that the scholarships should go to Japanese-Americans whose physical features clearly mark them and who value their ethnicity. Others will say that the scholarships should go to people who were probably, at one time or another, the victim of discrimination based on their physically communicated ethnicity. Others will say, "What the hell! She meets the scholarships' formal criterion. Go for it!"

Whatever the outcome of the discussion—and I've been surprised that the majority of students to whom I've posed this dilemma say "apply for the scholarships"—students will be introduced to several key facts. Ethnicity is manipulable, and it serves various purposes for people.

The Uses of Identity

As with all aspects of one's identity, ethnicity can be manipulated to serve one's needs. "Manipulation" is not used here as a pejorative term. At various times, people project those aspects of their identity that increase the probability of achieving their goals. When people go for a job interview, they dress in attractive clothes to meet the demands of that situation and to increase the chances of making a favorable impression. Manipulation, in this case the choice of clothes, is used in this sense to increase the probability of success. Clothes, speech patterns, hairstyles, mannerisms, and other observable behaviors can be used to emphasize or de-emphasize one's ethnic origins and may vary depending on the situation.

The manipulation of ethnicity can proceed according to varying degrees of specificity. A good example is the region of the country-of-ancestry, such as northern versus southern Italy or Ireland. The specification of ethnicity can proceed according to tribal origins, as among Black South Africans. It can be determined by mother tongue, as among Cebuano, Tagalog, and Ilocano, all names of ethnic groups indigenous to the Philippines (Bautista, 1982); these people will proudly claim Filipino as their ethnicity on some occasions, and will claim the more specific group on others. If such distinctions seem arcane, they are not in their implications. The continued support for the deposed Filipino dictator, Ferdinand Marcos, comes not from all Filipinos but primarily from Ilocanos, Marcos's own ethnic group. In fact, the support is best described even more specifically as Ilocanos from the same province as Marcos.

The manipulation can proceed according to customs, as among Islamic women who do or do not wear the traditional veil over their faces. It can proceed according to the goals of a given encounter: During World War II, Scotsmen and Englishmen found it more important to emphasize their feelings of fighting for the British Isles against Germany than to continue their historical squabbles. Currently in Israel, feelings of being Israeli sometimes take precedence over more specific designations (e.g., religiously observant versus non-religiously observant Jews) when confrontations with Arab nations arise (Schwarzwald and Amir, 1984). Feelings of ethnicity can develop due to political considerations, as when members of a certain ethnic group unify behind a candidate to have their voice heard in the nation's capital city. The consideration of politics brings up an interesting point. Ethnicity may be more important in urban than rural areas (Cohen, 1978). In cities, there are many desirable commodities and resources: good schools, jobs, services, patronage positions, roads, sewage disposal, demands for low cost housing, food stamps, and so forth. But there are too few resources for everyone demanding them and too few tax dollars to provide the best services to all. Thus, various political interest groups will form to encourage the delivery of resources to their constituents. Many times, these constituencies will form on the basis of ethnicity. A good example is the demand for bilingual education in many parts of North America. Members of many ethnic groups believed that their school systems were inattentive to the needs of their children and that instruction in various mother tongues other than English (e.g., Spanish, Chinese, French) would increase the chances of their children's success in school. The formation and maintenance of political action groups is time-consuming, frustrating, often boring, and always demanding of compromise. But such action is preferable to armed conflict (Crick, 1982), which too often is the result of ethnic tensions in various parts of the world.

Ingroups and Outgroups

Returning to the concept of identity, ethnicity serves the function of providing one basis for ingroup formation. Ingroups refer to people who value each other's presence; feel emotionally close; and look to each other for help in troubled times, confident that this help will be forthcoming. Outgroups refer to those people with whom a given individual does not seek interaction and who are kept at a physical and emotional distance. Often, outgroup members are looked down upon as having an incorrect set of religious beliefs, unintelligent customs, or irritating personal traits. The distinction between ingroups and outgroups is universal, having been found in societies all over the world (LeVine and Campbell, 1972). Apparently, a very basic human need is satisfied through the presence of familiar and similar others whom one can trust, share personal information with, and count on in times of need. Perhaps the desire to have an ingroup reaches back to our distant past when the demands of an oppressive physical environment were lessened if people lived in groups. Ethnicity provides an important basis for ingroup formation: Similarities in language allow obvious ease in communication. Similarities in experiences typical of an ethnic group allow the sharing of emotions because fellow group members understand the relative importance of those experiences. A sense of shared heritage also provides affective bonds among people, which leads to the formation of ingroups.

Exercise /: People's Use of Ethnic Markers

At this point, students may not be convinced that they pay much attention to ethnicity in their interactions with people. Students may feel that ethnicity is important for other people in other parts of the world, but not for them. Or students may feel that they have matured so much that they are beyond any concern with ethnicity and its potential associations with prejudice, stereotyping, and discrimination. To show that they are aware of ethnic markers, ask them to imagine this scenario. They see a person who may be from another ethnic group. This other person is in sight for about 30 seconds but is not speaking during this time. What markers might be used to place the person in another specific ethnic group? As with Exercise 5, answers will come slowly but surely. Students might make a list like this.

skin color	height
dress	weight
eye shape	broad gestures such as
nose shape	the way a
lips	person walks
other facial features	hair

Then, have the students assume that they hear the other person speak for about 30 seconds. What additional markers might this add?

language	topic of conversation
accent within society's	hand gestures while speaking
language of commerce	terms or jargon used

Finally, assume that the students have a chance to interview the person for about 10 minutes and can engage the person in discussions on any topic. What additional markers might this add?

last name	rituals taken seriously
neighborhood in which	food and drink preferences
person lives	club memberships
attendance at certain	holidays observed
events which the person	jokes shared with people
enjoys (e.g., movies in	from similar
a language besides	backgrounds who can
English; first birthday	recognize the jokes'
party of friend's child)	references

| religion | attention to particular |
| leisure time activities | world events |

The length of the eventual list should convince students about their attention to and knowledge of ethnicity, even though such knowledge may have gone unrecognized. The last entry on the list, world events, may encourage more self-insight. Students might be asked if they remember a test question, class discussion, or term paper on which they did well because their ethnicity gave them a special interest in the topic. For instance, Blacks may be more knowledgeable about specific developments in South Africa than Whites. Jewish students could be far better informed concerning the history of Israel than non-Jews.

Exercise 8: Friendship Choice

Another way to demonstrate the importance of ethnicity is to show that major ethnic boundaries are infrequently crossed when forming friendships. This exercise is an adaptation of research by Brislin (1983). Ask students to name their ten best friends (as in Exercise 2, which some instructors may want to combine with this one). Friends are those people with whom a given student feels closest and with whom the student shares personal information not divulged to everyone. Then, ask students to list the ethnic background of those other people. How many are from the same or a similar ethnic background? If consistent with previous research (Brislin, 1983; Taylor, Dubé, and Bellerose, 1986), most students will report that most of their friends are from a similar background. The boundaries shown by the unchangeable aspects of ethnicity, such as skin color and language (see discussion following Exercise 5), will be crossed infrequently. There will certainly be sixth generation German-Americans who interact with Irish-Americans, but this will be seen as a minimal if not trivial barrier. People keep a comfortable social distance from ethnically different others.

Exercise 9: An Interaction With Someone Different

Professors can either (a) ask students to remember their most recent interaction with an ethnically different other or (b) can assign students to initiate an interaction with such a person; students would also be asked (c) to recall their most recent interaction or (d) would be assigned to interact with an ethnically similar other. They then would report back the following information. Intimacy in the last question refers not to sex but to the amount and depth of personal information shared. The opposite end of that scale, formality, suggests interactions where people are proper and careful in each other's presence.

---

1. How long did the interaction last? _____ minutes

2. How agreeable or pleasant was the interaction?

very agreeable	agreeable	neither agreeable nor disagreeable	disagreeable	very disagreeable
_____	_____	_____	_____	_____

3. How important was the interaction?

very important	important	neither important nor unimportant	unim-portant	very unim-portant
_____	_____	_____	_____	_____

4. How intimate was the interaction?

very intimate	intimate	neither intimate nor formal	formal	very formal
_____	_____	_____	_____	_____

This exercise is an adaptation of research reported by Taylor et al. (1986) in their review of studies concerned with the interaction between English and French speakers in Quebec. They reported an interesting finding. Interactions between ethnically dissimilar people were perceived to be as agreeable as those between similar people, but the interactions were judged less important and less intimate. Another prediction would be that the ethnically dissimilar people's interactions would be shorter in length. Students can compare their results with those of this research finding (their interactions in condition (a) or (b) versus (c) or (d), above). Professors can remind students that both a formal encounter with a shopkeeper that lasts two minutes and a 60-minute chat with a close friend can be agreeable, but the latter will surely be thought of as more important and intimate. Taylor et al. (1986) concluded that individuals in a community may perceive that positive relations exist among people from different ethnic groups, but that such a perception is based on quite different sorts of interactions than between ethnically similar people: "It is argued here that one mechanism for insuring that cross-ethnic contacts are harmonious is to limit them to relatively superficial encounters" (p. 113). Further, the researchers found that when people did interact with ethnically dissimilar others, they were attentive to similarities along other dimensions such as age, sex, occupation, social class, attitudes, and personality traits. "So contact seems to be much more selective when it is with a member of the 'other' group and appears to be designed to enhance the probability that there will be compatibility" (Taylor et al., 1986, p. 113).

Stephan and Stephan (1984) argued that much prejudice is based on ignorance concerning outgroups. If people have few friends from other ethnic groups (Exercise 8) and have relatively superficial encounters (Exercise 9) with ethnically dissimilar others, then there will be little firsthand information shared that might combat the ignorance. Another reason for ignorance is difficulty in understanding the culture of people from other ethnic groups, a topic to which we now turn.

Culture

Ethnicity is part of people's identity as human beings and is determined by both subjective and objective factors. Within an ethnic group, there are ways to behave, acceptable and unacceptable attitudes, and knowledge that is considered important. These attitudes, behaviors, and bodies of knowledge constitute a group's culture. One link between ethnicity and culture already touched upon is that outsiders use observations of cultural practices in making judgments about a person's ethnicity.

More formal definitions of culture number in the hundreds. I have found the contributions of five anthropologists and psychologists especially helpful. Kroeber and Kluckhohn (1952) have a very technical definition, and I will paraphrase several elements. They argue that culture consists of patterns of behavior. This means that regularities in behavior over time, performed by large numbers of people, are keys to understanding culture. For instance, American Roman Catholics celebrate the following events in the lives of their children: Baptism at approximately 2 months, First Communion at about 8 years, and Confirmation at about 14 years. Jewish people will celebrate a Consecration at about the child's sixth birthday, the Bar (male) or Bat (female) Mitzvah at about 13 years, and a Confirmation at 15 or 16 years. There is not a widely accepted distinction regarding the appropriate size of the celebration and party for the three Catholic events. There *is* a distinction for Jews: The Bar or Bat Mitzvah leads to the biggest celebration. Many students will know this latter fact, which means they are sensitive to patterns of behavior. Other patterns of behavior might be used as examples. Who usually makes the offer of a first date in American society, the male or female? What are the typical years during which people go to college (18–22 years of age in the United States, but 16–20 in the Philippines)? What is a comfortable distance to keep from another person while speaking in a face-to-face interaction (it is shorter in many Latin American and Middle-Eastern cultures than it is in the United States; Hall, 1959)?

Another aspect in Kroeber and Kluckhohn's definition (1952) is that culture involves "ideas and their attached values" (p. 181). People have to work hard to understand the key ideas that allow members of a culture to communicate effectively. Because these ideas are used and seen frequently and contribute to the smooth functioning of society, they become highly valued. For instance, a central idea in the government of the United States is that there should be a separation of powers. The founding fathers distrusted any one person or group of people who possessed an inordinate amount of power because they were concerned that the power might be abused. A key idea they placed in the American Constitution was that power should be shared by various branches of government that would have a series of checks on each other's use of power. This key idea is now a central tenet in American society. Imagine what would happen if there were a proposal to abolish one of the three branches of American government.

Herskovits (1948) suggested that "culture is the man-made part of the human environment" (p. 17). Mountains are not a part of culture, but an engineering team's reservoir to collect rainwater falling on the mountain would be a part of culture. Note that such a reservoir would reflect a valued idea: Human intervention to improve upon Nature is appropriate. Triandis (1972) made a distinction between physical and subjective culture. The former would include objects made by people such as houses, tools, gardens, and books. The latter would include the less visible cognitions, attitudes, and behaviors associated with those objects. For instance, some cultures have norms concerning which sex typically tends the family garden. In many cultures, only certain people are allowed to touch certain religious objects. Returning to the example of family celebrations, in a Bar Mitzvah the young man reads from the Torah. The young woman, as part of her Bat Mitzvah, reads from the Haf Torah. This practice reflects the traditional Jewish distinction, part of their subjective culture, in the religious involvement of men and women.

Almost all definitions of culture include the component that culture is transmitted generation to generation by parents, teachers, and other respected adults (e.g., Geertz, 1973). I have found this image useful in explaining culture to students. Children are socialized in a certain society, and the major socializing agents are their parents. Culture consists of what parents hand down to their children, sometimes through direct instruction but more often through their example, so that the children are considered acceptable members of society. If respected elders say, "Yes, that person is one of us," then that person has been adequately socialized into the culture.

An important aspect of culture is that much of it is taken for granted by its members. If a set of values, for instance, is central to a culture, then there is no purpose in discussing them. People have been socialized over a number of years to accept the values, and consequently there is little reflection, questioning, or doubt about them. Because there is no perceived need to discuss the values, a culture's members seldom explain themselves to people from other ethnic groups. The resulting lack of knowledge is another reason why there is little interaction across ethnic boundaries.

Exercise 10: A Culture's Values

Triandis, Bontempo, Leung, and Hui (1987) developed this exercise to show the difference between widely accepted values that need no discussion and less-widely-accepted values that can be the source of disagreements. Professors can divide the class into small groups of 3, 5, or 7 people. The groups should consist of an odd-sized number of people and should be equal in size if possible. Each group should consist of people from as similar backgrounds as possible. If there are three Hispanics, for instance, they should be in the same group. Ask how many people have a mechanism to indicate the number of seconds on their watches. Assuming that a fairly large percentage do, assign one such person per group.

Each group is to decide whether or not the following list of values is central to their culture. Each value statement will be read aloud by one person. The owner of the watch begins to keep time as soon as the reader finishes a statement. People in the group then begin to discuss whether or not the value is central to their culture. As soon as the group decides by majority vote "yes" or "no," the timekeeper records the number of seconds that had been spent discussing that value. The value statements are the following (professors can add or subtract as they wish):

obedience to parents
equal treatment under law
   for rich and poor
consulting with extended
   family members, such
   as uncles, aunts, and
   cousins, regarding
   important decisions
protecting oneself through
   ownership of handguns
freedom of speech that
   does not put others in
   direct danger

equality of the sexes
respect for the elderly
children ages 13–16
   should be allowed to make
   some of their own choices
government has right
   to enter private homes
   at any time
people can live in any part of
   the country that they choose
innocent until proven guilty
women's right to abortion
   on demand

The major prediction is that widely held values, or values clearly not held at all, will demand little discussion and agreement will be reached quickly, perhaps within a few seconds. For instance, most groups of Americans will agree that "equality of the sexes" and "freedom of speech" are values, and that "government's right to enter homes at any time" is clearly not a value. Little time is needed to discuss the obvious aspects of culture. Other values are not widely held and will demand more discussion. For instance, "protecting oneself through ownership of handguns" is a controversial issue, and the presence of controversy indicates that it is not a cultural value. Many groups will not think that "obedience to parents" is a value, given the American ideals of independence and individualism. For those fortunate classrooms with multiple representatives of more than one ethnic group, there may be the opportunity to discuss cultural differences. A discussion group of Hispanics, for instance, might report that they needed little time to decide that "consulting with extended family members" is a value. Many groups of Caucasian Americans will argue either that it is clearly not a value, or that they needed time to discuss the matter. This could begin a discussion of cultural differences in the value placed on a nuclear versus an extended family.

As a result of this exercise, students should begin to understand that cultural values central to a society are not discussed frequently. Yet those values that are not discussed are central to their lives.

Colleagues and I have been interested in developing materials to help people understand the nature of culture and to prepare them to interact effectively with people from different ethnic groups (Brislin, Cushner, Cherrie, and Yong, 1986). The interactions might take place within a pluralistic society such as the United States, or they might take place if people travel to another country. Because culture is so pervasive it becomes much like the air we breathe: We don't think much about culture—or air—until they are taken away from us. One of the best ways to understand this point is to empathize with people from another ethnic group who are trying to understand American culture. The following is one of 100 critical incidents meant to help people understand culture and cultural differences and how both affect interpersonal relations (Brislin et al., 1986, pp. 203–204).

Exercise 11: Diagnosing the Difficulties in Critical Incidents

The professor reads the following critical incident to students as well as the alternative explanations. He then asks for a vote on which alternative(s) contribute to an understanding of the difficulty depicted in the incident. Students may vote for more than one alternative, because several factors are often involved in intercultural difficulties. Students can also ponder the question, "What are some aspects of American culture depicted in this incident that a person from a very different culture would have difficulty understanding?"

Informal Gatherings of People

After a year in the United States, Fumio, from Japan, seemed to be adjusting well to his graduate-level studies. He had cordial relations with his professors, interacted frequently with other graduate students at midday coffee breaks, and was content with his housing arrangements in the graduate student dormitory. Fumio's statistical knowledge was so good that professors recommended that certain American students should consult him for help in this area. He seemed to be excluded, however, from at least one type of activity in which many of the other American graduate students participated. This was the informal gathering of students at the local pub at about 5:00 on Friday afternoons. People did not stop and invite him to these gatherings. Since he was not invited, Fumio felt uncomfortable about simply showing up at the pub. Fumio wondered if the lack of an invitation should be interpreted as a sign that he was doing something wrong—that he was offending the American students in some way.

What is a good analysis of the situation involving the lack of invitations to the pub gatherings?

(1) The Americans were rude in not inviting Fumio, a guest in their country.

(2) The pub gatherings are meant to be an activity in which people who are very familiar with each other (an ingroup) can relax on a very informal basis.

(3) Japanese rarely drink beer. Realizing this, the Americans did not invite Fumio.

(4) The Americans resented the fact that Fumio knew more statistics than they did, and this made the Americans feel inferior because they had to ask Fumio for help.

(5) Pub gatherings on Friday afternoons, like this one, are largely based on pairings of specific males with specific females (or vice versa). Because Fumio had no girlfriend, he was not invited.

The most appropriate answer is number 2: The activities in the pub are ingroup oriented. Even people who make excellent adjustments to another culture find that there are always certain ingroup activities from which they are excluded. In many parts of the world, such activities would include home visits. People's homes, for instance in Japan or Spain, are for family and very close friends of many years. Citizens of these countries may invite sojourning Americans for a meal, but the sharing of food will be done at a restaurant. In the story, Fumio might be uncomfortable at the gathering since one of the primary activities is joke-telling. He might be unable to understand the references in many of the jokes and stories. The other explanations of the incidents may receive a few votes. Many will reject explanation number 1 by saying, "People just show up and nobody invites anybody, and so there is no purposeful rudeness." Few Americans will vote for number 5, however. A good question to ask is whether or not there are aspects of cultural knowledge used in rejecting this explanation. Successful interpersonal interactions in any culture involve both recognizing correct explanations about behavior as well as incorrect analyses. One aspect of American culture found on college campuses is that there is a distinction between Friday and Saturday night gatherings that involve males and females. It is far more likely that Saturday night gatherings would be based on pairings of specific males and females. How do Americans know this subtle distinction? Did someone tell them? Probably not. They simply learned this by observing others in their culture over a period of time.

In addition to empathizing with people crossing cultural boundaries, another good way to understand culture is to analyze "well-meaning clashes." I use this term to refer to behaviors in one culture that are perfectly proper and show social skills, but if performed in another culture are seen as inappropriate and boorish. What we find, then, are cultural differences in the desirability of the same behavior. Here is an incident dealing with this problem (Brislin et al., 1986, p. 93).

Social Ease

Daureen was thrilled to have been asked by some of her new friends at school to attend a birthday party in honor of one of the girl's sisters. She had only recently arrived in Indonesia from the United States as a part of a student exchange program and was excited to be meeting new friends.

When she arrived at the party she found many new things to experience. The food was certainly different, the drinks seemed to taste strange, and even the birthday greeting was done in a way she was not accustomed to. She was even aware that she was the only one dressed in typically Western clothes. This made her feel uneasy as she had gone to all the trouble to look her best. It didn't seem right that she should feel so awkward. She didn't seem to know how to act appropriately. She began feeling more and more uneasy as the night wore on.

Deciding that perhaps some food would help to relax her, Daureen approached a food table and began to help herself. Upon leaving the table, she inadvertently tripped on the leg of a chair and spilled her drink on the floor. Immediately, one of the girls nearby stooped down to begin mopping up the spill and everyone else in the room began laughing out loud. Daureen, uncertain of what to do next, quietly moved out of the way with her head lowered in shame. She kept to herself for the remainder of the evening, hoping to avoid more trouble.

What is a good explanation of the reaction to the spilled drink in this incident?

(1) Daureen had obviously been acting in an inappropriate manner all evening. The spilling of the drink was the straw that broke the camel's back, so to speak. Everyone simply found her actions amusing and could hold the laughter back no longer.

(2) Laughter is a means to disperse tension in Indonesia.

(3) Daureen began the evening wrong by not bringing a gift to the host. This immediately put the others against her; thus the above incident.

(4) Daureen is experiencing a minor form of culture shock. The laughter is probably not due to anything she did.

The correct answer is number 2. In some countries, laughter in a situation such as this is employed to cover up a mistake. Everyone laughs and then forgets the problem. In the United States, especially at a party where people are somewhat unfamiliar with each other, individuals would show their concern and try to make light of the matter, but not through laughter.

The entire collection of 100 critical incidents (Brislin et al., 1986) also contains explanations of the various alternatives and a set of 18 essays that integrate points brought up in the incidents and explanations. The incidents deal with such varied issues in intercultural interaction as anxiety, prejudice, interpreting ambiguity, understanding attributions about behavior common in other cultures, group-individual distinctions, values, learning styles, and the demand for a sense of belonging.

Exercise 12: A Visitor From Another Culture

An encounter with a person from another culture can have a significant impact because it forces people to think about their own culture in new ways. Through the assistance of the Foreign Student Adviser's Office, called the International Programs Office on some campuses, the professor might invite a foreign student to speak to the class (various suggestions for working with foreign students can be found in Mestenhauser, 1983). The guest might be asked to talk about cultural differences (s)he has observed. It is best that such a guest have lived in the host country for at least a year, either currently or on a previous sojourn. Possible cultural differences covered might include how people meet each other and how friendships are developed; student-faculty interactions at college; the importance or unimportance of punctuality; or the amount of purely social interaction that should occur before business people start negotiations on a serious contract. If the guest is from a country where arranged marriages are common, this is an excellent topic. There are few experiences more disconcerting to American students than observing an intelligent, articulate guest defend the practice of arranged marriages: "My parents know me, they know many potential marriage partners and their families, they know about the obligations of marriage after the honeymoon is over, and they know about life's difficulties when people are adults. They know better than I do when it comes to a lifelong partner." The confrontation with their own attitudes and values forces American students to think about the reasons why they are expected to choose their own mates. This will probably be a question that they will be asking themselves for the first time. Again, this is a major aspect of culture: Central values are not normally questioned or discussed.

With this understanding of class, ethnicity, and culture, we can now turn to a concept that has long and consistently been confused with all three.

Race

At this point, the professor might involve students in defining the term "race." This exercise should convince students of the confusion surrounding the term and the need for a more precise definition.

Exercise 13: What Does a Race Mean?

Class, ethnicity, and culture have been discussed. Ask students, "What does race mean and when is the term used?" Ask them to write down their thoughts, collect them in a separate place, and relate these new thoughts about race to previous discussions of the other concepts. The following is an example:

Student thought	**Relationship to other concepts**
Race involves prejudice between groups.	Prejudice was discussed as part of interethnic interactions, and it is common where there is an unchangeable barrier such as skin color.

Racial explanations are used when children from some groups drop out of school more than others.	Has the social class background of the children been taken into account?
A lot of Southeast Asian refugees are the valedictorians of their high school classes. We hear a lot about racial differences.	Have the importance of education and the belief that hard work in the schools is the best way to get ahead in life been analyzed as cultural differences?

The results of this exercise should help students realize that race is an overused term and that other explanatory concepts are much more helpful when talking about various aspects of human behavior. Following a number of definitions suggested by anthropologists (Brues, 1977; Campbell, 1976) I believe that race should have a very limited meaning. A race is one of the major populations of human beings that differ in certain hereditary traits. For reasons of geography and culture, a race constitutes a breeding population in which members are more likely to mate and procreate with each other than with members of another race. People's membership in a racial category today reflects the mating behavior of their distant and recent ancestors. The only inevitable aspect of race, then, is a small set of inherited physical features. These characteristics reflect a history of adaptation to the environments in which the ancestors found themselves. All differences other than this small set of physical characteristics are better explained through the use of other concepts such as those covered in this chapter. Campbell (1976) captures this limited use of race well:

> The most obvious differences we see between the races are little more than skin deep. . . . Furthermore, they are of recent origin: present-day racial differences are far less than the differences between modern man and his . . . forebears. . . . Modern races were probably hardly recognizable more than 30,000 years ago. (p. 424)

The three major racial groups, all of which stem from the same *Homo sapiens* ancestors in Africa (Cann, Stoneking, and Wilson, 1987; Gould, 1987), are White, Black, and Oriental/American Indian (Brues, 1977).

Skin color happens to be the most visible physical characteristic. (As with all the following analyses of racial differences, the source is Overfield, 1985.) The original skin color of *Homo sapiens* was black. As people migrated to Northern Europe, their skin became lighter to better allow the synthesis of vitamin D on the less frequent sunny days. The skin color of people who remained in Africa remained black since dark skin provided better protection (e.g., less skin cancer) against the tropical sun.

Other differences have an adaptive basis. For example, Blacks have a far higher rate of sickle-cell anemia than members of the other races. About 9.5% of American Blacks and 20% of African Blacks have the sickle-cell gene. The presence of this disease reflects past adaptation to malaria. When the malaria parasite enters human cells, "cells with the sickle defect are destroyed before the parasite's reproduction is complete. This reduces the parasite load" (Overfield, 1985, p. 85). The incidence of the sickle gene in American Blacks is lower because of mating with Whites and because the disease is no longer adaptive given the infrequency of malaria in the United States.

Although any evolutionary advantage is unknown, there are racial differences in the processing of alcohol. Assume a person drinks 200 ml of whiskey, vodka, or gin. When ingested, alcohol is oxidized to acetaldehyde by a specific and known enzyme. This enzyme has two variants. The high-activity type converts the alcohol quickly, the low-activity type more slowly. Acetaldehyde is thought to cause the body's reactions associated with alcohol use, such as changes in vasomotor symptoms and the pleasure many people feel when intoxicated. Approximately 85–90% of American Indians and Orientals have the high-activity type, which means that alcohol quickly becomes acetaldehyde and intoxication follows. Members of this racial group also have a response to alcohol known as the facial flush, a reddening of the face obvious to any observer. The high-activity enzyme type is also associated with another enzyme that maintains the acetaldehyde level in the blood. Approximately 80–90% of Whites and Blacks, on the other hand, have the low-activity enzyme and also have an associated enzyme that hastens the oxidation of acetaldehyde into a less harmful substance. Asians and American Indians, then, experience a rapid onset and slow deterioration of the intoxicating element that follows alcohol ingestion.

No racial group has a biological inheritance that puts them at a greater advantage over the others with respect to health. Blacks have denser bones and less tooth decay than Whites but many have the sickle-cell anemia problem already discussed. Blacks and Orientals/ American Indians are much more likely than Whites to be lactose intolerant, leading to greater difficulty in obtaining enough calcium. Lactose intolerance can also lead to health problems associated with diarrhea if too many foods made with milk are eaten. Whites and Blacks are more likely to have an offensive body odor and consequently are the major consumers in the multimillion-dollar deodorant industry. Whites show aging lines in their faces faster than the other races and also have more gray hair in old age. They also have more skin cancer than the other races. People who claim racial supe-riority would do well to study the positive and negative aspects their ancestors have handed down to them. Other races have a different, but not a better or worse, pattern of advantages and disadvantages.

Exercise 14: Does Any of This Relate to Me?

Students might be asked to find a physical feature of their racial or ethnic group that differentiates them from others. Although not as great as racial differences, there are sometimes ethnic correlates of physical features because ethnic group members are more likely to marry within than outside their group. Some of these differences will have health implications and some will not, and some may be phrased in terms of probabilities (e.g., a 1 in 20,000 rate in the gen-eral population). Students could consult biochemistry texts, talk to doctors or medical students, and check with their parents about any inherited features, and so forth. They should make sure that other reasons, such as nutrition associated with social class, are taken into account. Some findings students may report include a greater inci-dence of sickle-cell anemia in people of Greek and Italian ancestry in contrast to Caucasians as a whole. People of Irish and Scottish ances-try are more likely (1 in 4,000 cases) than other Caucasians (1 in 20,000) to have phenylketonuria, a metabolic disorder that can cause toxic effects to the brain and central nervous sytem. Orientals/Ameri-can Indians are much more likely to have dry earwax (84%), whereas Whites and Blacks have wet earwax (97% and 99%, respectively). Breast cancer appears to be higher in White than in Oriental women.

This exercise should encourage students to give race a more lim-ited explanatory role than they may have previously used in their thinking about human behavior. The greater explanatory power of class, ethnicity, and culture will be explored further when combina-tions among the four concepts are used in explaining selected re-search findings.

Combinations of Concepts

The complexity of human diversity and the need to move beyond su-perficial stereotypes becomes evident as combinations of concepts are examined.

Culture and Class

A body of research concerned with child rearing practices in various cultures has yielded results which have surprised the investigators (e.g., Cashmore and Goodnow, 1986; Lambert, Hamers, and Frasure-Smith, 1979). The social class background of the parents predicts child rearing preferences as well or better than their cultural background. In a study of Australians from Anglo and Italian backgrounds, working-class parents from both groups emphasized "being neat," "having good manners," and "being obedient." Cultural differences were eliminated for the first two items when parents' educational level was taken into account. The "being obedient" item was more emphasized by Italian fathers in comparison to Anglo fathers, but this cultural difference was also reduced when social class variables were considered. Note that these findings are consistent with the previously reviewed research on social class and child rearing. Combined with Lambert et al.'s (1979) similar findings emphasizing class over culture, the implication is that future studies of child rearing will be unacceptable unless they take the social class background of parents into account.

Ethnicity and Culture

There are ethnic groups in many societies that have a clear minority status in terms of numbers and community influence. In Hawaii, people with Hawaiian ancestry are a minority compared to Caucasians and Japanese-Americans. In a study that included an analysis of their self-esteem, Howard (1974) found that cultural knowledge was more important than self-designated ethnic identity in predicting positive self-esteem among part-Hawaiians. The cultural knowledge was assessed by asking respondents about very detailed aspects of traditional Hawaiian life, and respondents would have to be deeply involved in Hawaiian society to answer even a few questions correctly. Why didn't ethnic identity predict positive self-esteem? The answer goes back to the manipulability of ethnicity to meet the demands of various situations. In Hawaii, part-Hawaiians have a variety of identities from which to draw. Some will be part Caucasian, for instance, and might draw on this in carrying out their responsible job demands in the industrialized city of Honolulu. Some will have the possibility of a Filipino identity because of marriages within their families several generations ago. Some will claim a Hawaiian identity because they like the opportunities to interact with friends in a given community. This mix of identities, and reasons for emphasizing one over another, means that any measure will include part-Hawaiians who identify themselves as such for many different reasons. A better measure of their Hawaiian values consists of questions demanding detailed knowledge of Hawaiian culture.

Race and Culture

The fact that many Orientals and American Indians have a facial flush after ingesting alcohol has been pointed out. This is a physiological reaction over which people have no control except to abstain from alcohol. Indeed, this is one possible response. Johnson (Johnson, Schwitters, Wilson, Nagoshi, and McClearn, 1985; Park et al., 1984; see also Sue, Zane, and Ito, 1979) has studied culturally influenced drinking practices among Orientals. For some Orientals, the flush is interpreted as a sign that they have had enough to drink. This flush may be a cultural signal that others might react to by, for instance, ceasing to serve alcoholic beverages. But things get complicated when there are other attitudes about the flush. Some Orientals believe that a light complexion is attractive. They feel they become unattractive when they flush to a dark red. This value associated with the flush may not be "It's a good idea to stop drinking," but rather "I will be unattractive and embarrassed." Other Oriental cultural values, such as the necessity not to lose control of oneself, may also enter the decision to limit one's alcohol intake. Students may want to ponder why one sign of adulthood (age 21) in North America consists of societal tolerance (and often peer encouragement) toward ingesting enough alcohol to cause a loss of self-control.

Another interrelation of race and culture occurs when, year after year, the same decisions about behavior are based on race within any given society. Here, race is used by people in a much broader way than I have recommended, but this broader use is far and away more common. Jones (in press) points out that in such cases, thinking in racial terms becomes part of a culture. Decisions about schooling, jobs, marital partners, housing, and religious affiliations are often made with race in mind. Similarly, judgments concerning who is intelligent, competent, responsible, and socially graceful can be made with race as a major determining factor. When people say, "The races have always behaved this way toward each other around here," this marks a deeply-held aspect of those people's culture. Exposed to such cultural influences during their socialization, children learn to think in racial terms as they grow into adolescence and adulthood. Influences of society's categories on thinking are an important topic to which we now turn.

The Four Concepts as Social Categories

One more body of research findings should be reviewed as it relates to the four concepts. Class, ethnicity, culture, and race are social categories (Gardner, 1985) that people use to think about themselves and others and to make decisions about their behavior. Consider the following episode, which might occur in an American community. A young Caucasian woman of 22, daughter of a bank executive and a medical doctor, brings a 24-year-old Black man home for dinner. The daughter tells her parents that they are thinking of getting married. During the evening's conversation, the young man mentions that his parents work in a factory. The woman's parents, at the end of the evening, express displeasure with the proposed marriage. What might be their reason(s)?

Students might bring up the possibility of racial or ethnic prejudice. Others might add that it could be class prejudice: The parents are concerned about the social background of the young man's parents. After participating in some of the exercises in this chapter, some students might appeal to culture. The parents may feel that interracial marriage is still not widely accepted in American culture, and they are concerned that the couple will be entering a life filled with the potential for discrimination.

All these reasons show that the four concepts are being used as categories in people's thinking. In the example, the young man and woman are individual members of well-established categories with which people in the United States are familiar. When individuals are members of widely used categories, all the information from that category can be called upon. The young man is Black: All of people's widely held fears, concerns, memories, emotions, and behavioral predictions can be applied to their thinking about this one Black individual. The category of social class contains the elements of social stratification and the belief that marriages between people from the high and the low strata could be problematic.

Another important research finding (Hewstone and Brown, 1986) is that some interactions between people can be category based. This means that the interaction is between people representing different categories, not between two individuals. If a prejudiced White talks with a Black, there might be a pleasant interaction (recall the discussion of superficial encounters in Exercise 9). But the White's feelings about the whole category of Blacks will not change. If the interaction is unpleasant, the negative view of the entire outgroup category will be reinforced. If the Black is especially attractive and the White has a pleasant interaction that is memorable, there may still be little impact on the entire category. Rather, the Black will be "split off" and placed in a *new* category of "the individual exception," and the old, broad category will remain untouched. Much research (Allport, 1954; Brislin, 1981; Hewstone and Brown, 1986; Miller and Brewer, 1984) has dealt with the improvement of intergroup relations, and a recent chapter in this series had dealt with empirical research on the topic (Aronson, 1987). Briefly, the recommended action for affecting the entire category is to have extended and intimate interaction with outgroup members where all the people involved have equal status. The social norms surrounding the contact, for instance community leaders' and school administrators' support in a newly desegregated school, should be supportive of improved intergroup relations. The contact should involve various people in the groups, not just the most attractive and articulate, and the contact should take place in a variety of settings. People should be interested in obtaining the same goals, and the goals should demand the efforts of all the people involved in the contact. There should be "cognitive boosters" (Cook, 1984), or opportunities to think about the nature of people's new intergroup experiences and to modify or add categories to their thinking about different others. The sorts of exercises presented in this chapter are the sorts of cognitive boosters that have been suggested by researchers, educators, and specialists in training for improved intercultural relations.

Further Considerations for Teaching

Much of the material presented in this chapter can be used as intact units in courses in social psychology. In addition, much of the material can be used when social psychology is covered during the introductory course. Another way to use the material in the introductory course is to cover different sections at different times. The material on race can be covered as one topic during the period devoted to the biological bases of behavior or to physiological psychology; the material on social class can be treated during coverage of developmental psychology, educational psychology, or learning. The material on ethnicity and ethnic identity can be used during treatments of personality. Finally, the material on culture can be treated as part of the unit on social psychology, or as part of the unit on psychology and society that is frequently part of current introductory courses.

References

Abelson, R. (1981). Psychological status of the script concept. *American Psychologist, 36,* 715–729.

Allport, G. (1954). *The nature of prejudice.* Reading, MA: Addison-Wesley.

Arbuckle, T. Y., Gold, D., & Andres, D. (1986). Cognitive functioning of older people in relation to social and personality variables. *Psychology and Aging, 1,* 55–62.

Argyle, M. (1980). Interaction skills and social competence. In M. P. Feldman & J. Orford (Eds.), *Psychological problems: The social context* (pp. 123–150). New York: Wiley.

Armstrong, A. J. (1985). Social skills training. *Bulletin of the British Psychological Society, 38,* 418–420.

Aronson, E. (1987). Teaching students what they think they already know about prejudice and desegregation. In V. P. Makosky (Ed.), *The G. Stanley Hall lecture series, Vol. 7* (pp. 65–84). Washington, DC: American Psychological Association.

Bardouille-Crema, A., Black, K. N., & Feldhusen, J. (1986). Performance on Piagetian tasks of Black children of differing socioeconomic levels. *Developmental Psychology, 22,* 841–844.

Bautista, L. S. (1982). Relations among three ethnic groups in the Philippines. In D. Wu (Ed.), *Ethnicity and interpersonal interaction* (pp. 109–135). Singapore: Maruzen Asia, and Bridgeport, CT: Book Services International.

Boykin, A. W. (1986). The triple quandary and the schooling of Afro-American children. In V. Neisser (Ed.), *The school achievement of minority children: New perspectives.* Hillsdale, NJ: Erlbaum.

Brislin, R. (1981). *Cross-cultural encounters: Face-to-face interaction.* Elmsford, NY: Pergamon.

Brislin, R. (1983). The benefits of close intercultural relationships. In J. Berry and S. Irvine (Eds.), *Human assessment and cultural factors* (pp. 521–538). New York: Plenum.

Brislin, R., Cushner, K., Cherrie, C., & Yong, M. (1986). *Intercultural interactions: A practical guide.* Beverly Hills, CA: Sage.

Brownell, K. D. (1982). Obesity: Understanding and treating a serious, prevalent, and refractory disorder. *Journal of Consulting and Clinical Psychology, 50,* 820–840.

Brues, A. M. (1977). *People and races.* New York: Macmillan.

Campbell, B. G. (1976). *Humankind emerging.* Boston: Little, Brown.

Cann, R. C., Stoneking, M., & Wilson, A. C. (1987). Mitochondrial DNA and human evolution. *Nature, 325,* 31–36.

Casino, E. (1983). Consultants and competence in the development of cross-cultural programs. In D. Landis & R. Brislin (Eds.), *Handbook of intercultural training: Vol. 2. Issues in training methodology* (pp. 218–240). Elmsford, NY: Pergamon.

Cashmore, J. A., & Goodnow, J. L. (1986). Influence of Australian parents' values: Ethnicity versus socioeconomic status. *Journal of Cross-Cultural Psychology, 17,* 441–454.

Cohen, R. (1978). Ethnicity: Problem and focus in anthropology. *Annual Review of Anthropology, 7,* 379–403.

Cook, S. (1984). Cooperative interaction in multiethnic contexts. In N. Miller & M. B. Brewer (Eds.), *Groups in contact: The psychology of desegregation* (pp. 155–185). Orlando, FL: Academic Press.

Crick, B. (1982). *In defence of politics* (2nd ed.). Middlesex, England and New York: Penguin.

Denmark, F. L. (1983). Integrating the psychology of women into introductory psychology. In C. J. Scheirer & A. M. Rogers (Eds.), *The G. Stanley Hall lecture series, Vol. 3* (pp. 33–71). Washington, DC: American Psychological Association.

Dunn, N. E. (1981). Children's achievement at school-entry age as a function of mothers' and fathers' teaching sets. *The Elementary School Journal, 81,* 245–253.

Freedman, J. L. (1978). *Happy people.* New York: Harcourt Brace Jovanovich.

Gardner, H. (1985). *The mind's new science: The history of the cognitive revolution.* New York: Basic Books.

Geertz, C. (1973). *The interpretation of cultures.* New York: Basic Books.

Gilbert, D., & Kahl, J. A. (1982). *The American class structure: A new synthesis.* Homewood, IL: Dorsey.

Gould, S. J. (1987). Bushes all the way down. *Natural History, 96*(6), 12–19.

Graue, M. E., Weinstein, T., & Walberg, H. J. (1983). School-based home instruction and learning: A quantitative synthesis. *Journal of Educational Research, 79,* 351–360.

Grunberg, N. E. (1982). Obesity: Etiology, hazards, and treatment. In R. J. Gatchel, A. Baum, & J. E. Singer (Eds.), *Handbook of psychology and health: Vol. 1. Clinical psychology and behavioral medicine: Overlapping disciplines* (pp. 103–120). Hillsdale, NJ: Erlbaum.

Gullo, D. F. (1981). Social class differences in preschool children's comprehension of Wh— questions. *Child Development, 52,* 736–740.

Hall, E. (1959). *The silent language.* Garden City, NY: Doubleday.

Henderson, G. (Ed.). (1979). *Understanding and counseling ethnic minorities.* Springfield, IL: Charles Thomas.

Herskovits, M. (1948). *Man and his works.* New York: Knopf.

Hewstone, M., & Brown, R. (Eds.). (1986). *Contact and conflict in intergroup encounters.* Oxford and New York: Basil Blackwell.

Howard, A. (1974). *Ain't no big thing: Coping strategies in a Hawaiian-American community.* Honolulu, HI: University Press of Hawaii.

Hui, C. H., & Triandis, H. C. (1986). Individualism-collectivism: A study of cross-cultural researchers. *Journal of Cross-Cultural Psychology, 17,* 225–248.

Johnson, R. C., Schwitters, S. Y., Wilson, J. R., Nagoshi, C. T., & Mc-Clearn, G. E. (1985). A cross-ethnic comparison of reasons given for using alcohol, not using alcohol or ceasing to use alcohol. *Journal of Studies on Alcohol, 46,* 283–288.

Jones, J. (in press). Racism in Black and White: A bicultural model of reaction and evolution. In P. Katz and D. Taylor (Eds.), *Eliminating racism: Profiles in controversy.* New York: Plenum.

Jones, P. A., & McMillan, W. B. (1973). Speech characteristics as a function of social class and situational factors. *Child Development, 44,* 117–121.

Kagan, J. K. (1985). The human infant. In A. M. Rogers & C. J. Scheirer (Eds.), *The G. Stanley Hall lecture series, Vol. 5* (pp. 55–86). Washington, DC: American Psychological Association.

Katz, I. (1973). Negro performance in interracial situations. In P. Watson (Ed.), *Psychology and race* (pp. 256–266). Chicago: Aldine.

Kohn, M. L. (1977). *Class and conformity* (2nd ed.). Chicago: University of Chicago Press.

Kroeber, A., & Kluckhohn, C. (1952). *Culture: A critical review of concepts and definitions.* Cambridge, MA: Peabody Museum.

Lambert, W. E., Hamers, J. F., & Frasure-Smith, N. (1979). *Child-rearing values: A cross-national study.* New York: Praeger.

LeVine, R., & Campbell, D. (1972). *Ethnocentrism.* New York: Wiley.

Lindgren, H. C., & Suter, W. N. (1985). *Educational psychology in the classroom* (7th ed.). Monterey, CA: Brooks/Cole.

Lundberg, M. L. (1974). *The incomplete adult: Social class constraints on personality development.* Westport, CT: Greenwood Press.

McGuire, W. J., McGuire, C. V., Child, P., & Fujioka, T. (1978). Salience of ethnicity in the spontaneous self-concept as a function of one's ethnic distinctiveness in the social environment. *Journal of Personality and Social Psychology, 36,* 511–520.

McKeachie, W. J. (1986). Teaching psychology: Research and experience. In V. P. Makosky (Ed.), *The G. Stanley Hall lecture series, Vol. 6* (pp. 154–191). Washington, DC: American Psychological Association.

Mestenhauser, J. A. (1983). Learning from sojourners. In D. Landis & R. Brislin (Eds.), *Handbook of intercultural training: Vol. 2. Issues in training methodology* (pp. 153–185). Elmsford, NY: Pergamon.

Miller, N., & Brewer, M. B. (1984). *Groups in contact: The psychology of desegregation.* Orlando, FL: Academic Press.

Overfield, T. (1985). *Biological variation in health and illness.* Reading, MA: Addison-Wesley.

Park, J. Y., Huang, Y., Nagoshi, C. T., Yuen, S., Johnson, R. C., Ching, C. A., & Bowman, K. S. (1984). The flushing response to alcohol use among Koreans and Taiwanese. *Journal of Studies on Alcohol, 45,* 481–485.

Pettigrew, T. F. (1986). The intergroup contact hypothesis reconsidered. In M. Hewstone & R. Brown (Eds.), *Contact and conflict in intergroup encounters* (pp. 169–195). Oxford and New York: Basil Blackwell.

Rodin, J. (1981). Current status of the internal-external hypothesis for obesity: What went wrong? *American Psychologist, 36,* 361–372.

Saegert, S. (1986). Environmental psychology and the world beyond the mind. In V. P. Makosky (Ed.), *The G. Stanley Hall lecture series, Vol. 6* (pp. 129–164). Washington, DC: American Psychological Association.

Sarason, I. G. (1983). Contemporary abnormal psychology: Developments and issues. In C. J. Scheirer & A. M. Rogers (Eds.), *The G. Stanley Hall lecture series, Vol. 3* (pp. 75–115). Washington, DC: American Psychological Association.

Schlossberg, N. K. (1984). Exploring the adult years. In A. M. Rogers & C. J. Scheirer (Eds.), *The G. Stanley Hall lecture series, Vol. 4* (pp. 101–154). Washington, DC: American Psychological Association.

Schwarzwald, J., & Amir, Y. (1984). Interethnic relations and education: An Israeli perspective. In N. Miller & M. Brewer (Eds.), *Groups in contact: The psychology of desegregation* (pp. 53–76). Orlando, FL: Academic Press.

Stephan, W. G., & Stephan, C. W. (1984). The role of ignorance in intergroup relations. In N. Miller & M. B. Brewer (Eds.), *Groups in contact: The psychology of desegregation* (pp. 229–255). Orlando, FL: Academic Press.

Stokols, D. (1982). Environmental psychology: A coming of age. In A. G. Graut (Ed.), *The G. Stanley Hall lecture series, Vol. 2* (pp. 155–205). Washington, DC: American Psychological Association.

Sue, S., Zane, N., & Ito, J. (1979). Alcohol drinking patterns among Asian and Caucasian Americans. *Journal of Cross-Cultural Psychology, 10,* 41–56.

Taylor, D., Dubé, L., & Bellerose, J. (1986). Intergroup contact in Quebec. In M. Hewstone & R. Brown (Eds.), *Contact and conflict in intergroup encounters* (pp. 107–118). Oxford and New York: Basil Blackwell.

Thurow, L. M. (1987). A surge in inequality. *Scientific American, 256*(3), 30–37.

Triandis, H. C. (1972). *The analysis of subjective culture.* New York: Wiley.

Triandis, H. C., Bontempo, R., Leung, K., & Hui, H. (1987). *A method for extracting cultural, societal, and personal constructs.* Manuscript submitted for publication.

Trower, P., Bryant, B., & Argyle, M. (1978). *Social skills and mental health.* London: Methuen.

What works: Research about teaching and learning (1986). Washington, DC: United States Department of Education.

Wu, D., & Foster, B. (1982). Conclusion. In D. Wu (Ed.), *Ethnicity and interpersonal interaction.* Singapore: Maruzen Asia, and Bridgeport, CT: Book Services International.

Yando, R., Seitz, V., & Zigler, E. (1979). *Intellectual and personality characteristics of children: Social-class and ethnic-group differences.* Hillsdale, NJ: Erlbaum.

WILLIAM E. CASHIN

USING EVALUATION DATA TO IMPROVE COLLEGE CLASSROOM TEACHING

William E. Cashin is Director of the Center for Faculty Evaluation and Development at Kansas State University. He is primarily responsible for research on and administration of the Instructional Development Effectiveness Assessment (IDEA) system, a student rating of teaching system developed at Kansas State. He also consults and gives seminars at colleges and universities across the country on faculty evaluation and development, particularly the improvement of instruction.

Cashin received his PhD in counseling psychology from Catholic University in Washington, DC. He has counseled and taught undergraduate and graduate courses in psychology and education. During most of the 1960s he was at La Salle College in Philadelphia. Before coming to Kansas State in 1975, when the Center was created, Cashin was Coordinator of Testing and Evaluation at the University of Delaware, where he did institutional research. While there, he revised faculty evaluation procedures and student rating forms and initiated an all-university course and series of public colloquia on college teaching.

His research interests currently focus on differences in student ratings for various academic fields. He has written several of the center's IDEA papers dealing with improving teaching. He also serves on the editorial boards of *Teaching of Psychology* and the *Journal of Educational Psychology*.

WILLIAM E. CASHIN

USING EVALUATION DATA TO IMPROVE COLLEGE CLASSROOM TEACHING

To improve teaching we need three things: first, models of effective teaching; second, data about our present teaching; and third, if our teaching falls short of our models, some new strategies to achieve our instructional goals. The emphasis of this chapter is on the first two elements, especially on gathering data about our present teaching. I will focus on two major approaches to gathering data: classroom observation techniques (in which I will include videotaping of teaching) and student rating systems.

I shall discuss the use of evaluation data because both classroom observation techniques and student ratings produce data that need to be interpreted. We must interpret the data and put it into the context of the course. Initially the data are only descriptive, not evaluative.

This chapter has evolved from the Center for Faculty Evaluation and Development's seminars, "Instructional Development" and "Improving College Teaching." Primary credit for the design and content of the original seminar belongs to Judith D. Aubrecht (1979b) who developed the seminar while we were colleagues at the Center. I am pleased to acknowledge her significant contribution to this chapter. I would also like to thank the many seminar participants who provided feedback over the years.

Someone must make the evaluative judgment. Since I am talking about improvement or formative evaluation, the individual instructor should certainly help make those judgments.

I think my comments will be helpful in teaching psychology not only in college but also in high school. However, I suspect that high school teachers, because they are teaching students who are required to attend school, face a host of attitudinal and motivational concerns not faced by college-level teachers. I will not address the additional concerns of high school teachers. (See Aubrecht & Hanna, 1982, for a student rating form that does address these concerns.)

One or two comments about the use of the word "improve" are also in order. This chapter concerns formative evaluation, or the professional development of the instructor—that is, the improvement of teaching and the enhancement of student learning. It is not concerned with summative evaluation or using the data to make personnel decisions.

In addition, people often interpret the word "improve" as implying that there is a deficiency in a person seeking to improve. In my judgment, improvement is appropriate for all people, unless they are perfect. A few great teachers may be born, but there are things the other 99 percent can learn that may improve their teaching.

Using evaluation data, either from classroom observation techniques or from student rating systems, has three advantages. The most important advantage is that evaluation data provide us with a way to distance ourselves from our own behavior. Such data can bestow some objectivity on what we have done; we can stand back and view it from another's perspective. Secondly, the data provide a kind of permanent record. We have the protocol, rating summary, videotape, and so on, and we do not have to rely solely on our own recall.

The third advantage is a mixed blessing: Evaluation data provide a focus. We can never attend to all of our or the students' behavior; no observation technique, videotape, or student rating system can capture a course or class in its entirety. All of these techniques are necessarily selective. To the extent that they focus on relevant behavior—something the instructor wishes to improve or needs to improve—this focusing is an advantage. But an observation technique can also focus on the wrong aspect or on something that is not especially helpful. There is limited advantage to gathering extensive data about something we are already doing especially well.

Views of Effective Teaching

As with many issues in higher education, there is no agreed-upon definition of effective teaching. Based on my reading, neither the research literature nor the speculations of theorists have produced a definition of effective teaching that can be presented with any authority. Since 1969 the *Annual Review of Psychology* has included seven reviews of instructional psychology, the most recent by Pintrich, Cross, Kozma, and McKeachie (1986). These reviews are of limited help in defining effective teaching at the college level, however. First, there is considerable variety in what the different authors have chosen to cover, and second, most of the research reviewed was done on teaching at the kindergarten through 12th-grade levels. The third edition of the *Handbook of Research on Teaching* (Wittrock, 1986) includes a chapter on "Research on Teaching in Higher Education" (Dunkin & Barnes, 1986) and a number of other chapters treating relevant topics. However, at least based upon my reading, the research has not yet coalesced sufficiently to make a case for an agreed-upon definition or description of effective teaching.

The most useful reading I found was a chapter by McCord (1985), "Methods and Theories of Instruction" in *Higher Education: Handbook of Theory and Research.* The section on modes of instruction (lecture, discussion, and so on) was particularly relevant. However, McCord concludes:

> There are several criticisms, however, that can be raised of instructional models as they currently exist. One of the criticisms is the failure of these models of instruction to be stated in terms that are understandable to the instructor. The average college instructor will not be able to study most models of instruction and draw from them a meaningful conceptual framework to use in designing or planning an approach to instruction in the classroom. (p. 123)

Perhaps this is simply my rationalization to continue using the approach that I have been using for several years: You, the instructor, must decide what criteria to use to define effective teaching.

The approach that Judy Aubrecht and I used in our seminars was a card exchange exercise that contained many different statements or assumptions about teaching and learning (see Bergquist & Phillips, 1975). We had a total of 72 statements. Each participant is given a set of six cards, each containing a different statement. The participants keep the statements they like and try to trade the others. There are several iterations in the exercise that I will not describe, but the exercise is effective in generating discussion about what is good teaching or good learning.

Following are three sets of three statements each. Take a few moments to read them and then, from each set of three, choose the statement you agree with most.

Set 1

A. The teacher's primary role in the classroom is as "information dispenser."
B. Teaching is primarily the cultivation of rational activity.
C. Learning comes primarily from student experience.

Set 2

A. Effective teachers are, first and foremost, masters of their academic disciplines.
B. Students should understand the principles or reasons for various practices or procedures.
C. Too many teachers teach only intellects, not total people.

Set 3

A. The instructor has knowledge that the students need, and the instructor is able to transmit that knowledge.
B. How students learn is more important than what they learn.
C. One of the most important things a student can learn is to tolerate some ambiguity in the search for understanding of course material.

Not only does considering statements like these result in lively discussions about what is effective teaching; more importantly, for most participants it leads to the conclusion: it depends. It depends upon the level of the course, the academic field, the students, the instructor, and so forth. Perhaps some of you may have had that feeling just in reading the preceding nine statements. This ambivalence almost always occurs when faculty in groups of twos or fours are asked to agree upon the ranking of the statements. This implies that you (the individual instructor or departmental or college committee) must decide specifically what you are trying to achieve in a given course and in the many subunits within the course. Until this is done, it is futile to discuss improvement.

Aubrecht and I added the five instructional dimensions or continua, which are ways of looking at the instruction tasks, as a context for the statements (Table 1).

What we are suggesting is: first, that there are many different ways we can look at our teaching (five are suggested here); second, that these represent continua, and there can be wide variations along each of the continua; and third, and most importantly, that no given teaching approach is necessarily better than another in the abstract. What instructors must do is to decide for any given course or class where they think their instructional goals best fit. Will the class emphasize content or process and to what extent? Who will be more active—the teacher or the students? Will the goals and pace be the same for all students? Will the rewards to the student be extrinsic (coming

Table 1
Instructional Dimensions, Educational Taxonomies, and Instructional Methods

Instructional Dimensions

Content-oriented	——— TEACHING ———	Process-oriented
Teacher most active	——— LEARNING ———	Student most active
Same for all	——— GOALS/OBJECTIVES ———	Individual
Same for all	——— PACE OF LEARNING ———	Self-paced
Extrinsic to student	——— REWARDS ———	Intrinsic to student

Educational Taxonomies

COGNITIVE	Knowledge	Comprehensive	Application	Higher-order objectives
AFFECTIVE	Receiving	Responding	Valuing	Organizing
PSYCHOMOTOR	Imitation	Manipulation, Precision, Articulation, Naturalization		

Instructional Methods

LISTENING	LECTURE	RECITATION	DIALOGUE	DISCUSSION
TALKING				GUIDED PURE
READING	TEXTBOOK ———	PROGRAMMED TEXTS ———		
		INDEPENDENT READING———		
WRITING		OBJECTIVE EXAMS ———	ESSAY EXAMS ———	
		PAPERS ———		
DOING		JOURNALS———	PSI—CAI ———	
		DRILL LABS ———	PROJECTS ———	PRACTICUMS
			ROLE PLAYING ——	SIMULATION GAMES
			CASE STUDIES ——	GUIDED DESIGN ——
MULTI		FIELD TRIPS———		
		AUDIO-TUTORIAL ——		
SEEING		(MODELS, PHOTOGRAPHS, FILMS, DIAGRAMS, ETC.)[a]		
HEARING		(LANGUAGE TAPES, MUSIC, ETC.)[a]		

Note. [a]Position probably depends upon how materials are introduced and followed up: See Weston and Cranton (1986) for an elaborate and useful discussion of the use of these and other instructional materials.

primarily from the teacher's behavior) or intrinsic (coming primarily from the student's behavior)?

When we generated the 72 statements about teaching and learning, we tried to place the statements used in the card exchange at varying positions along the continua. For example, we think that the "A" statements tend to fall to the left side of the continua, the "B" statements more in the middle, and the "C" statements to the right. So, if you chose the "A" statements, you tend to think that you should be more content-oriented, more active than the students, and so on. We cannot claim any special empirical or theoretical bases for these dimensions, but our experience has been that many college instructors have found them a useful context in which to consider their teaching.

Many teachers have also found the classical taxonomies of Bloom useful: the cognitive domain (Bloom, Engelhart, Furst, Hill, & Krathwohl, 1956) and the affective domain (Krathwohl, Bloom, & Masia, 1964). Because most psychologists are familiar with these taxonomies, I have simply listed them in Table 1 without explanation.

In the cognitive domain, I have combined analysis, synthesis, and evaluation under the label "higher-order objectives." I have omitted "characterization" from the affective domain because I do not think that in any given course or even all of college, instructors have the capability of developing an all-pervasive value system or lifestyle. I have also omitted the various taxonomies for the psychomotor domain because the typical introductory psychology course does not include such goals.

Both in my own teaching and in working with other faculty, I have found the preceding instructional dimensions and the various taxonomies useful. You may also find it useful to look for another frame of reference. Gagne's (1984) learning outcomes have wide applicability: intellectual skills, verbal information, cognitive strategies, motor skills, and attitudes. Axelrod's (1973) four types of evocative teachers—discipline-centered, instructor-centered, student-as-mind, and student-as-person—and the thirteen questions Axelrod raises for each may also be useful (see also Dressel & Marcus, 1982, for a discussion of these four types). Finally, you may want to use the dimensions or factors found in student rating systems as a framework in which to consider their teaching (e.g., Abrami, 1985; Frey, Leonard, & Beatty, 1975; Marques, Lane, & Dorfman, 1979). You must select and make explicit some frame of reference to improve your teaching, then choose teaching methods fitted to your goals.

In Table 1 I attempt to pull together the instructional dimensions and educational taxonomies and show their relationship to various instructional methods. I suggest that the objectives of different courses or classes will fall on different parts of the continua and that no one position is necessarily better than another. You, the instructor, must decide what is appropriate. In general, however, if the class is content-oriented, the teacher will tend to be more active, the goals and pace will tend to be the same for all students, and the rewards will be more extrinsic than intrinsic to the student. Moving down the left side of Table 1, I am suggesting that the left ends of the five continua fit the more basic categories of the taxonomies. As your course objectives move to the right, you can achieve higher levels on the taxonomies.

The instructional methods are positioned roughly under the appropriate part of the dimensions' continua and taxonomy categories. For example, lectures are most appropriate and effective for teaching classes that fall at the left end of the continua and for achieving the basic level of the taxonomies. If the class or course objectives fall to the right, then discussions, essays, practicums, and so forth are more appropriate. The positioning is crude at best and should not be over-interpreted. The dashed lines suggest that a given instructional method is capable of covering a range of positions when it is properly developed and used. Although some studies suggest, for example, that discussions are more effective than lectures in teaching higher-level cognitive and affective objectives (see McKeachie, 1985, for a review of some of the literature), the positions are *not* based on the results of extensive empirical studies but on my armchair reflections and the suggestions of past seminar participants. (See also Eble, 1976; Fuhrmann & Grasha, 1983; Hyman, 1974; Lowman, 1984; and Milton and Associates, 1978.)

I had hoped to find a recent reference that would discuss the goals of the introductory psychology course, but neither I nor several knowledgeable colleagues were aware of any. There are articles in the *Handbook for Teaching Introductory Psychology* (Benjamin, Daniel, & Brewer, 1985) and in the February 1982 issue of *Teaching of Psychology* that discuss ways to organize the content, but they do not really address process. Walker and McKeachie's (1967) publication, *Some Thoughts About Teaching the Beginning Course in Psychology,* is still the most relevant reference of which I am aware. They list ten course goals, including communication of elementary concepts, communication of the intrinsic interest of the subject matter, and development of selected intellectual skills. In their judgment, lectures are appropriate for the achievement of only two of the ten goals: communication of the intrinsic interest of the subject matter and presentation of the newest developments of the field. To achieve most course goals, we need something in addition to a lecture. Thus, you need to make explicit what your course goals are for introductory psychology.

The intent of the foregoing discussion has been, first, to convince you that there is no such thing as effective teaching in the abstract; second, to provide you with one or more contexts to use to decide what is effective teaching for any given course or class; and finally, to suggest some instructional methods appropriate for a given objective or set of objectives.

Classroom Observation

Classroom observation has been with us for several decades. Evertson and Green (1986) reviewed research on classroom observations. However, the focus of that review was primarily on using classroom observation for research rather than for improving teaching. Evertson and Holley (1981) focused on the practical applications of classroom observations, specifically for teacher evaluation and improvement. Classroom observations systems are necessarily selective. Your first task is to decide which aspect of teaching you wish to focus upon, realizing that a great deal of information will be lost.

Our seminar participants usually have no difficulty understanding the focus a given observational system provides for a class. But when they begin to examine the data, their reaction almost always is to point out everything that has been omitted. Concentrate first on the information the data provide. Later you can decide whether you want additional data.

Second, you must either find a system that fits your needs or develop one. (See Borich & Madden, 1977; Simon & Boyer, 1974; and Stallings, 1977, for sample instruments.) For an instrument applying Flanders' system to college level teaching, see Lewis (1986). If you develop your own instrument, try to list a number of mutually exclusive categories that will encompass all of the aspects of the behavior you want to focus on. They must be mutually exclusive to avoid unreliability resulting from the possibility of coding given behaviors into more than one category. The data must be collected and summarized or analyzed into patterns and the like, as appropriate for the particular observation system being used. Then the data must be interpreted, because no behavior or pattern of behavior should be assumed to be good or bad in the abstract. Often, you will decide that you need additional observations of the same behavior or other kinds of data before you can decide upon an improvement strategy. Finally, having decided upon an improvement strategy, all of the steps in problem solving become appropriate: Try the strategy, evaluate its effectiveness, perhaps modify the strategy, reevaluate, and so on.

In order to make the discussion of classroom observation more meaningful, I would like to use some examples. Three brief excerpts from actual college classes are presented in Appendix A. Read each of them, observing whatever you like. We will then apply one or two systems to these excerpts, illustrating aspects of observation systems and ways the data might be used to improve instruction. After reading each segment, take a moment or two and jot down, at least mentally, your reactions.

If the reactions of past seminar participants are any indication, you probably had more negative than positive reactions. I am not sure why this is—perhaps graduate school trains us to look for what is wrong with research. Not only are we instructors negatively critical of others' teaching, but we also tend to react negatively to our own teaching.

In the following sections, I have put my recommendations for improvement entirely in capital letters. They are stated as prescriptions but should be considered only as suggestions.

FIRST, DELIBERATELY LOOK FOR *POSITIVE* ASPECTS OF THE TEACHING, THINGS THAT IN YOUR JUDGMENT ENHANCED STUDENT LEARNING. THEN LOOK FOR THINGS THAT MIGHT BE IMPROVED. Many instructors have found this kind of approach helpful. It may strike some readers as subjective. I prefer to think of it as clinical; after all, we have some expertise as teachers. (One observation form that may be useful in this endeavor but is not listed in any of the standard references focuses solely on positive aspects of teaching at the college level; Helling, 1979.)

At first glance, the three teaching segments strike people as being fairly different. To what extent is that true? Turn back to Table 1 and look at the five instructional dimensions. Where would you place each of the three classes? Most seminar participants think that the Professor Davies (chemistry) and Professor Levin (statistics) segments are basically to the left on all five dimensions. They are primarily concerned with covering a body of content, the teachers are more active, the instructional goals are basically the same for all students, the pace of learning in the segments is the same (there is little pausing to allow questions), and the source of rewards comes primarily from an interesting or entertaining presentation. However, Professor Zarefsky's class (rhetorical history) is seen by most people as basically to the right. He is trying to teach process—rhetorical criticism, critical thinking, and so forth. The students are more active. The goals tend to be individual, at least insofar as different students can demonstrate skill in rhetorical criticism in different ways, and the students can influence the pacing of the class by their own questions and comments. Finally, the students' own behavior in this class is much more likely to be rewarding or satisfying compared to the first two classes.

In terms of the cognitive taxonomy, the lecturing method used in the first two classes is appropriate for the basic levels of knowledge and comprehension. (Based upon the segments, I believe that this is correct. However, both classes would require that the students do problems, the chemistry class at least would have a lab, and so on. Depending on the quality of the feedback provided to the students, these classes could also help the students achieve application and higher-order cognitive objectives.) For the rhetorical history class, we see in the segment itself the students practicing application, analysis, synthesis, and evaluation.

Think about your introductory psychology course. What are your instructional goals? You probably want your students to achieve something more than mastery of specific content; you want the students to develop some cognitive skills, or to use the course material to achieve some personal goals. These last two goals cannot be achieved effectively by merely lecturing. Ask yourself what have you built into the course *specifically* to help the students achieve these goals.

Language of the Classroom

What are some other ways that we can view these three classes? One approach is Bellack, Hyman, Smith, and Kliebard's (1966) Language of the Classroom, which was developed to analyze the linguistic behaviors of teachers and students in the classroom. The system assigns codes to several categories. One identifies the speaker: Teacher (T); Pupil (P)—I will use Student (S); and Audio-visual Device (A)—not used in our three segments.

Another category codes pedagogical move. There are four possible moves: Structuring, Soliciting, Responding, and Reacting. The Structuring Move (STR) sets the stage, lets everyone know what they are going to do next, or introduces new content. The Soliciting Move (SOL) includes all questions, commands, requests, and directions. The Responding Move (RES) is a direct answer to another's Soliciting Move. The Reacting Move (REA) is a comment on any of the other Moves or even on a preceding Reacting Move.

The coding by speaker and move for the three segments included in Appendix A can be summarized as follows (Table 2):

Table 2
Coding by Speaker and Move of Linguistic Behaviors for the Three Segments in Appendix A

Segments	I	II	III	Segments	I	II	III
T/STR	8	9	1	S/STR	0	0	0
T/SOL	1	6	6	S/SOL	0	1	0
T/RES	0	1	0	S/RES	1	1	5
T/REA	3	5	2	S/REA	0	0	10
TOTAL	12	21	9	TOTAL	1	2	15

Note. T—Teacher, S—Student, STR—Structuring Move, SOL—Soliciting Move, RES—Responding Move, REA—Reacting Move.

Viewed from the Bellack system, all those segments, even I and II, appear to be different. In Segment I, the professor is doing almost all of the talking, introducing content (T/STR) or elaborating upon it (T/REA). In Segment II, the instructor is also checking (T/SOL) to see whether the students are following him. In Segment III, the students are doing more talking than the teacher. Whether these differences reflect those in teaching effectiveness must be judged by the instructor or someone else; again, the data in and of themselves are simply descriptive.

An example from an entire class might better illustrate the use of this kind of coding. Following is a summary of the coding (Aubrecht, 1979b; see also Aubrecht, 1976) for an entire class of about 50 minutes (Table 3). The class was a physics recitation class; the students also took 2 hours of lecture and a lab. The purpose of the recitation section was to clear up any difficulties the students were having with the lecture material or the assigned problems.

Table 3
Coding by Speaker and Move of Linguistic Behaviors
in a Physics Recitation Class (I)

T/STR	4	S/STR	0
T/SOL	17	S/SOL	7
T/RES	7	S/RES	15
T/REA	17	S/REA	7
TOTAL	45	TOTAL	29

Note. T—Teacher, S—Student, STR—Structuring Move, SOL—Soliciting Move, RES—Responding Move, REA—Reacting Move.

Pause a moment and examine the data. Do you think that the instructor was satisfied or dissatisfied with his teaching effectiveness in this class? Why do you think so? If these data were for a psychology recitation or quiz section, how satisfactory would they be?

The pattern that struck the instructor most was: T/SOL (17), S/RES (15), T/REA (17). What this pattern suggested (and the instructor's recall of the class confirmed) was that most of the class time was spent in his asking questions, the students responding, and his giving them feedback on the quality of their responses. The instructor's reaction was that the recitation class was being used to answer his questions, when it should have been used to answer the students' questions. This instructor was dissatisfied with what the data revealed, and I think that such data would be equally unsatisfactory for a recitation section in introductory psychology.

The same instructor was observed later, again for the entire class period, and the summary of the coding for the second recitation section was as follows (Table 4):

Table 4
Coding by Speaker and Move of Linguistic Behaviors in a Physics Recitation Class (II)

T/STR	5	S/STR	3
T/SOL	16	S/SOL	21
T/RES	18	S/RES	8
T/REA	24	S/REA	19
TOTAL	63	TOTAL	51

Note. T—Teacher, S—Student, STR—Structuring Move, SOL—Soliciting Move, RES—Responding Move, REA—Reacting Move.

Although the instructor was still asking many questions, the students were now asking more. There was also a better balance between the total number of teacher moves (63) compared to student moves (51). For this instructor, who was actually a graduate teaching assistant (GTA), simply becoming aware of the problem led to a change in teaching approach. Working with other GTAs (see Aubrecht, 1976), examination of these kinds of data led to discussions about the quality of the questions being asked, for example, whether they were general or specific, the levels of the questions, and how much wait time the instructor allowed after asking a question. What may seem an interminable time to the instructor is often only 3 to 5 seconds as shown on a video- or audiotape.

Verbal Flow

Let me briefly discuss one other classroom observation approach, Verbal Flow (Acheson & Gall, 1980), before commenting on videotaping. Essentially, Verbal Flow is a graphic system that shows primarily who is talking to whom and what the nature of the communication is. A concrete example is shown in Figure 1, Verbal Flow for Segment III. A line between two individuals indicates that they talked to one another (I have drawn a line from the professor to the center to indicate comments addessed to the entire class). Thus, the professor addressed three questions (a line with a single arrow— see key) to the entire class. Jim responded (line with perpendicular slash) twice to the professor, and the professor asked Jim one question and responded (line with X) once to Jim. The longest interaction in the four-minute segment was between Tricia and Student D, six exchanges of student talk (line with double arrows). Verbal Flow can be useful in identifying such things as group members who never interact or the instructor's favoring one side of a class or certain groups or individuals over others.

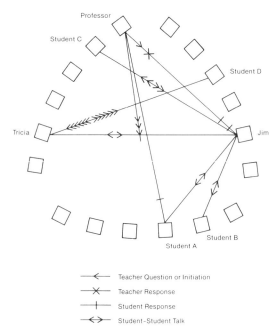

Figure 1. Verbal Flow for segment III (Professor Zarefsky, rhetorical history).

Videotaping

At the University of Delaware and at Kansas State University, I have used videotaping of teachers to help them improve their teaching. Both the participants and I found videotaping to be effective. However, a literature search turned up relatively few references on videotaping (for example, see Cohen, Ebeling, & Kulik, 1981).

The Professional and Organizational Development Network, a professional organization of people interested in faculty development, conducted a survey in 1984 of four-year colleges and universities about their faculty development practices (Erickson, 1986). I mailed a one-page survey to the 246 institutions that indicated they used videotaping, and 59 (24%) usable responses were received. Some people responded that videotaping was available, but they did not know of any faculty who used it; these responses have not been included. In response to a question about approximately how much faculty use videotaping, 69% of the respondents indicated that fewer than 5% of the faculty used videotaping. However, in response to a question about the estimated effectiveness of videotaping, 61% indicated that it was effective or very effective. Thus, few faculty use videotaping to improve instruction, but those who do find it effective or very effective, findings similar to Centra's (1976) earlier survey on videotaping.

USE VIDEOTAPING (OR AUDIOTAPING); BUT TAPE THE STUDENTS' BEHAVIOR, NOT JUST THE INSTRUCTOR'S. You will find such tapes data rich. They will permit you to be more objective about your behavior, and you can rewind the tape to double-check anything you wish. Even if you only react clinically to the data, they are helpful, and they can be analyzed further by using classroom observation techniques.

Student Ratings

There have probably been more studies of student ratings (over 12,000) than of all the other data used to evaluate faculty combined (see Centra, 1979, and Seldin, 1980, for general discussions of the faculty evaluation and development literature). The volume of reviews of the student ratings literature[1] is impressive, and unlike discussants of some issues in higher education, reviewers of the student rating research tend to agree on many important conclusions. For example, Marsh (1984) states:

> Based on this overview, class-average student ratings are (a) multidimensional; (b) reliable and stable; (c) primarily a function of the instructor who teaches a course rather than the course that is taught; (d) relatively valid against a variety of indicators of effective teaching; (e) relatively unaffected by a variety of variables hypothesized as potential biases; and (f) seen to be useful by faculty as feedback about their teaching, by students for use in course selection, and by administrators for use in personnel decisions. (p. 707)

[1]See the following for reviews of the student rating literature: Aleamoni, 1981; Aubrecht, 1979a, 1981; Benton, 1982; Braskamp, Brandenberg, & Ory, 1984; Cohen, 1980, 1981, 1986; Costin, Greenough, & Menges, 1971; Doyle, 1975, 1983; Feldman, 1976a, 1976b, 1977, 1978, 1979, 1983, 1984, 1986, in press; Kulik & Kulik, 1974; Kulik & McKeachie, 1975; Marsh, 1984; McKeachie, 1979; Menges, 1973; and Murray, 1980. For the reader wishing to read only a single review, I recommend Marsh, 1984. For those interested in an in-depth review on a particular facet of student ratings, I suggest scanning the titles of the nine reviews by Feldman.

Desirable Characteristics in Student Rating Systems

I will now discuss two desirable characteristics in student rating systems: the need for flexibility and the need for comparative data.

Need for flexibility. Experience suggests that most student rating forms used today are "homegrown" forms, developed either by the individual institution or, more likely, by an academic subunit or an individual instructor. Most of these forms use what Menges (1973) termed an "intuition or consensus" approach. In other words, a group, or the individual instructor, agreed or concluded that certain factors—mostly teacher behaviors—constitute effective teaching. The kinds of items chosen tend to be similar; for example, the instructor should speak clearly, be well organized, use discussion, and respect the students. In fact, most factor analyses of student rating forms turn up very similar factors (Kulik & Kulik, 1974). The seven factors described by Frey, Leonard, and Beatty (1975) are a good example of the factors frequently found in student rating forms: clarity of presentation, organization and planning, personal attention, class discussion, work load, grading, and student accomplishment.

Implicit in all such instruments is the assumption that there is a single, correct way to teach; that every instructor in every class should speak clearly, be well organized, and so on. I question this assumption. In a course primarily devoted to developing critical thinking, problem-solving ability, or decision-making, discussion or student–student interaction may be very appropriate, but an onlooker (or the students themselves) may consider the class disorganized, with the instructor letting the students flounder around sharing their ignorance rather than telling them the right answers. In such a course, the ideal might not be the instructor's speaking clearly, but the instructor's hardly speaking at all!

USE A STUDENT RATING FORM THAT IS FLEXIBLE, ONE THAT FITS YOUR COURSE GOALS AND INSTRUCTIONAL OBJECTIVES. Because instructional goals vary considerably from course to course, and even from class to class within a given course, it is essential that your student rating form can be adapted to what you are trying to teach. One approach to achieving flexibility is a "cafeteria" system. (Appendix B lists eight student rating systems—including all of the ones mentioned here—available to the public.) Perhaps the earliest system was Purdue University's CAFETERIA System (Purdue Research Foundation, 1974). This system uses five general or summary items and then permits the instructor to choose up to 35 additional items (from a pool of about 200). The Instructor and Course Evaluation System (ICES) from the University of Illinois (1977) is a more recent and refined cafeteria system. It now uses two common summary items and lets the instructor select an additional 23 items from a pool of over 400 (personal communication, D. C. Brandenburg, July 10, 1987). Both of these systems solve the flexibility problem by allowing the instructor to choose items that are appropriate for his or her course. If it is a large, introductory lecture with limited opportunity for student discussion, as introductory psychology courses tend to be, then the instructor should think twice before selecting items that ask the students to rate the quality of the discussions. Another approach of flexibility is the Instructional Assessment System (IAS) used by the University of Washington (Gillmore, 1975, 1980); it could be viewed as a modified cafeteria system. The IAS has seven separate forms, one for a large lecture, one for a discussion, and so forth.

A third approach to the flexibility problem is that taken by Kansas State's Instructional Development and Effectiveness Assessment (IDEA) system (Hoyt & Cashin, 1977). IDEA emphasizes student learning rather than teacher behaviors. Student learning is measured by the students' reports of their progress on ten general course objectives, such as gaining factual knowledge; learning rational thinking and problem solving; or developing a sense of responsibility. Flexibility is achieved by having the instructor (or a departmental committee or the like) weight the importance of each of the ten course objectives on a 3-point scale: essential, important, or of no more than minor importance. Course objectives weighted to be of minor importance are not included in a diagnostic summary or in an overall evaluation composite score.

Thus, flexibility in a student rating system can be achieved in a variety of ways, but it must be achieved for the system to be maximally useful. Providing instructors with ratings on items that are not relevant to their courses is counterproductive.

Need for comparative data. One reason comparative data are needed is *rating inflation.* On a 5-point scale, 3.0 is usually considered average. This is rarely the case for any student rating item. The Student Instructional Report (SIR; Educational Testing Service, 1979) is probably the most widely used student rating form in the United States. In the data from over 8,000 classes, the average mean for the eight SIR items which use a 5-point scale is 3.6, about one standard deviation above 3.0. All of the IDEA items use a 5-point scale. In data from over 23,000 classes (Cashin & Perrin, 1978), the average mean rating for the 38 IDEA items is 3.7, again about one standard deviation above 3.0. What this suggests is that on many 5-point student rating items, a rating of 3.0 is not around the 50th percentile but closer to the 20th!

Not only do students tend to rate most items high on the average, there is also considerable *variability* in the way they rate individual items. Looking at the 20 teaching methods items on IDEA (Cashin & Perrin, 1978), there is 1.0 point difference between the means of the highest rated item and the lowest, a difference of about 1.7 standard deviations. The mean of the highest rated item—the instructor "seemed enthusiastic about the subject matter"—is 4.3. The mean on the lowest rated item—the instructor "explained the reasons for criticisms of students' academic performance"—is 3.3.

A final reason that we need comparative data is to control for *possible sources of bias.* Faculty often ask, do instructors who receive higher student ratings actually teach more effectively? A corollary question is, to what extent are student ratings influenced by factors not primarily reflecting the instructor's teaching effectiveness? The good news is that, in general, many variables (student's age, sex, grade level; instructor's sex) show little or no relationship to student ratings (Feldman, 1977; McKeachie, 1979; Menges, 1973). The bad news is that there are other variables that do appear to bias ratings, for example, student motivation, size of class, and academic field. More motivated students tend to give higher student ratings (Costin, Greenough, & Menges, 1971; Feldman, 1978; Kulik & Kulik, 1974; Kulik & McKeachie, 1975; Marsh, 1984; McKeachie, 1979). IDEA (Hoyt & Cashin, 1977) uses one item to control for student motivation, "I had a strong desire to take this course." That one item picks up from 10% to as much as 42% of the variance in the other IDEA items (Cashin & Perrin, 1978).

A modest relationship has also been found between the size of the class and student ratings. Smaller classes tend to receive higher ratings (Kulik & Kulik, 1974; Kulik & McKeachie, 1975; Feldman, 1978, 1984; McKeachie, 1979). IDEA controls for class size by using comparative data for four class sizes, ranging from less than 15 students to 100 or more students. IDEA also controls for five levels of student motivation at the same time.

One variable that is not directly controlled by any student rating system is academic field. There is growing evidence that humanities and fine arts courses receive higher ratings than social science courses, which in turn receive higher ratings than math and science courses (Kulik & Kulik, 1974; Kulik & McKeachie, 1975; Feldman, 1978; McKeachie, 1979). Presently SIR provides the most comprehensive comparative data with tables for 33 fields, including psychology, for four-year colleges (Educational Testing Service, 1979) and tables for 31 fields, again including psychology, for two-year colleges (Educational Testing Service, 1977).

A recent analysis of IDEA data from over 87,000 classes (Cashin & Clegg, 1978) from more than 300 two-year and four-year institutions showed large differences among the student ratings of 44 academic fields. The first phase of the analysis only considered three summary items, reporting the data in scaled scores with approximate means of 50 and standard deviations of 10. On the "Overall Evaluation (Progress on Relevant Objectives)" composite item, there was a difference of 9.3 between the highest mean rating (fine and applied arts, 58.7) and the lowest (economics, 49.4). On the "Would Like Instructor Again" item the difference was 8.1 between the highest (foreign languages, 54.9) and lowest (physics, 46.8) ratings. On the "Improved Attitude Toward Field" item the difference was 12.4 between the highest (health professions, 57.4) and the lowest (physics, 45.0) ratings. The ratings for psychology courses—all courses in the data pool (4,133), not just introductory psychology courses—were 54.1, 50.9, and 52.0 respectively. These ratings for psychology courses are about a half to a whole standard deviation above the mean for the entire data pool. On average, the student ratings for all 38 IDEA items for psychology courses ranked 5th among the ten academic fields analyzed. The rankings from highest to lowest were: foreign languages, art, letters and humanities, English, psychology, sociology, biology, mathematics and accounting (tied), and economics.

USE A STUDENT RATING SYSTEM THAT PROVIDES COMPARATIVE DATA. There are practical, significant differences in student rating items related to several variables, such as student motivation, class size, and academic field (psychology courses tend to receive somewhat higher ratings when compared to a data base containing all academic fields). We need to take this into consideration when we interpret student rating data for psychology courses. It is possible that when we receive high ratings, this is not solely due to our teaching effectiveness, but may also reflect the intrinsic interest of psychology to our students. Psychologists may also know more about teaching and learning than the average college instructor.

Sample Student Rating Data

There are many parallels between student rating data and classroom observation data. Both types of data are selective, and you, or an interested faculty committee, need to decide what you want to focus on. These data need to be interpreted. Ratings should not be assumed to be good or bad until they are put into the context of the specific course.

I will illustrate the use of student rating data by applying sample items from ICES (University of Illinois, 1977) and IDEA (Cashin & Perrin, 1978) to the professors in the three segments discussed in the section on classroom observation. I have selected sample items that fit the seven dimensions identified by Frey, Leonard, and Beatty (1975), but I have omitted personal attention, work load, and grading because we did not view those aspects of the three classes. The sample ratings will be fictitious, but I will make a case for their applicability or inapplicability. Some of my comments are based upon interviews of the students that are included in the Northwestern tapes (Menges, 1977, 1979) but not in this chapter. The ICES system provides varying descriptors for each end of a 5-point scale; these will be indicated for those items.

1. Clarity of presentation (ICES item 281): The instructor presented material at a level appropriate for me (1=Almost never, 5=Almost always). Based on the interviews, the students of both Professors Davies (D) and Levin (L) found the material understandable. I think Professors D and L would receive ratings of 4 or 5. Professor Zarefsky's (Z) students should probably omit this item because he did not make any presentations in the seminar segment. (His course also included lectures we did not see in which he did make presentations.)

2. Organization–planning (ICES item 7): Did the instructor present topics in a logical sequence? (1=No, almost never, 5=Yes, almost always). The students would probably rate Professors D and L with 4s and 5s. We could see elements of organization in both segments. We do not know for Professor Z; he might well receive high ratings for logical presentation of the sequence of readings and discussion topics.

3. Class discussion (ICES item 32): Class discussion seemed to lack direction and purpose (1=Almost always, 5=Almost never). Professor D's and Professor L's students would omit this item based on the segments we saw because there were no discussions, but Professor Z would probably receive very positive ratings.

4. Student accomplishment (IDEA item 22): Progress on learning fundamental principles, generalizations, or theories. (Students rate their progress compared to other courses, with 5 being the highest point rating.) Professors D and L were actually rated 3.8 and 4.0; these instructors had used IDEA, and data on this item were included in the materials supplied by Northwestern (Menges, 1977). Professor Z would be rated low because he was teaching process, not content, but this objective would be appropriate for the lecture portion of his class.

The above are a few examples of the wide range of information that an instructor can gain from student rating data. The examples reinforce the notion that not every item is appropriate for every class.

Using the Data to Improve

Because college faculty use student ratings far more frequently than classroom observations, most of the following recommendations are derived from experience with student ratings. However, many of the recommendations are probably equally appropriate when using classroom observation data. Assuming that you have selected classroom observation techniques or student rating items appropriate for your course and that some of your results are less than satisfactory, what might you do to improve your teaching?

PUT THE ITEM IN THE CONTEXT OF YOUR COURSE; ASK YOURSELF HOW YOU TYPICALLY BEHAVE RELATED TO THAT SITUATION. For example, one of the IDEA items is concerned with how frequently the instructor found ways to help the students answer their own questions. If an instructor were to receive low ratings on this item, he or she should ask, "What do I do when a student asks a question?" I suspect that many of us simply answer it, which is very effective if we are teaching content, but often counterproductive if we want to teach process. Or perhaps we respond to different students differently. For example, if a nonmajor asks a question, we answer it; but if a major asks a question, we enter into a brief Socratic dialogue, trying to ask questions that will help the student to arrive at the answer on his or her own.

The graduate teaching assistant teaching the physics recitation class mentioned previously was dissatisfied with his data. The same data might be acceptable to a foreign language instructor who was asking questions in the foreign language, having the students respond in that language, and then reacting to the quality of the students' responses.

READ THE STUDENTS' RESPONSES TO THE OPEN-ENDED QUESTIONS. If, by simply searching our memories, we instructors are unable to find useful clues as to why we received low ratings, reading the students' responses to questions such as "What would you suggest the instructor do to improve this course?" can be useful. Often these student comments will help us remember what we did that might have led to a low rating.

INTERVIEW THE STUDENTS. Even though the data may have been collected during the previous term, you can use these data to interview your current students. If you are teaching the same course this term, a few weeks into the course, you could approach the class and say something like, "Last term the students in this class gave me low ratings on. . . . Can any of you suggest what I might be doing that would cause those low ratings and what changes might help solve that problem?"

COLLECT FEEDBACK FROM STUDENTS DURING THE TERM. Classroom observation data must be collected during the term. Most student rating data is collected near the end of the term, probably because it is used for personnel decisions as well as teacher improvement. You do not have to collect student rating data during the term on a long, quantitative, diagnostic form. A few qualitative items about the instructor, the course, and the amount of material the students have learned as well as some open-ended questions may suffice. I have used these three open-ended questions:

1. Describe one or more aspects of this class that you found helpful and that you would recommend be included in future classes. Why?
2. Describe one or more aspects of this class that you did not find helpful and that you recommend be changed or dropped. Why?
3. Give additional comments.

These data need to be interpreted just like other student rating data.

DISCUSS THE RESULTS WITH YOUR STUDENTS. I recommend that you take the time to discuss with the students what you will try to change and what you will not or cannot change (because they are prerequisites to later courses and so forth) and why. Students do not require that we accept all of their suggestions—sometimes suggestions are diametrically opposed—but they want some evidence that we have considered their feedback.

CONSULT WITH YOUR COLLEAGUES. Besides talking to your students, you could discuss the data with a peer who teaches the same course or with a knowledgeable administrator. If your campus has mentors, master teachers, or instructional development consultants, they can help. Cohen's (1980; 1986) reviews of the literature strongly suggest that if we want to use student ratings (I would add classroom observations) to improve teaching, we need not just the data, but also consultation. The form of the consultation can vary, but you should talk to someone.

Summary

There is no agreed-upon definition of what constitutes effective teaching in the literature on educational or instructional psychology. I have taken the position that there is no single, correct way to teach, that it depends upon the course, academic field, students, instructor, and so on. Therefore, I suggest that the individual instructor or a faculty committee decide upon the criteria for effective teaching for each course and even for individual classes.

I believe that self-evaluation, the instructor's reflections about what worked or did not work in a given class, is beneficial. However, other kinds of evaluation data can be helpful in this endeavor, particularly classroom observation techniques and student rating systems. These approaches have an advantage over self-evaluation because they provide objectivity, a permanent record, and focus. Many classroom observation techniques are available that focus on various aspects of teaching and levels of complexity. I examined Bellack et al.'s (1966) Language of the Classroom, which focuses on cognitive aspects of a class, and Verbal Flow (Acheson & Gall, 1980), which is a graphic approach.

Despite the infrequent use of videotaping in higher education to improve teaching, I suggest that videotaping teaching can be especially helpful because videotapes are so rich in data. Those faculty who have used this technique report that it is effective.

Unlike many issues in higher education, there is a significant body of research about student ratings and a growing consensus among the reviewers of that research concerning the usefulness of student ratings. For improvement of teaching effectiveness, I believe that student rating systems should be flexible, provide comparative data, and be combined with consultation.

I have made a number of suggestions about how we can use student rating and classroom observation data to improve teaching. I have become convinced that the crux of the problem is in deciding what we want to teach or, more accurately, what we want students to learn. Once we have made these decisions, there are many kinds of data we can collect that will suggest ways to improve. Experience has shown that if we use these data, we will become better teachers.

References

Abrami, P. C. (1985). Dimensions of effective college instruction. *Review of Higher Education, 8,* 211–228.

Acheson, K. A., & Gall, M. D. (1980). *Techniques in the clinical supervision of teachers.* New York: Longman.

Aleamoni, L. M. (1981). Student ratings of instruction. In J. Millman (Ed.), *Handbook of teacher evaluation.* Beverly Hills, CA: Sage Publications.

Aubrecht, J. D. (1976). Teachers do change. How much? An empirical study; How and why? A clinical study. *Dissertation Abstracts International, 37,* 3440-A. (University Microfilms No. 76-27, 624)

Aubrecht, J. D. (1979a). *Are student ratings of teacher effectiveness valid?* (IDEA Paper No. 2). Manhattan: Kansas State University, Center for Faculty Evaluation and Development. (ERIC Document Reproduction Service No. ED 202 410)

Aubrecht, J. D. (1979b). *Instructional development seminar.* (Available from Center for Faculty Evaluation and Development, Kansas State University, 1623 Anderson Ave., Manhattan, KS 66502)

Aubrecht, J. D. (1981). *Reliability, validity and generalizability of student ratings of instruction.* (IDEA Paper No. 6). Manhattan: Kansas State University, Center for Faculty Evaluation and Development. (ERIC Document Reproduction Service No. ED 213 296)

Aubrecht, J. D., & Hanna, G. S. (1982). *IDEA Form H technical manual.*

Manhattan: Kansas State University, Center for Faculty Evaluation and Development.

Axelrod, J. (1973). *The university teacher as artist*. San Francisco: Jossey-Bass.

Bellack, A. A., Hyman, R. T., Smith, F. L., & Kliebard, H. M. (1966). *The language of the classroom*. New York: Teachers College Press, Columbia University.

Benjamin, L. T., Daniel, R. S., & Brewer, C. L. (Eds.). (1985). *Handbook for teaching introductory psychology*. Hillsdale, NJ: Lawrence Erlbaum Associates.

Benton, S. E. (1982). *Rating college teachers: Criterion validity studies of student evaluation-of-instruction instruments*. AAHE-ERIC Higher Education Research Report, No. 1. Washington, DC: American Association for Higher Education.

Bergquist, W. H., & Phillips, S. R. (1975). *A handbook for faculty development*. Washington, DC: Council for the Advancement of Small Colleges.

Bloom, B. S., Engelhart, M. D., Furst, E. J., Hill, W. H., & Krathwohl, D. R. (1956). *Taxonomy of education objectives: Handbook I, the cognitive domain*. New York: David McKay.

Borich, G. D., & Madden, S. K. (1977). *Evaluating classroom instruction: A source-book of instruments*. Reading, MA: Addison-Wesley.

Braskamp, L. A., Brandenberg, D. C., & Ory, J. C. (1984). *Evaluating teaching effectiveness: A practical guide*. Beverly Hills, CA: Sage Publications.

Cashin, W. E., & Clegg, V. L. (1987, April). *Are student ratings of different academic fields different?* Paper presented at the annual meeting of the American Educational Research Association, Chicago, IL.

Cashin, W. E., & Perrin, B. M. (1978). *IDEA technical report no. 4: Description of IDEA Standard Form data base*. Manhattan: Kansas State University, Center for Faculty Evaluation and Development.

Centra, J. A. (1976). *Faculty development practices in U.S. colleges and universities* (Report PR-76-30). Princeton, NJ: Educational Testing Service.

Centra, J. A. (1979). *Determining faculty effectiveness: Assessing teaching, research, and service for personnel decisions and improvement*. San Francisco: Jossey-Bass.

Cohen, P. A. (1980). Effectiveness of student-rating feedback for improving college instruction: A meta-analysis of findings. *Research in Higher Education, 13,* 321–341.

Cohen, P. A. (1981). Student ratings of instruction and student achievement: A meta-analysis of multisection validity studies. *Review of Educational Research, 51,* 281–309.

Cohen, P. A. (1986, April). *An updated and expanded meta-analysis of multisection student rating validity studies*. Paper presented at the annual meeting of the American Educational Research Association; San Francisco, CA.

Cohen, P. A., Ebeling, B. J., & Kulik, J. A. (1981). A meta-analysis of outcome studies of visual-based instruction. *Educational Communication and Technology, 29,* 26–36.

Costin, F., Greenough, W. T., & Menges, R. J. (1971). Student ratings of college teaching: Reliability, validity, and usefulness. *Review of Educational Research, 8,* 511–535.

Doyle, K. O. (1975). *Student evaluation of instruction.* Lexington, MA: D. C. Heath.

Doyle, K. O. (1983). *Evaluating teaching.* Lexington, MA: D. C. Heath.

Dressel, P. L., & Marcus, D. (1982). *On teaching and learning in college.* San Francisco: Jossey-Bass.

Dunkin, M. J., & Barnes, J. (1986). Research on teaching in higher education. In M. C. Wittrock (Ed.), *Handbook of research on teaching* (3rd ed.). (pp. 754–777). New York: Macmillan.

Eble, K. E. (1976). *The craft of teaching.* San Francisco: Jossey-Bass.

Educational Testing Service. (1977). *Student Instructional Report: Comparative data guide for two-year colleges and technical institutions.* Princeton, NJ: Author.

Educational Testing Service. (1979). *Student Instructional Report: Comparative data guide for four-year colleges and universities.* Princeton, NJ: Author.

Erickson, G. (1986). A survey of faculty development practices. In *To improve the academy: Resources for student, faculty, & institutional development.* (pp. 182–196). No place: The Professional and Organizational Development Network and the National Council for Staff, Program and Organizational Development.

Evertson, C. M., & Green, J. L. (1986). Observations as inquiry and method. In M. C. Wittrock (Ed.), *Handbook of research on teaching* (3rd ed.) (pp. 162–213). New York: Macmillan.

Evertson, C. M., & Holley, F. M. (1981). Classroom observation. In J. Millman (Ed.), *Handbook of teacher evaluation* (pp. 90–109). Beverly Hills, CA: Sage Publications.

Feldman, K. A. (1976a). Grades and college students' evaluations of their courses and teachers. *Research in Higher Education, 4,* 69–111.

Feldman, K. A. (1976b). The superior college teacher from the students' view. *Research in Higher Education, 5,* 243–288.

Feldman, K. A. (1977). Consistency and variability among college students in rating their teachers and courses: A review and analysis. *Research in Higher Education, 6,* 233–274.

Feldman, K. A. (1978). Course characteristics and college students' ratings of their teachers: What we know and what we don't. *Research in Higher Education, 9,* 199–242.

Feldman, K. A. (1979). The significance of circumstances for college students' ratings of their teachers and courses. *Research in Higher Education, 10,* 149–172.

Feldman, K. A. (1983). Seniority and experience of college teachers as related to evaluations they receive from students. *Research in Higher Education, 18,* 3–124.

Feldman, K. A. (1984). Class size and college students' evaluations of teachers and courses: A closer look. *Research in Higher Education, 21,* 45–116.

Feldman, K. A. (1986). The perceived instructional effectiveness of college teachers as related to their personality and attitudinal characteristics: A review and synthesis. *Research in Higher Education, 24,* 139–213.

Feldman, K. A. (in press). Research productivity and scholarly accomplishment of college teachers as related to their instructional effectiveness: A review and exploration. *Research in Higher Education.*

Frey, P. W., Leonard, D. W., & Beatty, W. W. (1975). Student ratings of instruction: Validation research. *American Educational Research Journal, 12,* 435–447.

Fuhrmann, B. S., & Grasha, A. F. (1983). *A practical handbook for college teachers.* Boston: Little, Brown.

Gagne, R. M. (1984). Learning outcomes and their effects: Useful categories of human performance. *American Psychologist, 39,* 377–385.

Gillmore, G. M. (1975). *Statistical analysis of the data from the first year of use of the student rating forms of the University of Washington Instructional Assessment System.* Seattle: University of Washington, Educational Assessment Center.

Gillmore, G. M. (1980). *A brief description of the student rating forms of the University of Washington Instructional Assessment System.* Seattle: University of Washington, Educational Assessment Center..

Helling, B. B. (1979). *Looking for good teaching: A guide to peer observation.* (Danforth Faculty Fellowship Project Report). Northfield, MN: St. Olaf College. (ERIC Document Reproduction Service No. ED 186 380)

Hoyt, D. P., & Cashin, W. E. (1977). *IDEA technical report no. 1: Development of the IDEA system.* Manhattan: Kansas State University, Center for Faculty Evaluation and Development.

Hyman, R. T. (1974). *Ways of teaching* (2nd ed.). Philadelphia: J. B. Lippincott.

Krathwohl, D. R., Bloom, B. S., & Masia, B. B. (1964). *Taxonomy of educational objectives: Handbook II, the affective domain.* New York: David McKay.

Kulik, J. A., & Kulik, C. C. (1974). Student ratings of instruction. *Teaching of Psychology, 1,* 51–57.

Kulik, J. A., & McKeachie, W. J. (1975). The evaluation of teachers in higher education. In F. N. Kerlinger (Ed.), *Review of research in education* (Vol. 3). Itasca, IL: F. E. Peacock.

Lewis, K. G. (1986). Using an objective observation system to diagnose teaching problems. *Journal of Staff, Program & Organizational Development, 4,* 81–90.

Lowman, J. (1984). *Mastering the techniques of teaching.* San Francisco: Jossey-Bass.

Marques, T. E., Lane, D. M., & Dorfman, P. W. (1979). Toward the development of a system for instructional evaluation: Is there consensus regarding what constitutes effective teaching? *Journal of Educational Psychology, 71,* 840–849.

Marsh, H. W. (1984). Students' evaluations of university teaching: Dimensionality, reliability, validity, potential biases, and utility. *Journal of Educational Psychology, 76,* 707–754.

McCord, M. T. (1985). Methods and theories of instruction. In J. C. Smart (Ed.), *Higher education: Handbook of theory and research* (Vol. I) (pp. 97–131). New York: Agathon Press.

McKeachie, W. J. (1979). Student ratings of faculty: A reprise. *Academe, 65,* 384–397.

McKeachie, W. J. (1985). *Teaching tips: A guidebook for the beginning teacher.* (8th ed.). Lexington, MA: D. C. Heath.

Menges, R. J. (1973). The new reporters: Students rate instruction. In

C. R. Pace (Ed.). *Evaluating learning and teaching: New directions for higher education.* No. 4. San Francisco: Jossey-Bass.

Menges, R. J. (Producer). (1977). *Helping students clarify ideas: College classroom vignettes* (Tape III) [Videotape]. Evanston, IL: Northwestern University, Center for the Teaching Professions.

Menges, R. J. (Producer). (1979). *Lecturing goals: Cognitive and affective: College classroom vignettes* (Tape IX) [Videotape]. Evanston, IL: Northwestern University, Center for the Teaching Professions.

Milton, O., & Associates. (1978). *On college teaching: A guide to contemporary practices.* San Francisco: Jossey-Bass.

Murray, H. G. (1980). *Evaluating university teaching: A review of research.* Toronto, Canada: Ontario Confederation of University Faculty Association.

Pintrich, P. R., Cross, D. R., Kozma, R. B., & McKeachie, W. J. (1986). Instructional psychology. *Annual Review of Psychology, 378,* 611–651.

Purdue Research Foundation (1974). *Instructor and course appraisal: Cafeteria System.* West Lafayette, IN: Author.

Seldin, P. (1980). *Successful faculty evaluation programs: A practical guide to improve faculty performance and promotion/tenure decisions.* Crugers, NY: Coventry Press.

Simon, A., & Boyer, E. G. (Eds.). (1974). *Mirrors for behavior III: An anthology of observation instruments.* Wyncote, PA: Communications Materials Center.

Stallings, J. A. (1977). *Learning to look: A handbook on classroom observation and teaching models.* Belmont, CA: Wadsworth.

University of Illinois. (1977). *ICES item catalog.* Urbana-Champaign: Author.

Walker, E. L., & McKeachie, W. J. (1967). *Some thoughts about teaching the beginning course in psychology.* Belmont, CA: Brooks/Cole Publishing.

Weston, C., & Cranton, P. A. (1986). Selecting instructional strategies. *Journal of Higher Education, 57,* 259–288.

Wittrock, M. C. (Ed.). (1986). *Handbook of research on teaching* (3rd ed.). New York: Macmillan.

Appendix A

Typescripts from "College Classroom Vignettes"

At the lecture presented in New York in August 1987, I used videotaped excerpts from "College Classroom Vignettes" from the Center for the Teaching Professions, Northwestern University (Menges, 1977, 1979). Segment I (Professor Davies) and Segment II (Professor Levin) were excerpted from Tape IX, "Lecturing Goals: Cognitive and Affective" (1979). Segment III (Professor Zarefsky) was excerpted from Tape III, "Helping Students Clarify Ideas" (1977; copyrighted by Northwestern University, Center for the Teaching Professions; excerpted and adapted by permission).

Along with the videotapes, Northwestern University provides accompanying printed materials, including a typescript of the tapes. The verbal material in this appendix is from those typescripts, except for a few minor corrections made by me. However, almost none of the nonverbal behavior was included in the typescripts. The nonverbal material in parentheses in this appendix has been added by me; it is inserted before the verbal behavior that accompanied it. In deciding on what nonverbal behavior to include in the parentheses, I was guided primarily by the comments that past seminar participants had made after viewing these tapes. I recommend to interested readers that, if at all possible, they view the actual videotapes, which are available from the Center for the Teaching Professions.

The coding from Bellack et al.'s (1966) Language of the Classroom (e.g., T/STR) is also included in the segments. These codes follow the verbal behavior being coded.

SEGMENT I

GENERAL CHEMISTRY (2 min. 35 sec.) Taught by Professor Geoffrey Davies. Taped during the tenth week of class; the students are primarily freshman biology majors.

(As the tape begins we see the instructor in shirt-sleeves walking towards the chalkboard and pointing to materials on the board; he has a British accent and speaks with animation.) PROF. DAVIES: Now when we come to molecules that only have two atoms in it like these have, it is very easy to talk about dipole moments. But, as soon as we start making bigger molecules, then it is harder to decide what kind of magnets we have or even if we have magnets at all. (Erases board and draws diagram for structure of methane—C with four Hs around it.) So let's just look at one such example. This molecule is the mother and father of all the millions of so-called organic molecules that you are coming across. This compound is called methane. (Writes "methane" on board, then walks away to left and looks at class; camera pulls back and shows large lab table across front of room with models on it.) Now, we could have worked out the Lewis structure of methane. (Walks back to board and points to diagram of methane molecule.) We would have concluded that the hydrogen atoms were around the outside and the thing was arranged in this way such that the carbon atom was in the middle (T/STR). (Walks away—always walks away to left—glances at class.) The way in which we have drawn this molecule is flat. (Walks back to board, and points.) It is shown to be flat. Right? It is in the plane of the blackboard (T/STR). (Walks away, glances at class, walks back to board.) But you must bear something in mind and that is there are electrons holding these nuclei together and these electrons are negatively charged. (Walks away, then back to board.) And you have to ask yourself, is there a better way of arranging the hydrogren atoms around the carbon. (Walks away looking at class.) Because mother knows best and so does nature, and nature knows what shape its molecules are going to be and it turns out it knows a better way of arranging the hydrogen atoms around the carbon (goes to lab table and picks up three dimensional model to show class; camera zooms in), and this is the way it does it. Right? (T/STR) Now you ask yourself, why? (Goes to diagram on board and points, then back to model and points to various atoms.) Well, I can show you why. If I wanted to make this molecule flat so that all five atoms were in the same plane then I'd have to rotate this part of the molecule around like this (demonstrates with model) and you can see what would happen. The distance between these two would get smaller. And the distance between these electrons would get smaller (T/STR), and this is not good. Mother Nature likes to make things of minimum energy. She's always looking to get rid of energy some way. Shove it somewhere else, (goes back to board and points) so this molecule isn't flat. (Goes back to model.) It is this shape, and this is the tetrahedron (T/REA). Now what are the characteristics of this tetrahedron? (Goes back to board.) Well, first of all it doesn't matter whether we draw it (points to board) this way or we draw it (points to model) that way. We'd all agree that the bond distance of each one of these is going to be the same (walks away from board) and that makes the tetrahedron a regular tetrahedron (T/STR). (Holds up a second 3D model from table.) Here is another representation that is just the same. All the distances are just the same. When we determine the shape of the molecule, what we are actually doing is locating the nuclei (T/STR). (Looks at class.) Why can't we locate the electrons (T/SOL)? (Mumbles from students.) (S/RES) Because anything we use to locate them will move them, right? We'll never be able to pinpoint the electrons (T/REA). So, when we look at the molecule, and we can do it, there's a machine across in the chemistry department which will show you the shape of the molecule. (Points to different parts of second model.) What you'd find is the hydrogen atom nucleus here, the carbon, hydrogen, so on, which defines the shape (T/STR). (Points to different parts of second model.) Okay. Well we ask ourselves, if this, all these, three atoms, four atoms are the same, is it true that the angle between these bonds, these are really straight lines that we draw between the nuclei, are going to be a certain value? They are all going to be the same. The answer of course is "yes." And the angle in a regular tetrahedron, however big it is, is about 109 degrees (T/STR). (Goes back to board and points.) Okay. Now what would it be in here? If it were flat, it would be 90 degrees. (Walks away from board; camera pulls back showing large lecture hall about one third full.) And you see, there's another indication that these electrons are further away from each other than they would be if the molecules were flat (T/STR). Okay. This is kind of interesting, now (T/REA).

SEGMENT II

SOCIAL STATISTICS (2 min. 10 sec.) Taught by Professor Jack Levin. Taped during the third week of class; the students are primarily sophomores from the colleges of Liberal Arts, Nursing, and Criminal Justice.

(At beginning instructor is standing behind long table in front of chalkboard looking at class, wearing coat and tie, large mustache and long hair—he reminds some viewers of Gene Shalit.)

PROF. LEVIN: In order to fulfill that function, I am very pleased to introduce you at this time (gestures broadly towards the chalkboard) to the mean deviation, mean deviation, and that does exactly that. (Writes "MD" on board.) Now, we're going to abbreviate this MD (T/STR). (Look at class and gestures several times to board.) This has no relationship to health care or hospital work or visiting a physician in his office. I just want to make sure that it is a coincidence, entirely a coincidence they are both MD, mean deviation, no relationship whatsoever (T/REA). And, let me give you the formula and tell you a little bit about the mean deviation because I think you're really going to like it. I think you're going to like it. (Starts to write formula on board, looks back at class.) Mean deviation is the sum of the absolute deviations (T/STR), (appears to be talking to individual student) just write it down and I'll explain it, okay (T/SOL); the sum of the absolute deviations divided by n, the sum of the absolute deviations divided by n (T/STR). (Finishes writing formula and points to individual symbols.)
STUDENT: End? (S/SOL)
PROF.: n–n, not end, E-N-D, but n, the number of people in the group (T/RES). (Pointed to board, now walking back to table, almost always looking at class.) The sum of the absolute deviations divided by n. Some of you, when I put that on the board, may have cringed a little bit. Please, (gesturing, laughs, shakes head) it is going to be so simple, it's really kind of fun. It's a lot more fun than the range—because the range is you know, what can you learn about the range—the highest-lowest scores, you already knew that, this is so much fun (T/REA). (Gestures pointing toward class several times.) In order to understand this, we'll have to go back to something that I talked about in a previous topic, Central Tendency. Remember, I asked you when we talked about the mean, I said it was a point of balance or a center of gravity in the distribution, (mumbled response from class; he points—apparently at individual) and I asked you to put big parentheses around something (T/STR). (Gestures making parentheses.) Do you remember? I said, "Did you really do that?" (T/SOL) (Prof. shrugs shoulders and laughs).
STUDENT: Yeah. (S/RES)
PROF.: Okay, now there was a concept that I introduced at that time, it was called deviation. (Erases a new part of board looking back and forth from board to students.) Do you remember (T/SOL)? Let me just refresh your memory a little bit (T/STR). (Writes on board.) Deviation was small x, remember? (Looking at class, Prof. raises his hand—apparently asking students for a show of hands.) How many people remember deviation, remember what I talked about (T/SOL)? Okay, that was the raw score minus the mean (T/STR). Do you remember that? (Scans class looking for student response.) Seriously (T/SOL)? Okay, that indicates both the distance and the direction that any raw score falls from the mean (T/STR).

(Gestures several times, points to class when mentions "notes.") You don't have to write that down, because you already have that in your notes, remember. We talked about it (T/REA). For example, let me go back to the example that I used last time. Joe, remember Joe. Joe was a rotten student (T/STR). Do you remember that? I don't want to say anything about Joe because he's a nice guy, it doesn't mean that he's not a nice person, and he spoke highly of me last time (T/REA), (writes on board) but it does indicate that Joe had a deviation score of minus ten. Do you remember that? I remember it very clearly because I remember that I think, (points index finger to his temple—"remembering") who was the person—Zelda? Had a plus ten? Joe had a minus ten, indicating that Joe's exam score fell ten points below the mean. Remember that? And if Zelda had a plus ten, it indicated that Zelda's score fell ten points above the mean (T/STR). Think a second, what does that tell us about Joe or Zelda (T/SOL)? (Throughout most of the tape the prof. gestures, varies inflection, and looks at class.)

SEGMENT III

RHETORICAL HISTORY OF THE UNITED STATES (4 min.) Taught by Professor David Zarefsky. The course consists of three lectures a week plus a number of options that the students can choose to contract for a given grade. The tape is one of a discussion group that meets once a week, attended by about 18 students.

(At beginning of tape we see students sitting at tables—arranged in a triangle—with professor sitting by one apex; he begins conversationally with question.)

PROF. ZAREFSKY: If you could imagine a segment of the American public with whom this particular editorial would be least persuasive, what segment might you pick (T/STR)? Jim (T/SOL)?

JIM: (Camera focuses on Jim who looks at professor.) Those that had, ah, contact with slavery, for a number of reasons. First of all, this particular . . . . (S/RES)

PROF.: Let me interrupt you for a second (T/REA), what do you mean when you say had contact with (T/SOL)?

JIM: Well, the abolitionists for one, okay, would be against it right off the bat. But also, I think, Northerners that weren't abolitionists but just felt, maybe having some contact with the slave trade that had come North, (camera focuses two male students who are apparently commenting to one another) the border states maybe would be the ones that would be most skeptical of it because of all the talk about equality and it seems like even though the divisiveness of the issue wasn't that apparent at the time, you could perhaps see it in the future as a serious problem that would have to be resolved (S/RES).

PROF.: Do you, do others of you agree (T/SOL)?

STUDENT A: (One of the students who was talking before answers, talking to Prof.) Well, I think that the abolitionists would of, would of agreed with the editorial because they would have seen the principle of equality being extended through their movement to the slaves. They would have seen the abolition of slavery as one more aspect of the principle of equality triumphing in America (S/RES).

JIM: (Addressing Student A, then looks at Prof., then back to student.) You're assuming that the abolish, abolitionists thought they would succeed and I don't really think you can make that assumption in 1840. I mean if they took a realistic look at the situation, besides the fact here it is all these promises that there's equality right now, it addresses what there is right now, what will happen, not necessarily what will only happen in the future. It's future, it's futuristic, but it also addresses what there is right now (S/REA).

STUDENT B: (This comment comes from second student who was earlier seen talking with Student A. He looks mainly at Jim.) But, James, it seems that um, you're ignoring one of the terms that we talked about in class today, namely social reality and in pure rhetorical terms it would seem that the argument of futurity would imply that there can, since we can expect perfection, any wrong that might occur can be resolved through the notion of futurity and destiny. Therefore, the abolitionists could turn that argument to their advantage, in the social sense at least, perhaps not in the completely real sense (S/REA).

STUDENT C: (Female student sitting next to Prof., looking at Jim.) In addition, he's not, I don't think he's saying that what we now have is totally perfect. At the last paragraph he goes, "we must honor the fulfillment of our mission," and so I think they could have easily read into it, yes, God is on our side, equality is important and we will go on to fulfill that (S/REA).

JIM: (Jim looking at Student C). I think he bases his whole argument on what will come in the future on the perfection of what we have right now, on the perfect equality, universality of the system right now. You know, what we have now determines what we will have in the future (S/REA).

PROF.: (Addressing Jim). So you're suggesting that O'Sullivan was assuming that we have already achieved moral perfection and as a result of that, the future holds these kinds of promises as opposed to the notion that says we're on the way towards moral perfection (T/REA). (Starts to address entire class, stops and looks to his right.) Well, let me just get . . . Tricia (T/SOL).

TRICIA: (Addressing Prof.) Well, I disagree with that because one of the things he says. . . . (S/RES)

PROFESSOR: With what (T/SOL)?

TRICIA: (Looking first at Prof., then at Jim) With James's statement, that is ah that it's a progression, because he mentions progress a lot and one of the things when he's talking about equality he's talking about the principle of equality upon which the nation is organized. It's not that we had equality now, it's that that's the basic principle. And his, all of his talk about progress and forward moving is talking about moving toward the fulfillment of the principle (S/RES).

STUDENT D: (Addressing Tricia) But, wouldn't the abolitionists have said, what is this principle of, principle of equality? I don't see it today. I mean, they could have easily seen that this is hypocritical. Anyone with any kind of racist regime could have said, well, we, we've, our regime is based on this principle of equality. Then an abolitionist would have said, you know it just doesn't, it just doesn't make sense, given what we have (S/REA).

TRICIA: (To Student D) But he was talking about it in relationship to say

various other governments, when he was talking about the uniqueness of America and the specific mission that they were to fulfill (S/REA).
STUDENT D: Right (S/REA).
TRICIA: So that he was talking about it being more equal than others and progressing, progressing towards perfect equality (S/REA).
STUDENT D: Ah, yeah I know, and I think the, I think that the point only is abolitionists would have, would have tended to see a fallacy there, not that others wouldn't (S/REA). (At end looks at Prof.)
TRICIA: Yeah, but all the same it wasn't ah, a perfect equality he was advocating at the time, that's all that I'm saying (S/REA).
PROF.: (To class, points to new student at end.) Would anybody pick an audience other than abolitionists, that you think might be the least likely to be persuaded by it (T/SOL)?

Appendix B

Available Student Rating Instruments

The following institutions make their student rating system available to off-campus clients.

System: CAFETERIA System

Contact:
Marjorie J. Cree
CAFETERIA Coordinator
Center for Instructional Services
Purdue University
West Lafayette, IN 47907
(317) 494-5100

System: (CIEQ) Arizona Course/
    Instructor Evaluation
    Questionnaire

Contact:
Lawrence M. Aleamoni
Division of Educational
    Foundations and Administration
College of Education, Room 605
University of Arizona
Tucson, AZ 85721
(602) 621-7832 or 7825

System: (IAS) Instructional
    Assessment System

Contact:
Gerald M. Gillmore
Educational Assessment Center
PB-30, University of Washington
Seattle, WA 98195
(206) 543-1170

System: (ICES) Instructor and
    Course Evaluation System

Contact:
Dale C. Brandenburg
Associate Head
1308 W. Green Street
307 Engineering Hall
University of Illinois
Urbana, IL 61801
(217) 333-3490

System: (IDEA) Instructional
    Development and
    Effectiveness
    Assessment System

Contact:
William E. Cashin
Center for Faculty Evaluation and
    Development
Kansas State University
1623 Anderson Avenue
Manhattan, KS 66502
(913) 532-5970

System: (SIR) Student
    Instructional Report

Contact:
Nancy Beck
Student Instructional Report
Educational Testing Service
Princeton, NJ 08541
(609) 921-9000

System: (SIRS) Student
Instructional Rating
System

Contact:
LeRoy A. Olson
Professor and Evaluation
Consultant
Computer Laboratory
Michigan State University
East Lansing, MI 48824
(517) 353-5296

System: Student Description
of Teaching

Contact:
Robert C. Wilson, Chief
Research on Teaching
Improvement and Evaluation
Teaching Innovation and
Evaluation Services
271 Stephens Hall
University of California, Berkeley
Berkeley, CA 94720
(415) 642-1811